MIWA UEDA Illustrations
上田美和［ピーチガール］イラスト集

# PEACH

MIWA UEDA Illustrations
上田美和［ピーチガール］イラスト集

MIWA UEDA Illustrations

上田美和「ピーチガール」イラスト集

PEACH

MIWA UEDA Illustrations

上田美和「ピーチガール」イラスト集

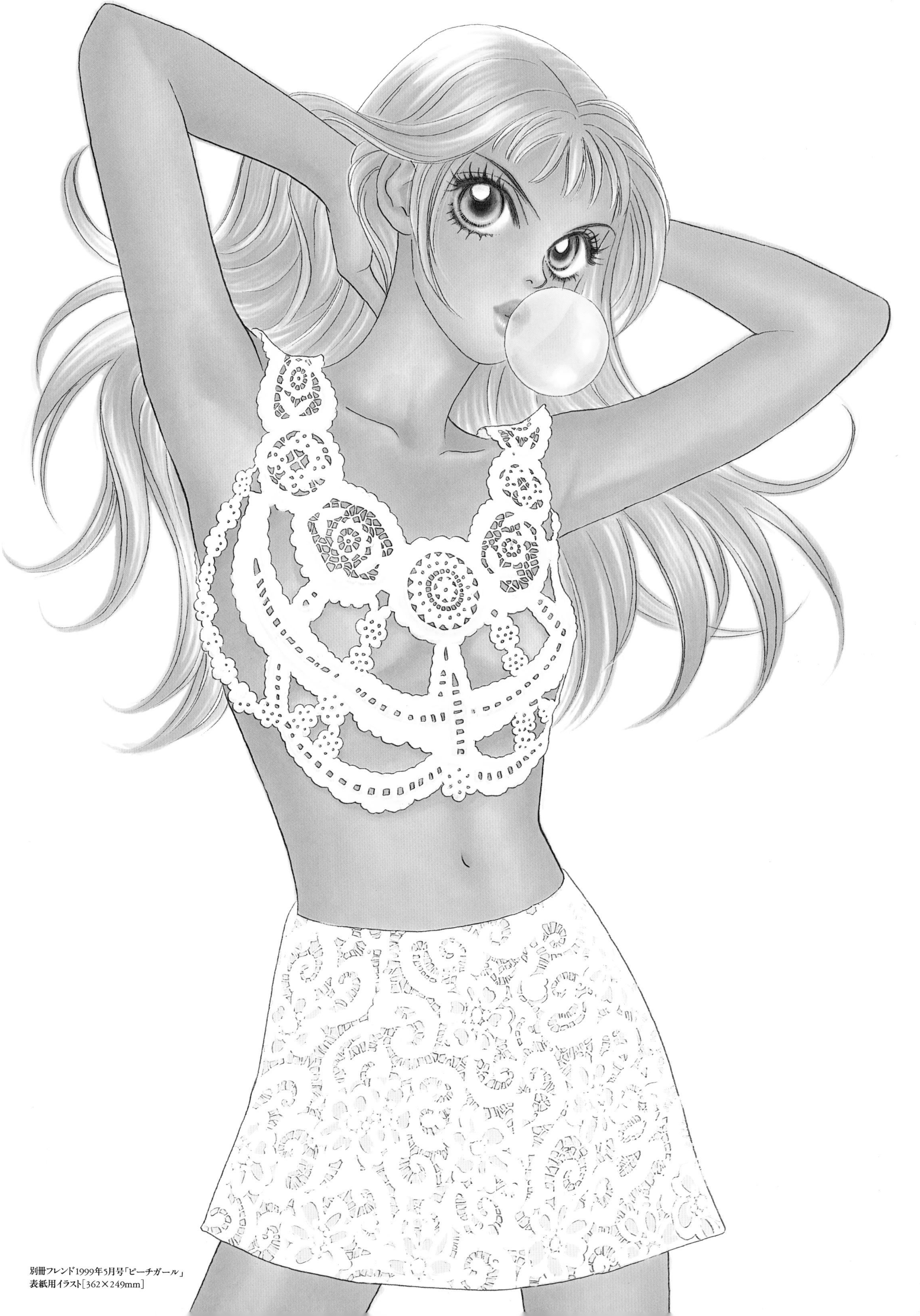

別冊フレンド1999年5月号「ピーチガール」
表紙用イラスト［362×249mm］

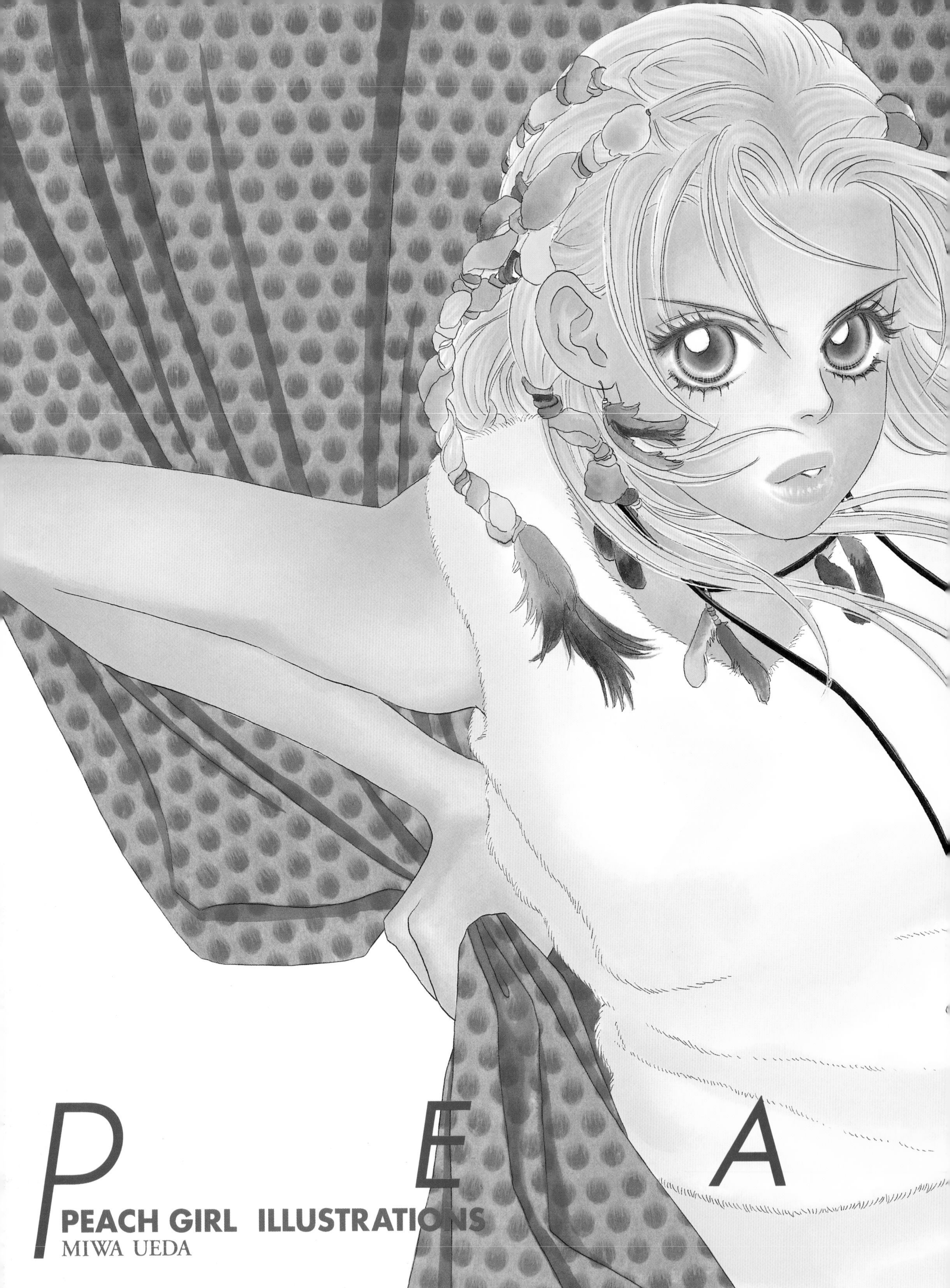
P E A
PEACH GIRL ILLUSTRATIONS
MIWA UEDA

別冊フレンド2000年3月号「ピーチガール」見開き扉用イラスト［338×517mm］

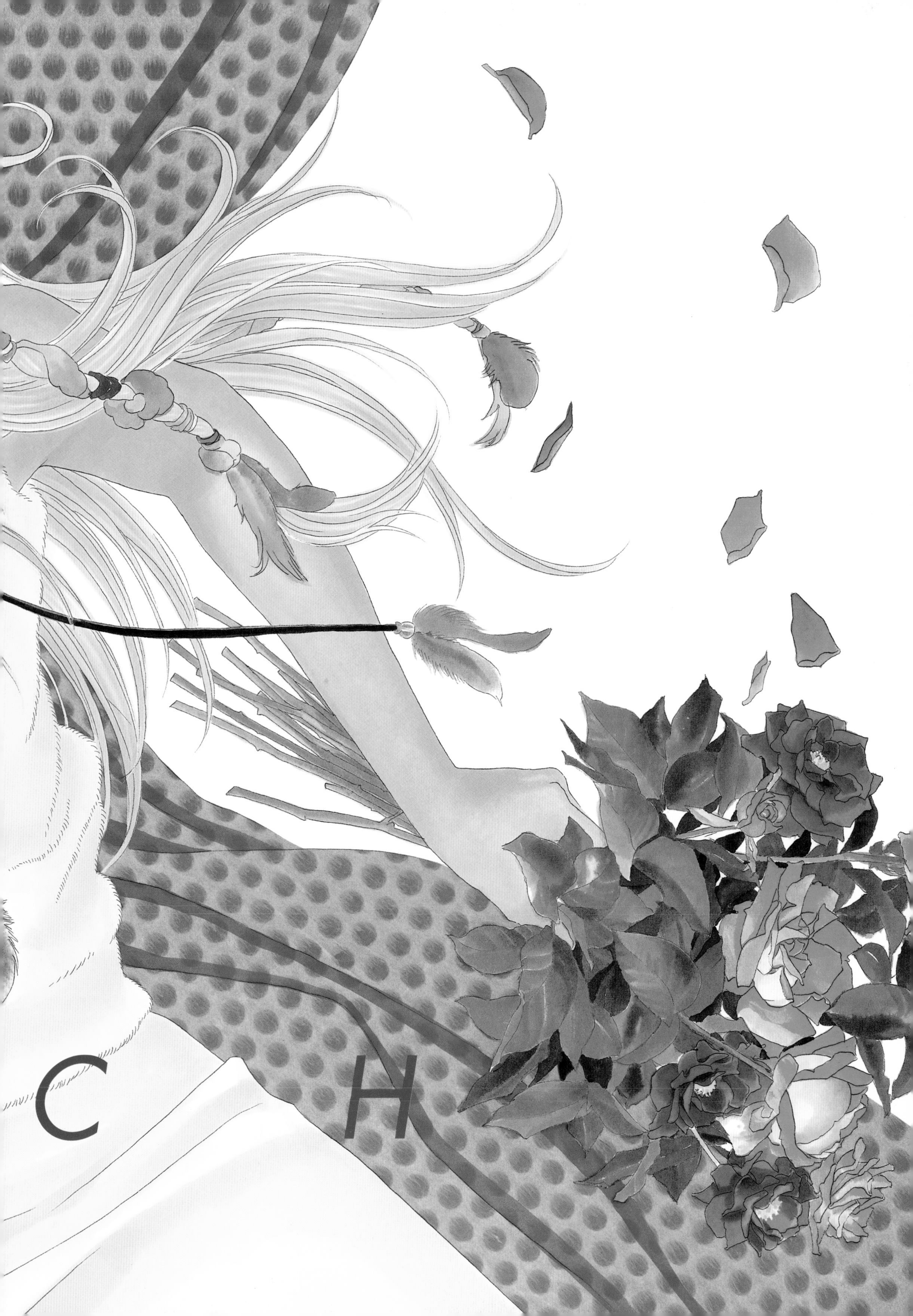
C H

# CONTENTS

別冊フレンド1997年11月号「ピーチガール」表紙用イラスト［349×261mm］

PEACH PREVIEW
# opening selection

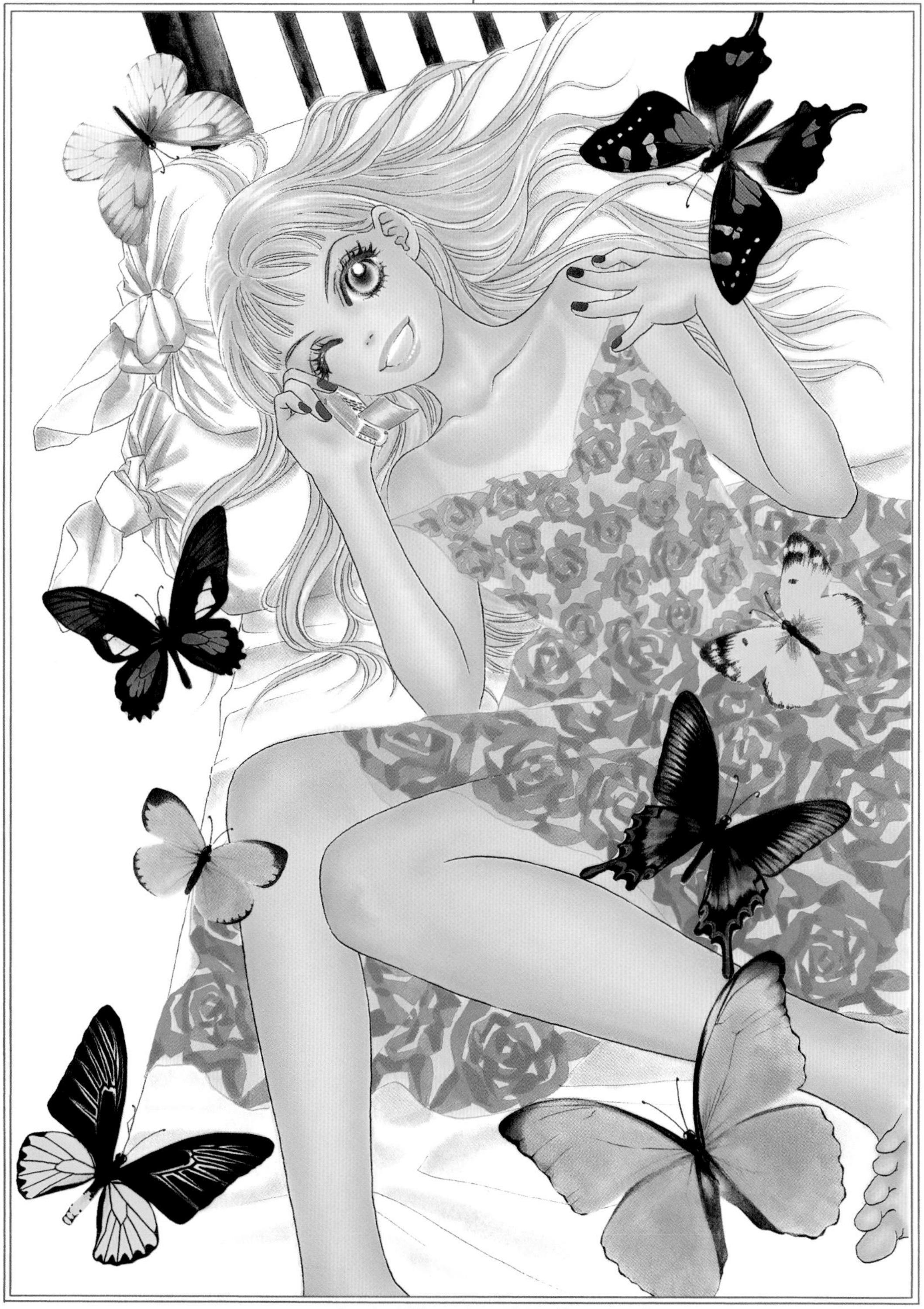

別冊フレンド1998年12月号「ピーチガール」扉用イラスト［367×260mm］

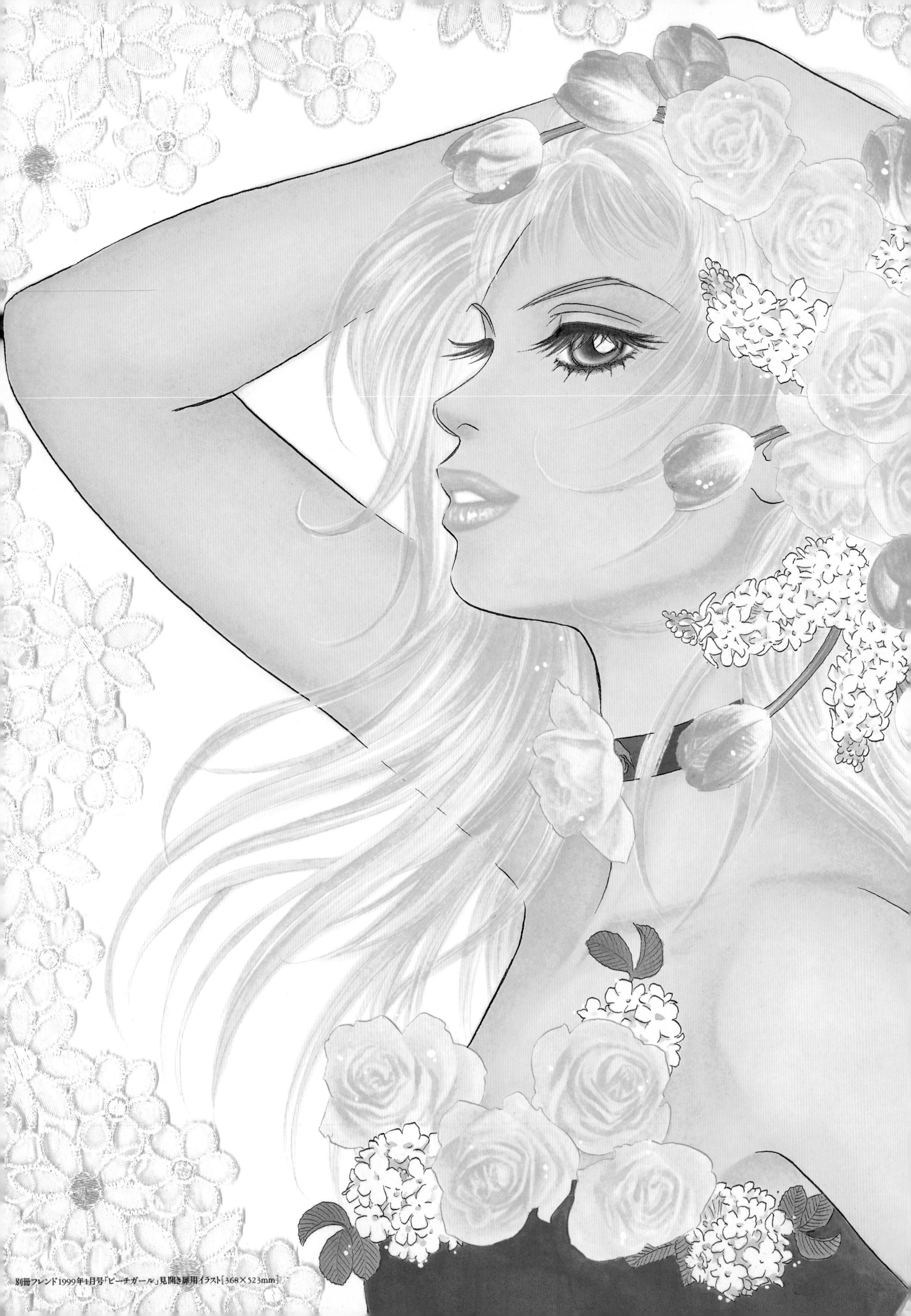

別冊フレンド1999年1月号「ピーチガール」見開き扉用イラスト[368×523mm]

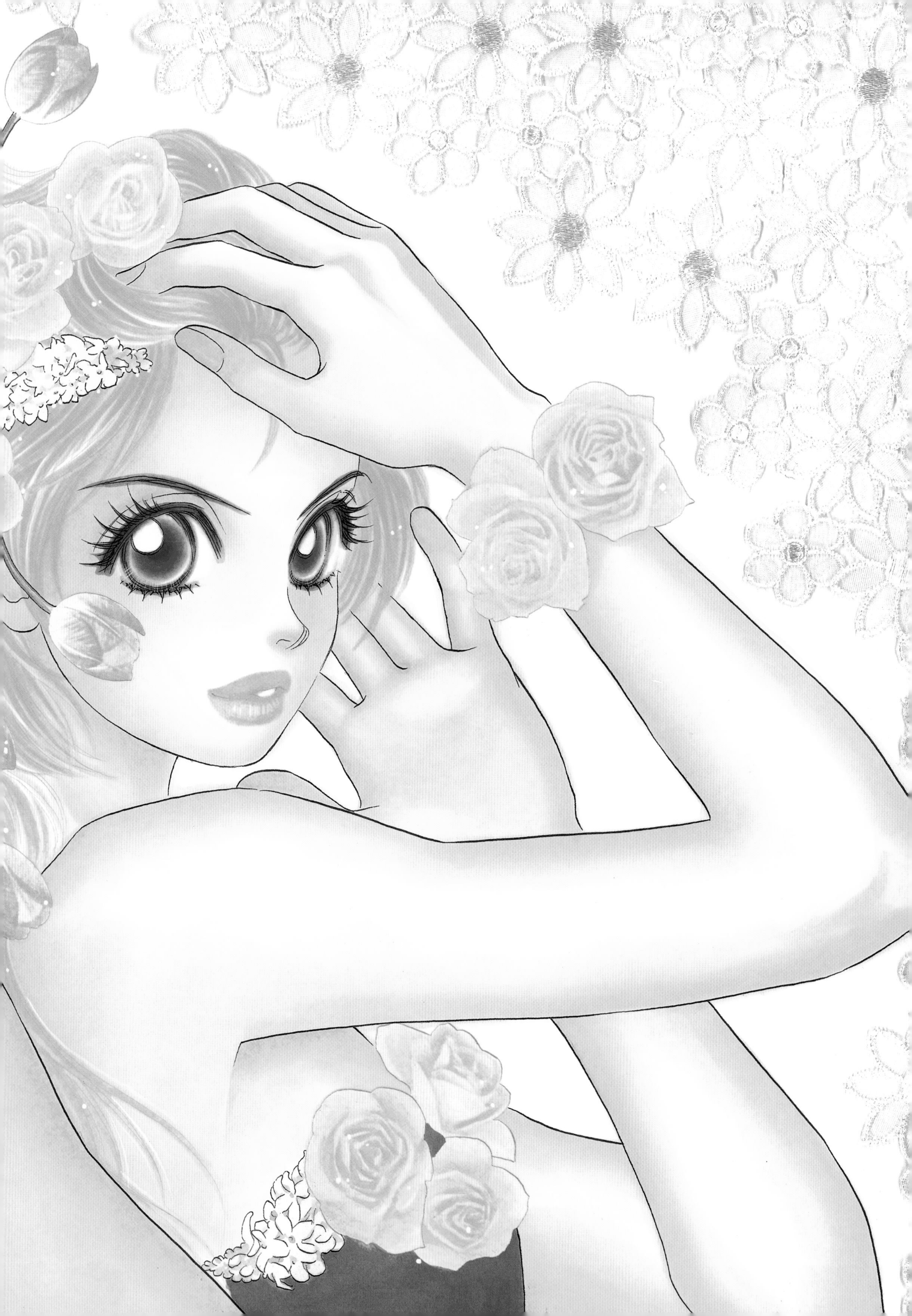

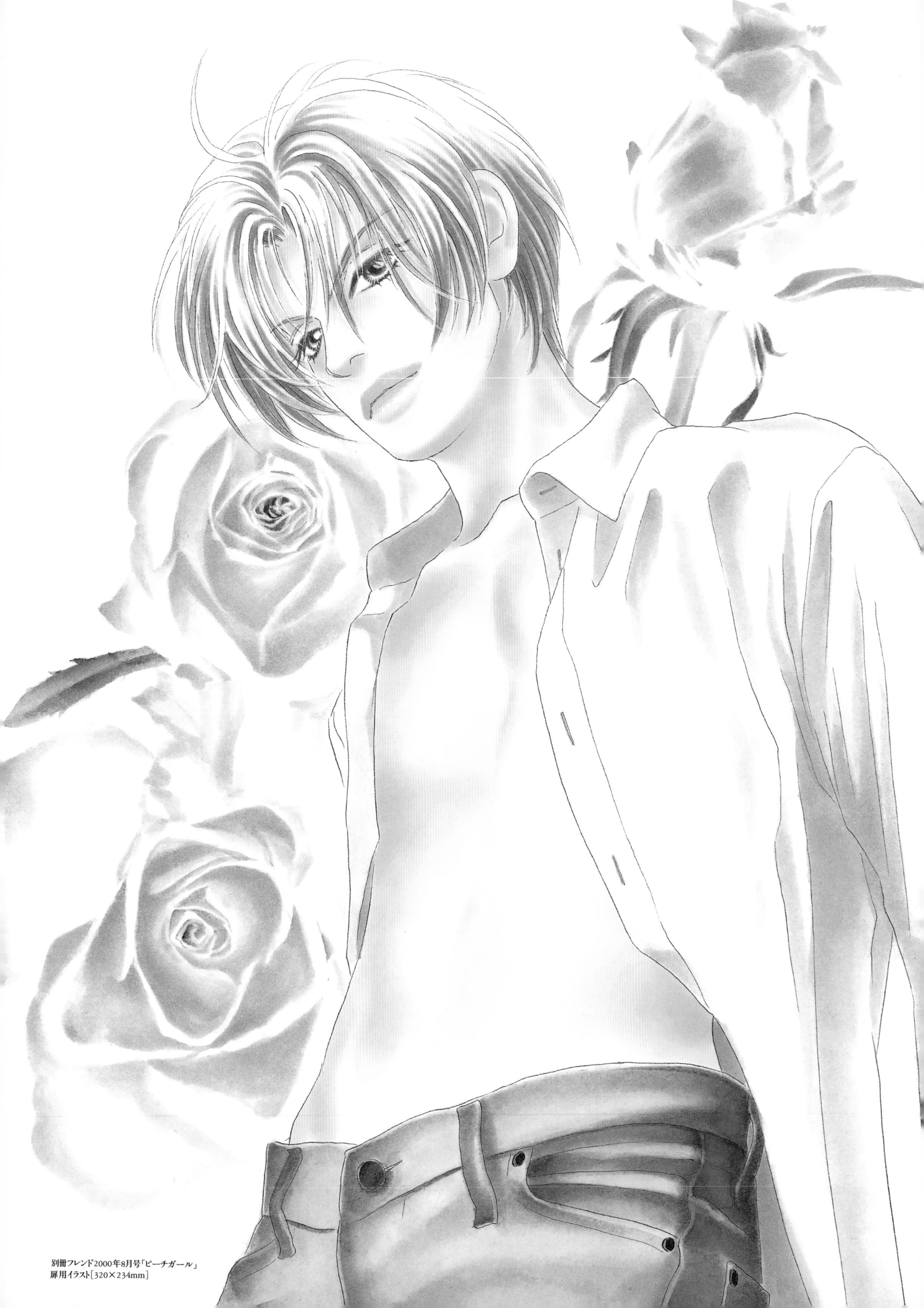

別冊フレンド2000年8月号「ピーチガール」
扉用イラスト［320×234mm］

PEACH GIRL

# 1997-1998 works

## October'97~December'98

「ピーチガール」別冊フレンド'97～'98年掲載のイラストを集めました。

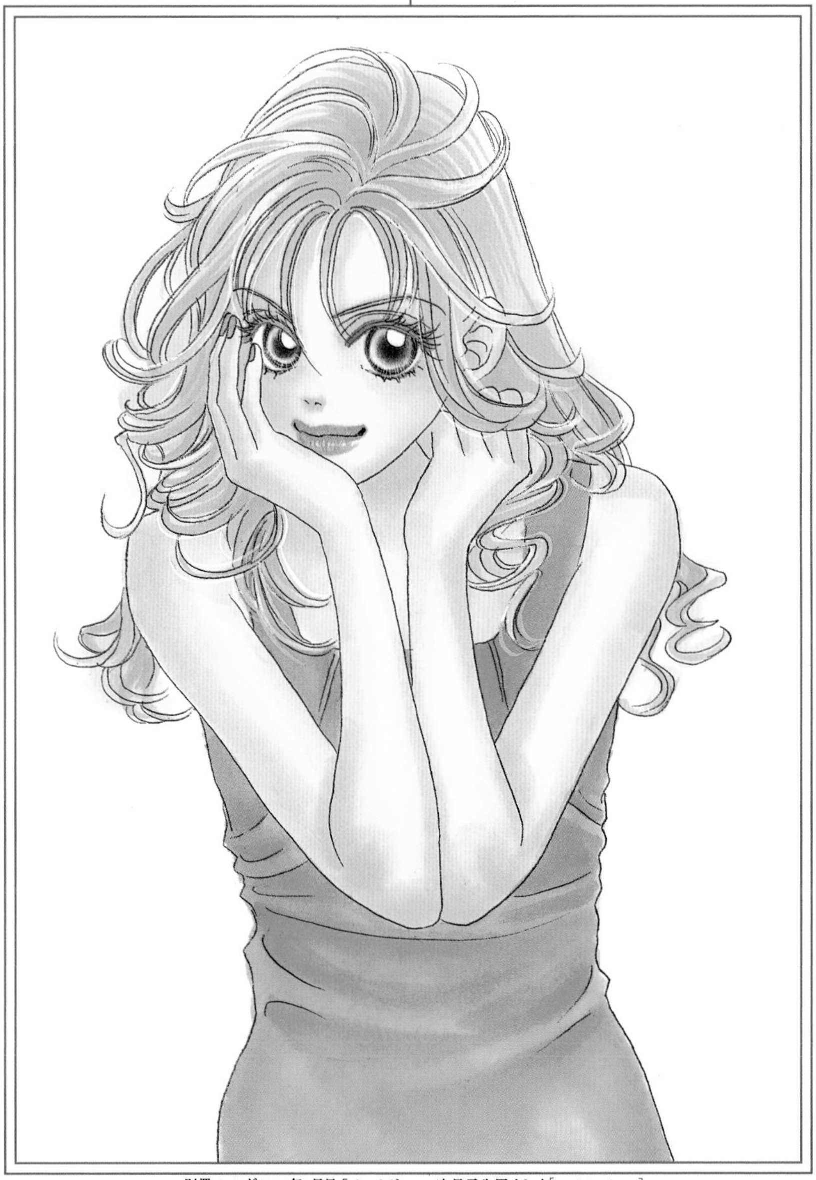

別冊フレンド1998年3月号「ピーチガール」次号予告用イラスト[178×114mm]

♥ Kogyaru style: A trendy high school student in Japan with tanned skin and red hair. Momo's archenemy Sae always interferes with Momo's love life! A storm is brewing when a girl's love and pride is on the line. We're in for a love battle of the century!

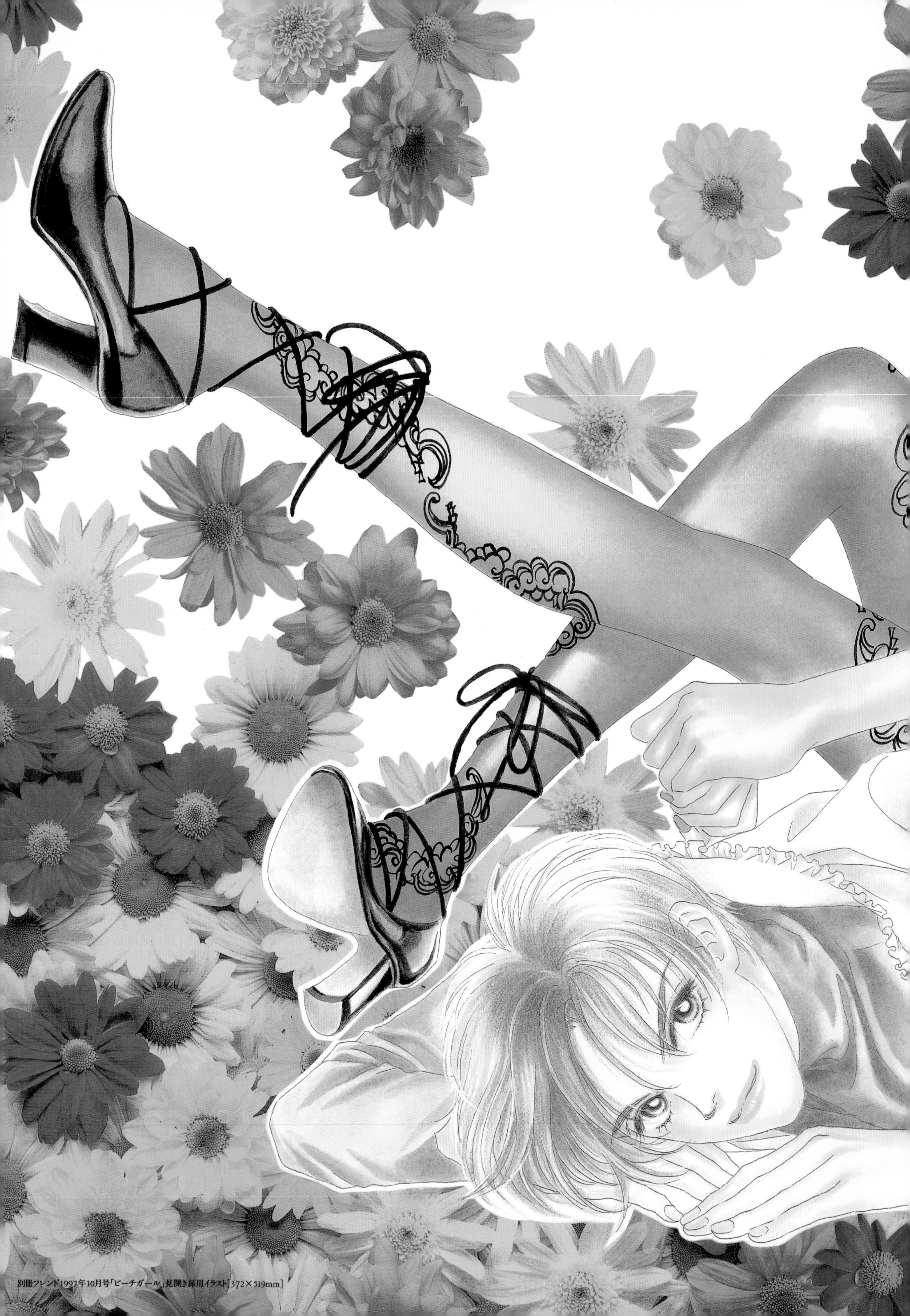

別冊フレンド1997年10月号「ピーチガール」見開き扉用イラスト［372×519mm］

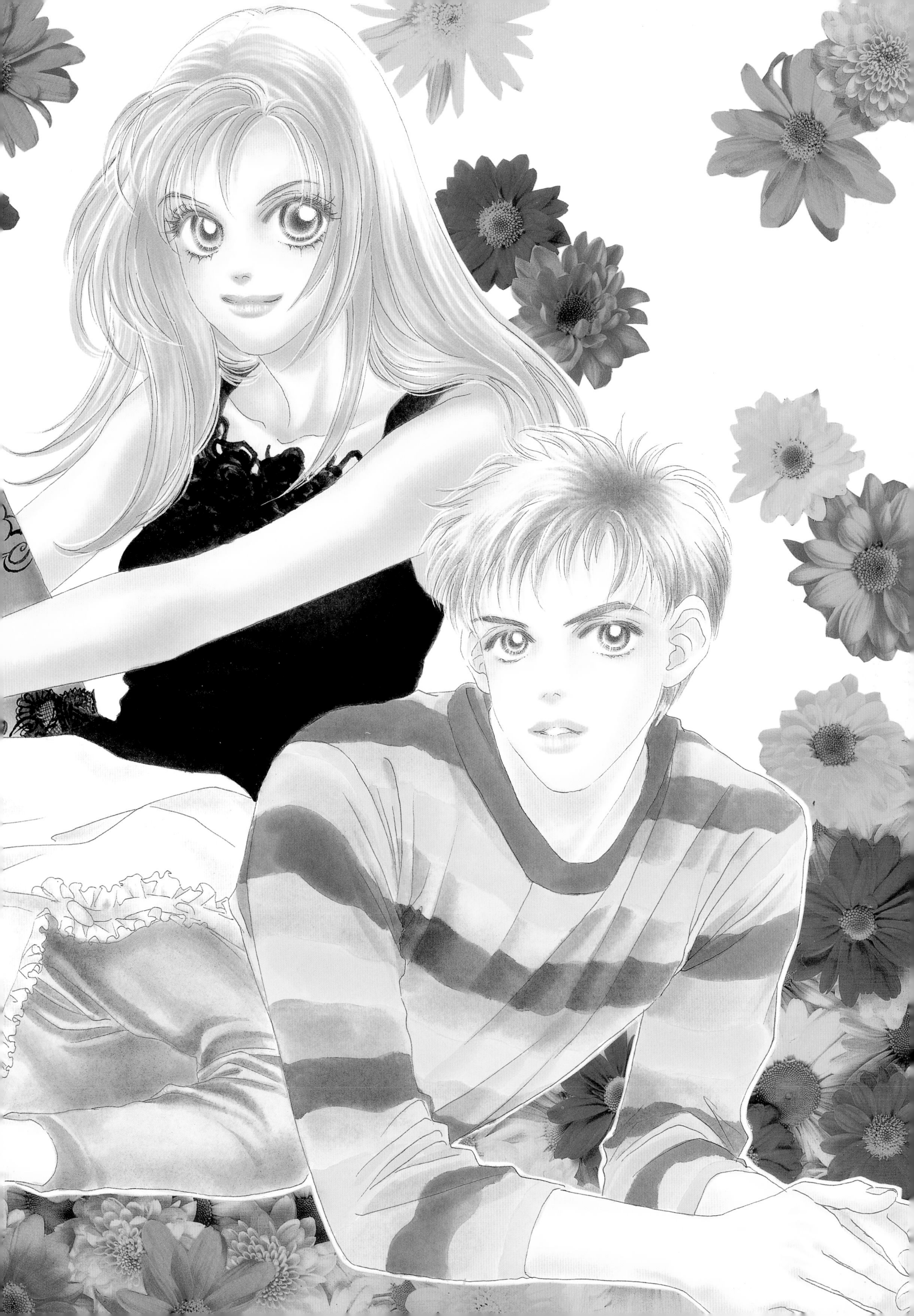

別冊フレンド1998年1月号「ピーチガール」BFオリジナルテレホンカードプレゼント用イラスト［203×171mm］

別冊フレンド1997年10月号「ピーチガール」次号予告用イラスト［260×205mm］

# PEACH PINK

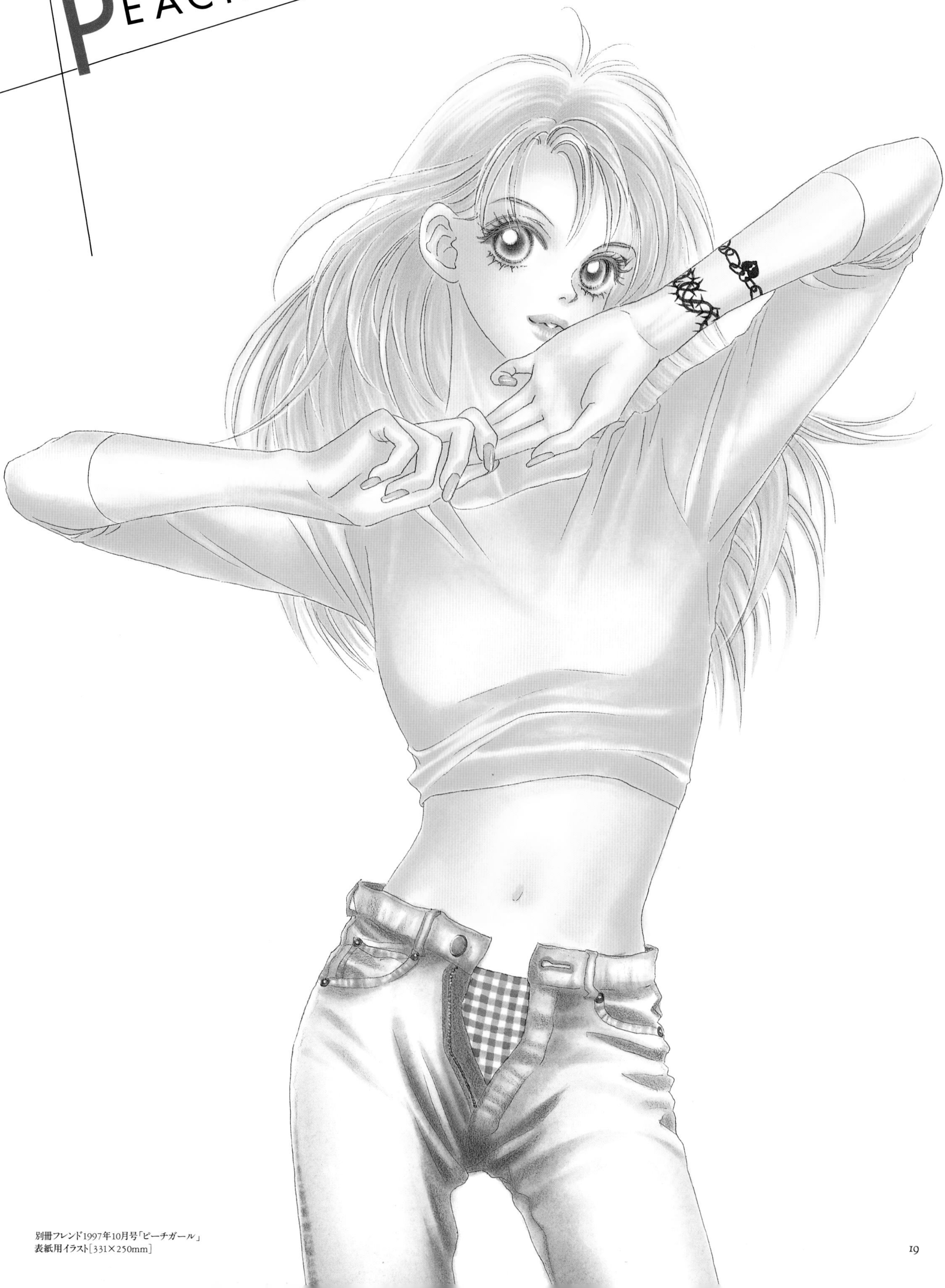

別冊フレンド1997年10月号「ピーチガール」
表紙用イラスト［331×250mm］

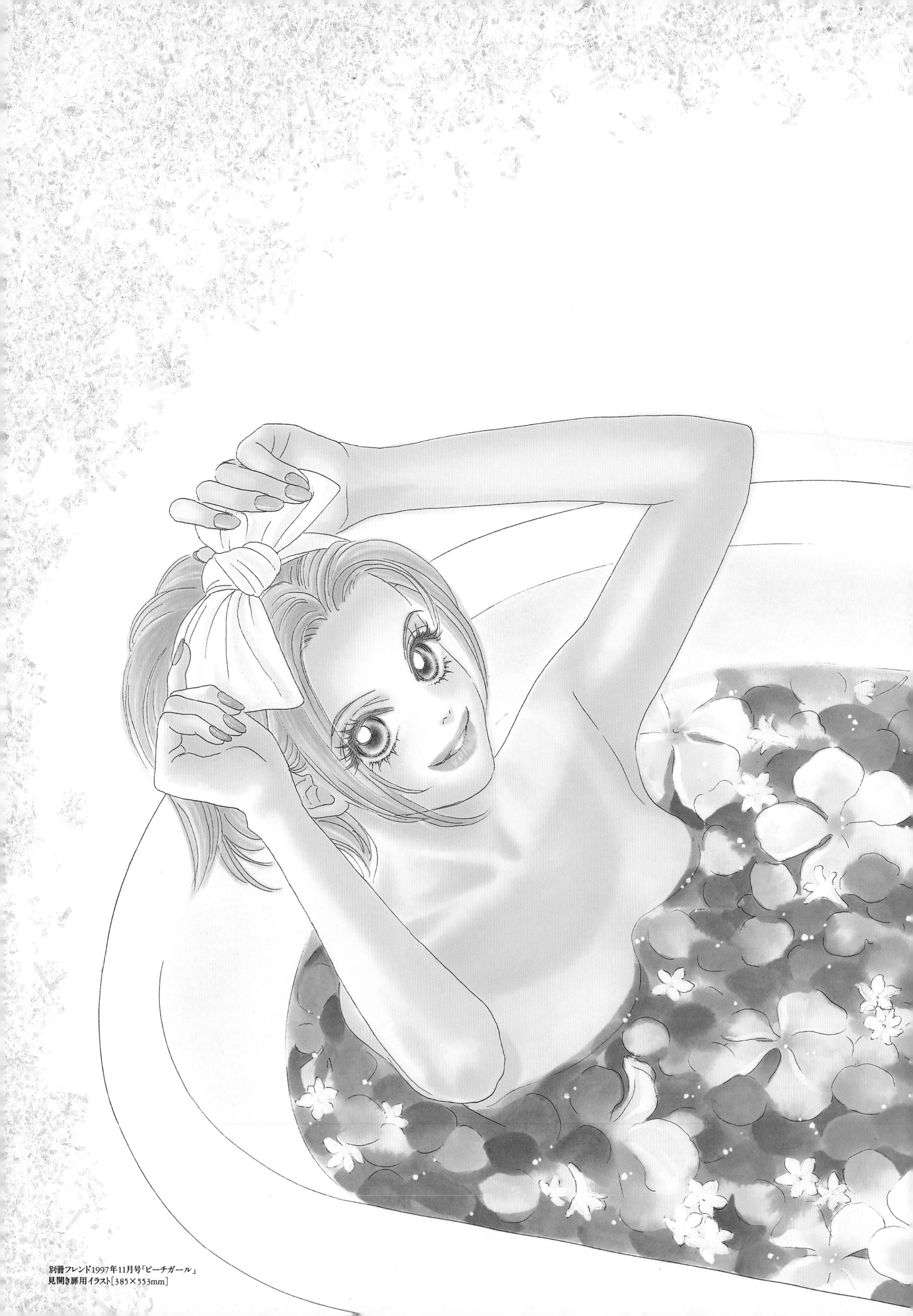

別冊フレンド1997年11月号「ピーチガール」
見開き扉用イラスト[385×553mm]

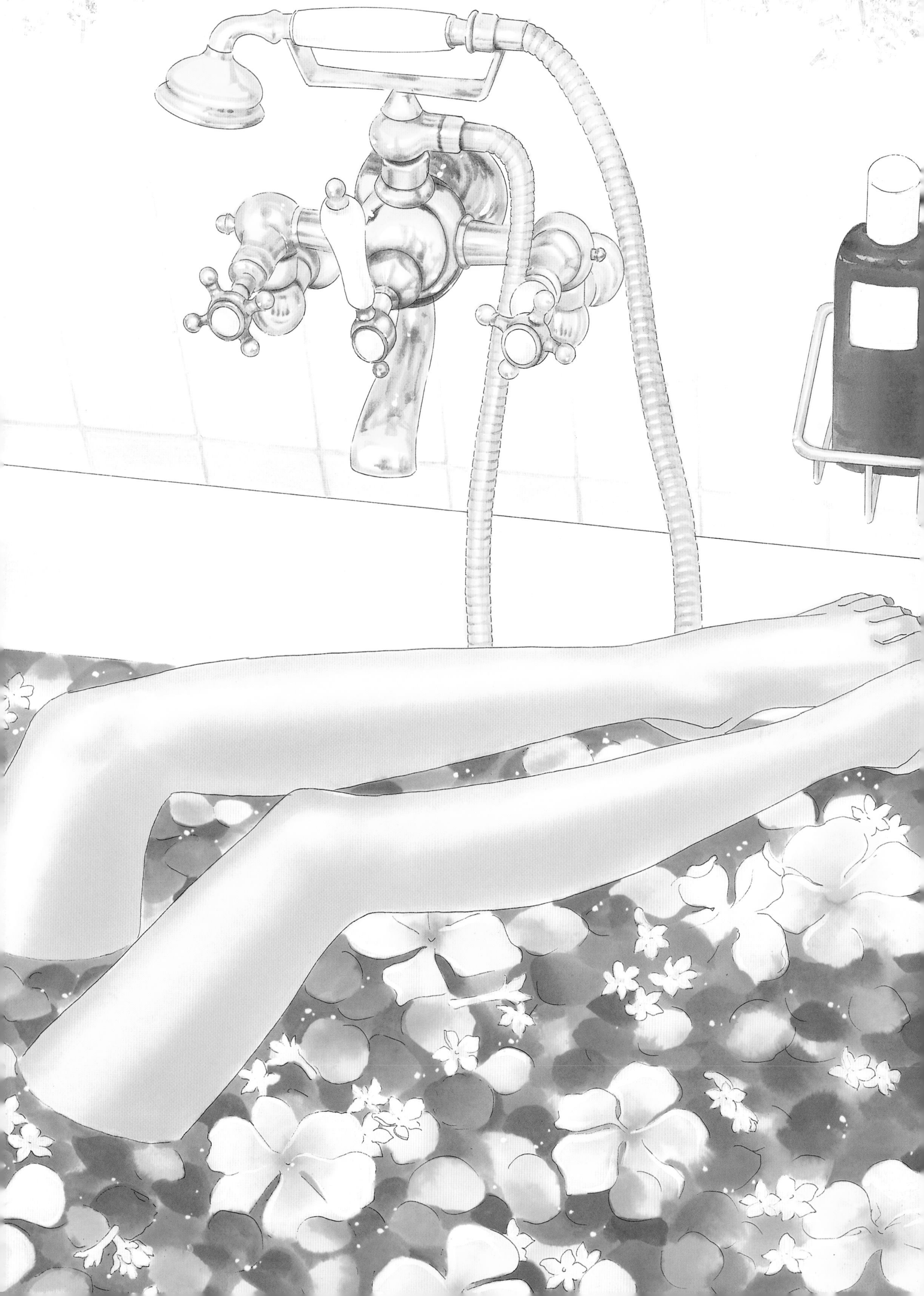

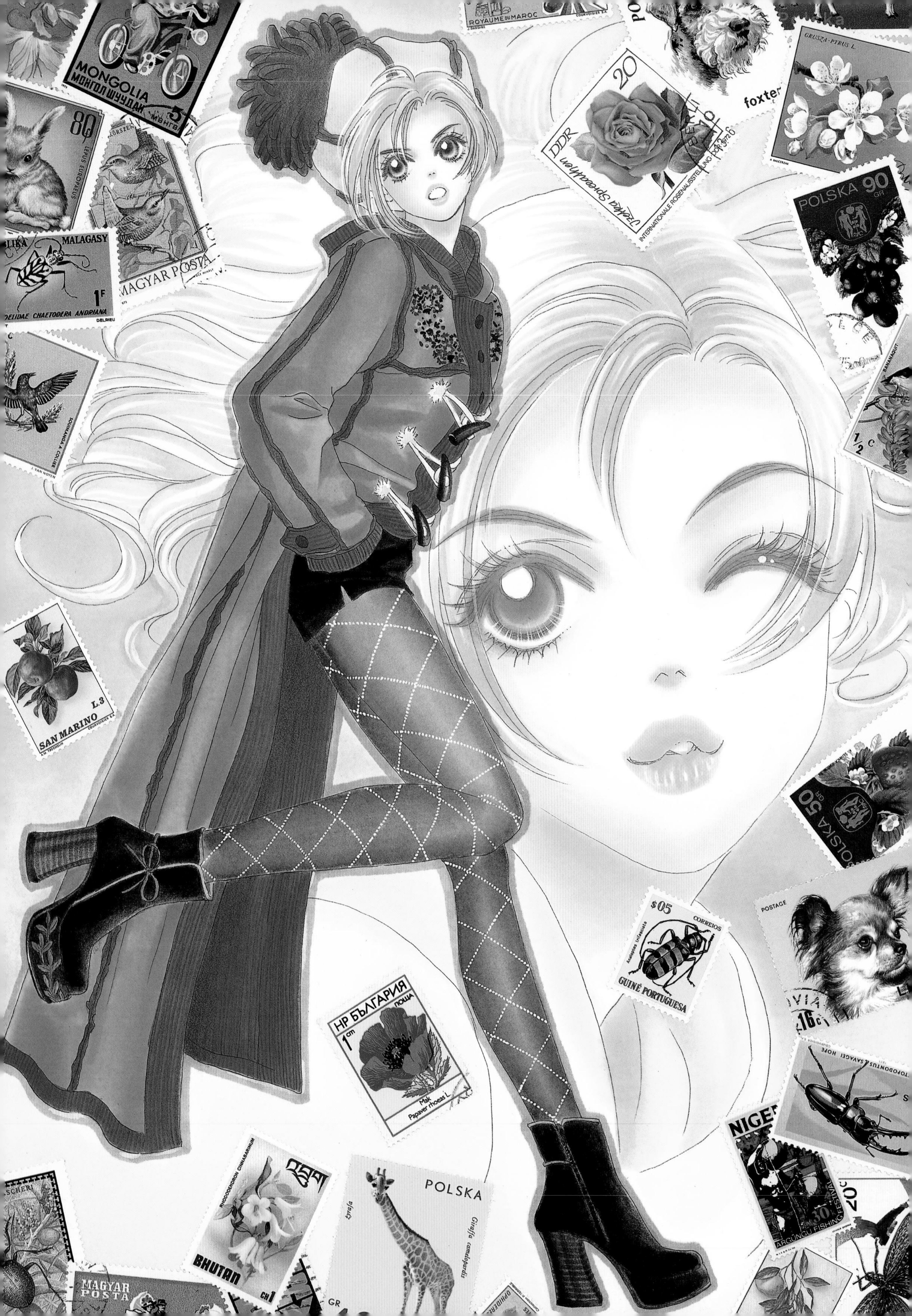
MONGOLIA
МОНГОЛ ШУУДАН
ROYAUME DU MAROC
DDR
20
INTERNATIONALE ROSENAUSSTELLUNG
GRUSZA · PYRUS L.
foxter
POLSKA 90 GR
80
LEPUS EUROPAEUS
MALAGASY
CHAETODERA ANDRIANA
MAGYAR POSTA
SAN MARINO
L.3
POLSKA 50
POSTAGE
$05
CORREIOS
GUINÉ PORTUGUESA
НР БЪЛГАРИЯ
ПОЩА
Mak
Papaver rhoeas L.
POLSKA
Giraffa camelopardalis
Żyrafa
BHUTAN
RHODODENDRON CINNABARINUM
MAGYAR POSTA
NIGER
ARGUNGU FISHING FESTIVAL

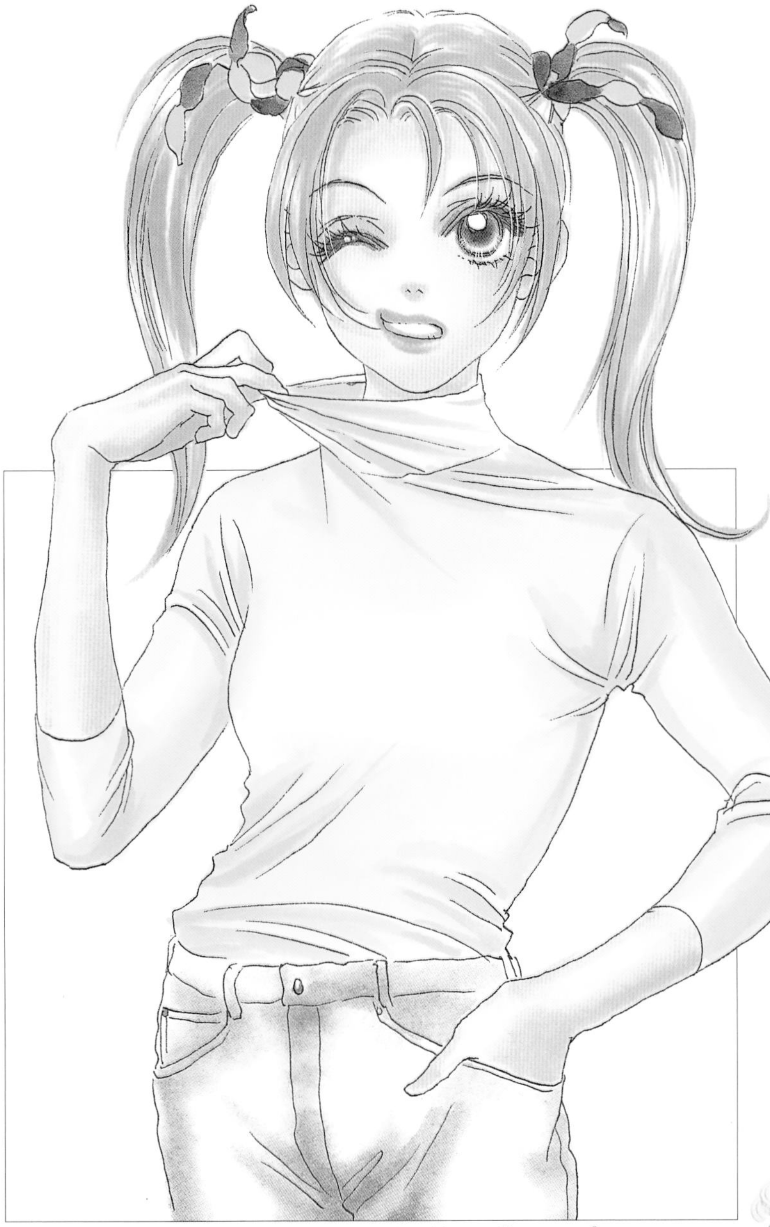

別冊フレンド1997年11月号「ピーチガール」次号予告用イラスト［164×114mm］

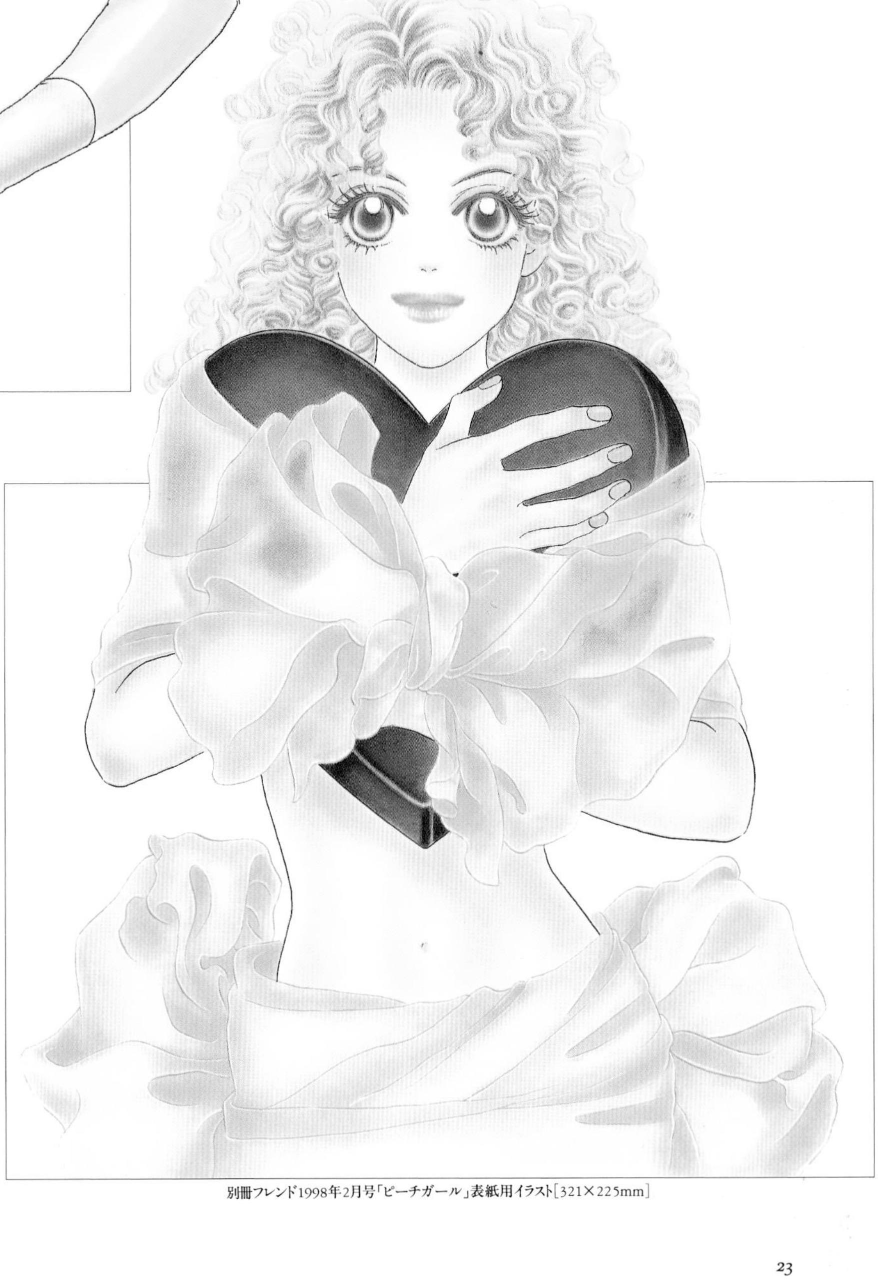

別冊フレンド1998年2月号「ピーチガール」表紙用イラスト［321×225mm］

別冊フレンド1997年12月号「ピーチガール」扉用イラスト［384×270mm］

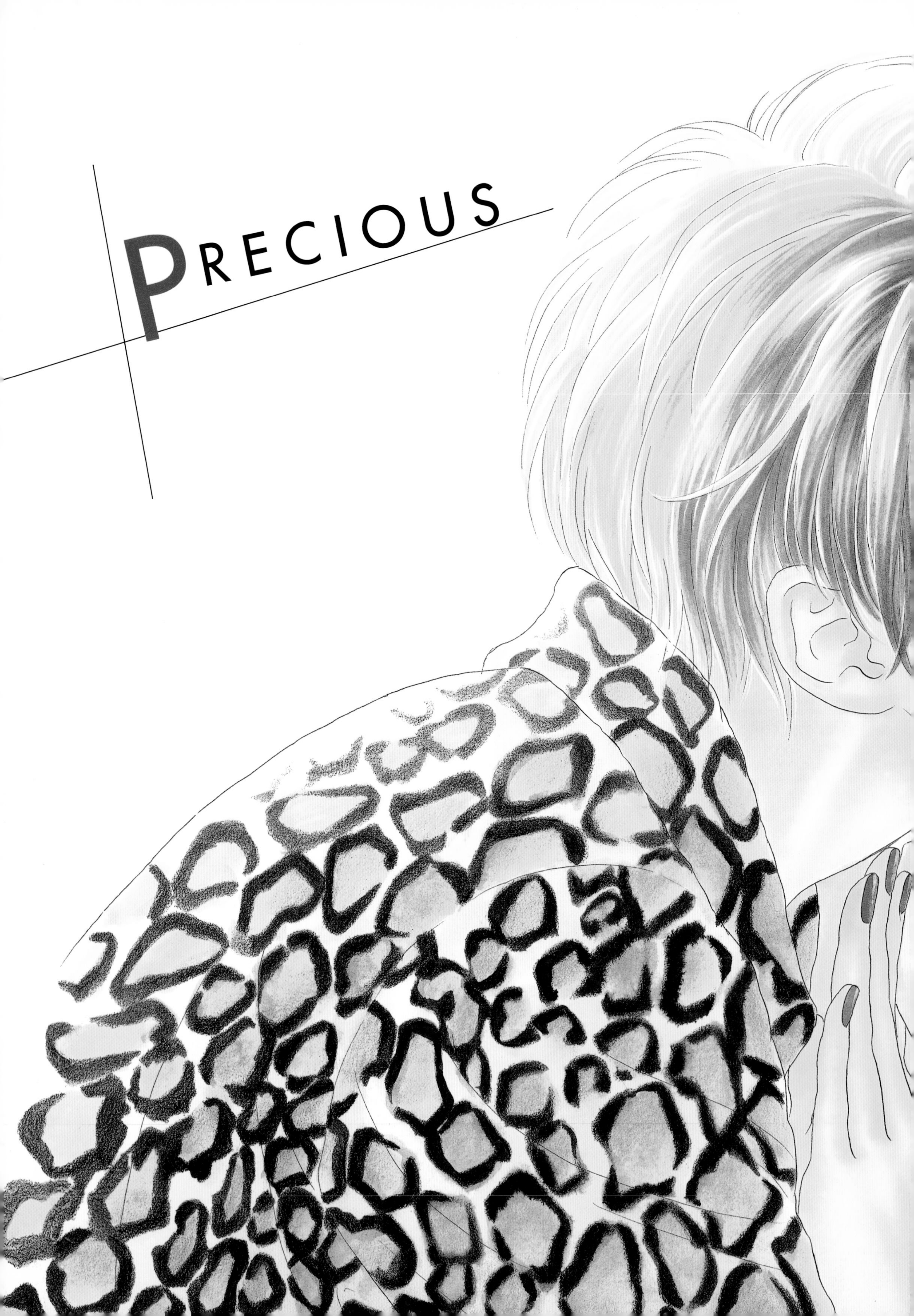
PRECIOUS

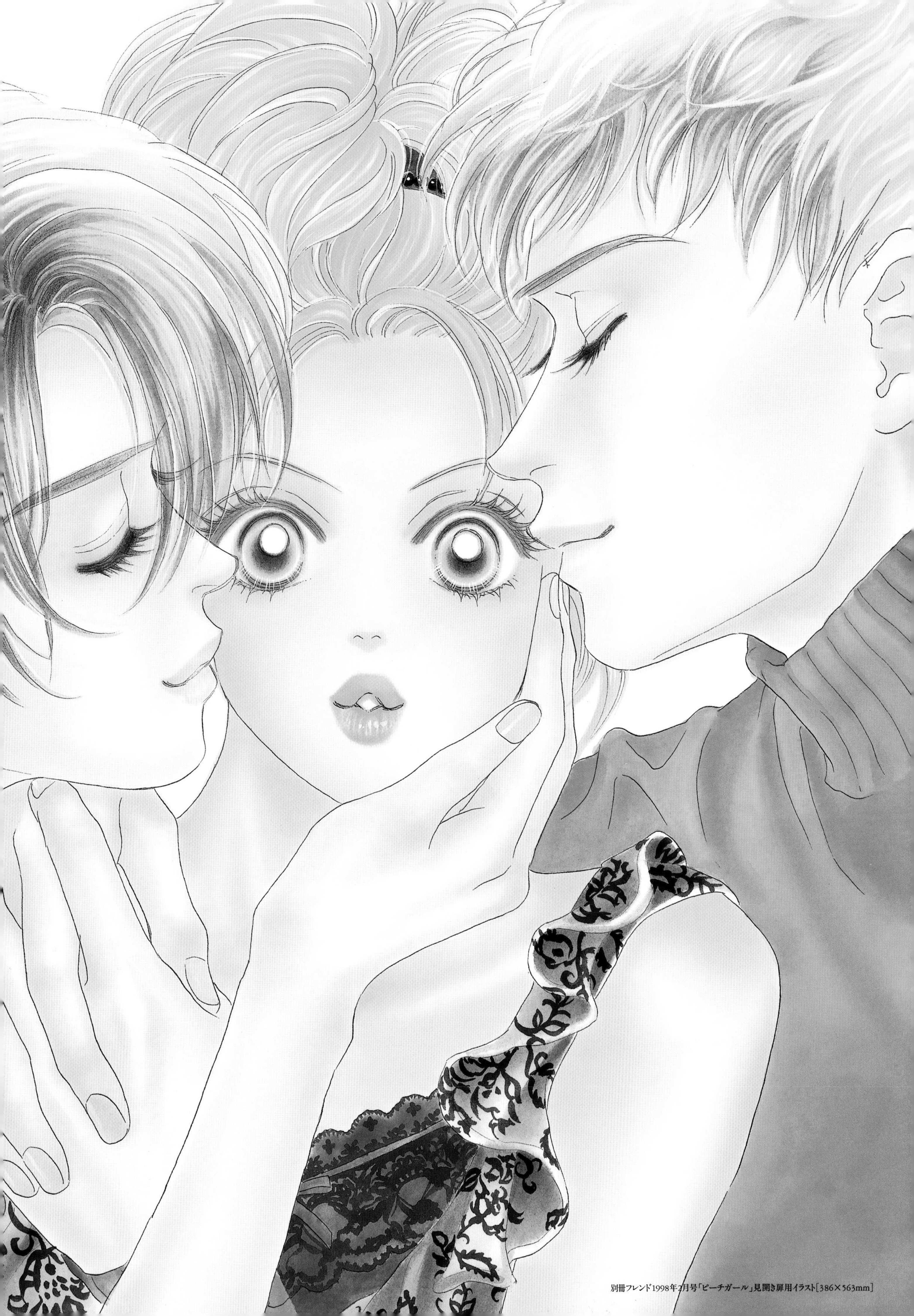

別冊フレンド1998年2月号「ピーチガール」見開き扉用イラスト［386×563mm］

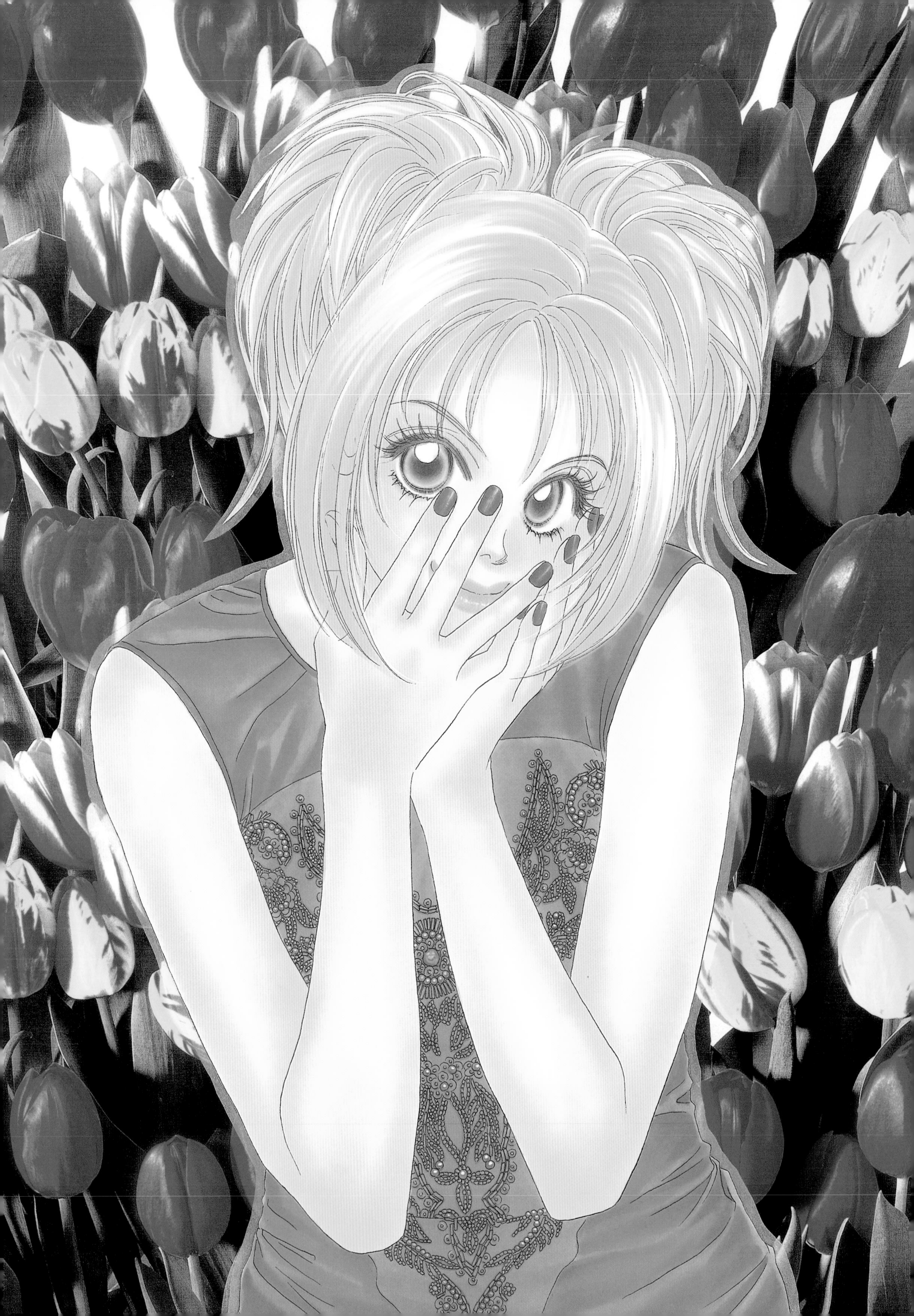

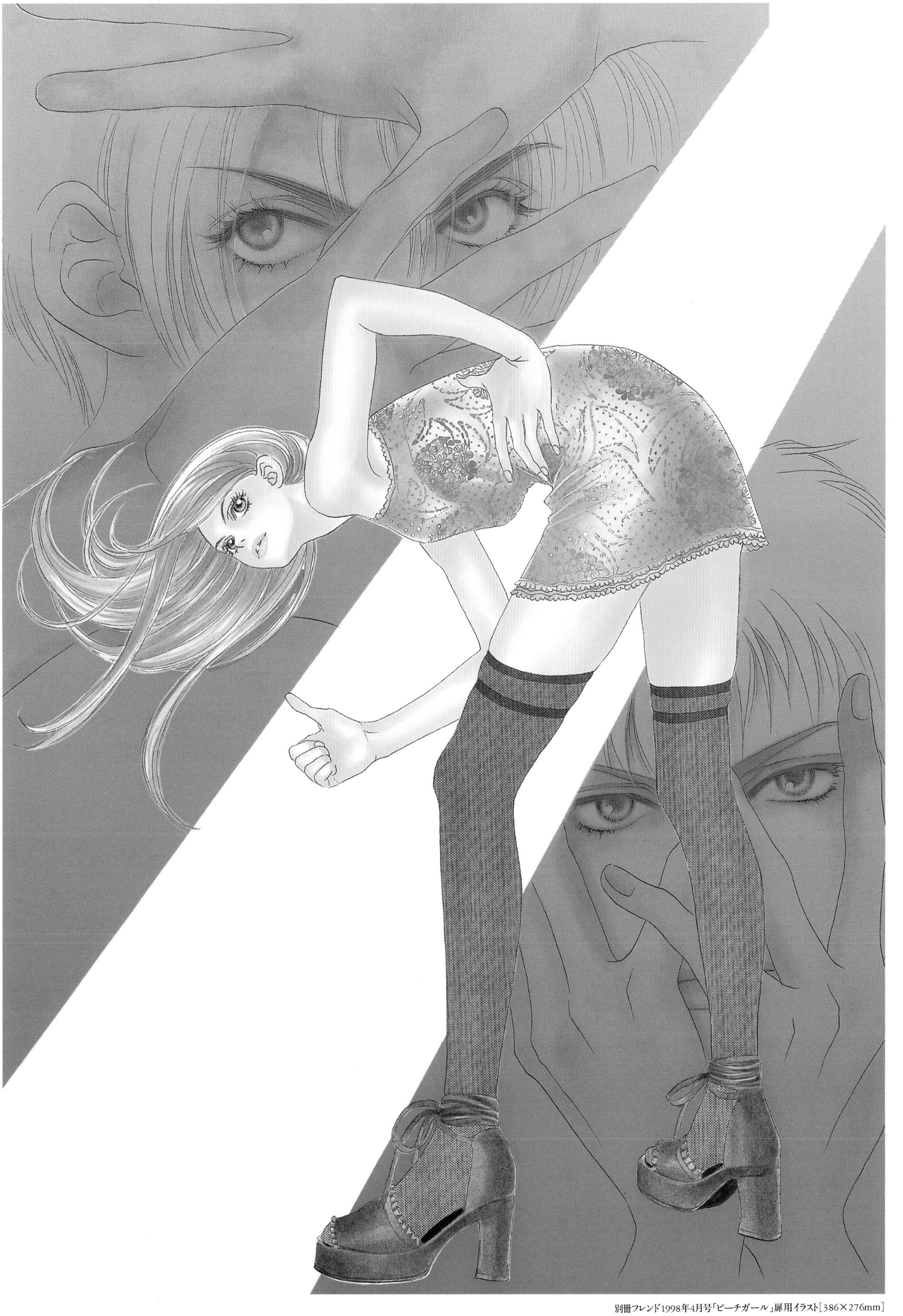

別冊フレンド1998年4月号「ピーチガール」扉用イラスト［386×276mm］

別冊フレンド1998年5月号「ピーチガール」扉用イラスト［382×284mm］

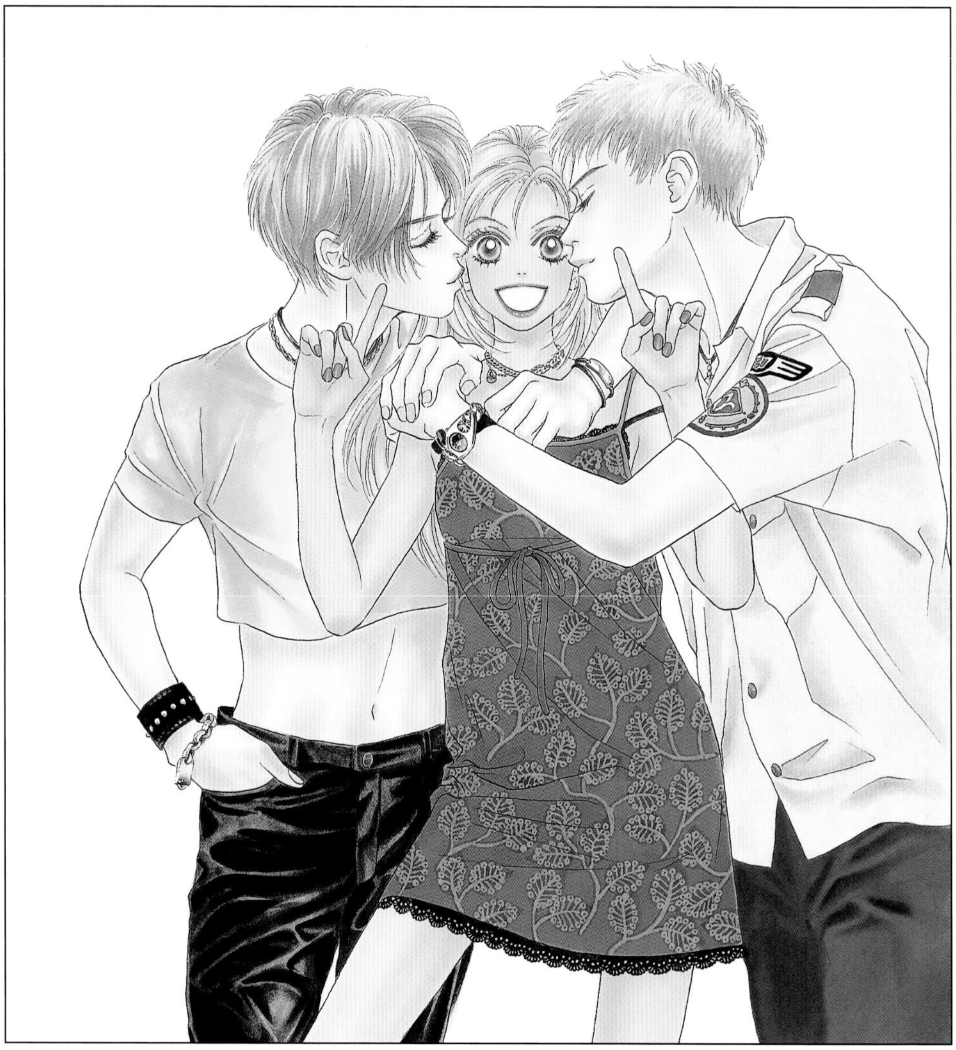

別冊フレンド1998年6月号「ピーチガール」表紙用イラスト[301×272mm]

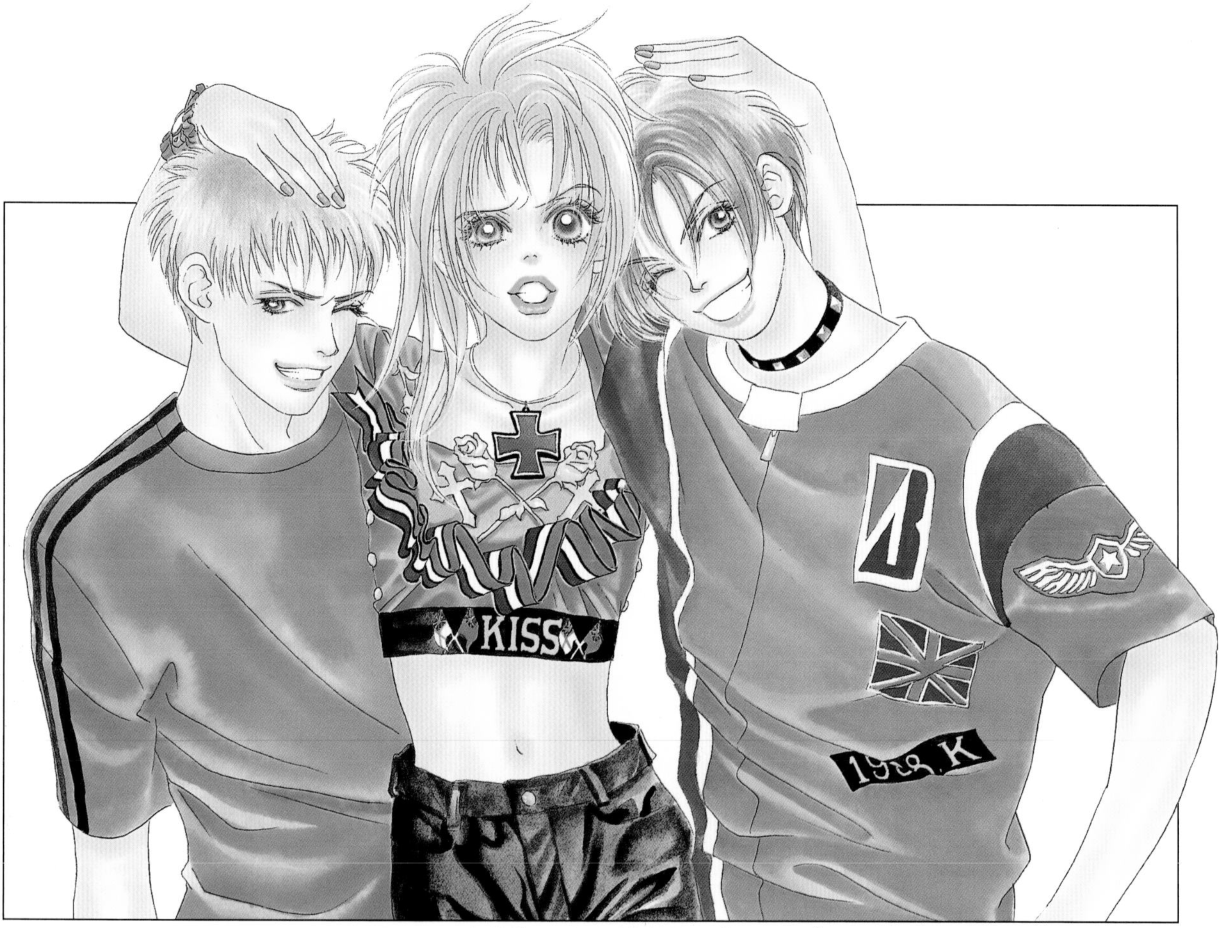
KISS

別冊フレンド1998年5月号「ピーチガール」次号予告用イラスト[210×275mm]



別冊フレンド1998年7月号「ピーチガール」表紙用イラスト[363×257mm]

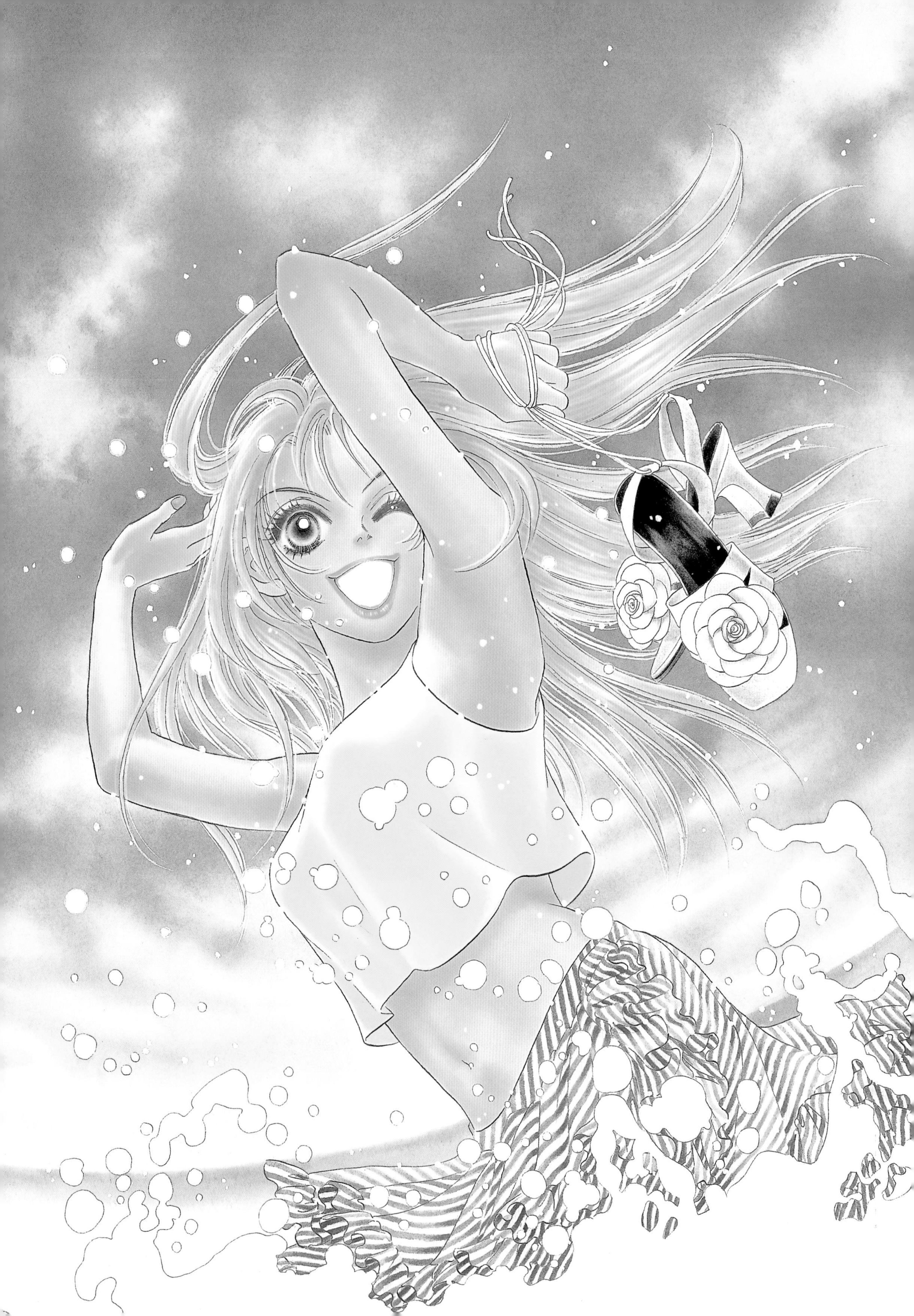

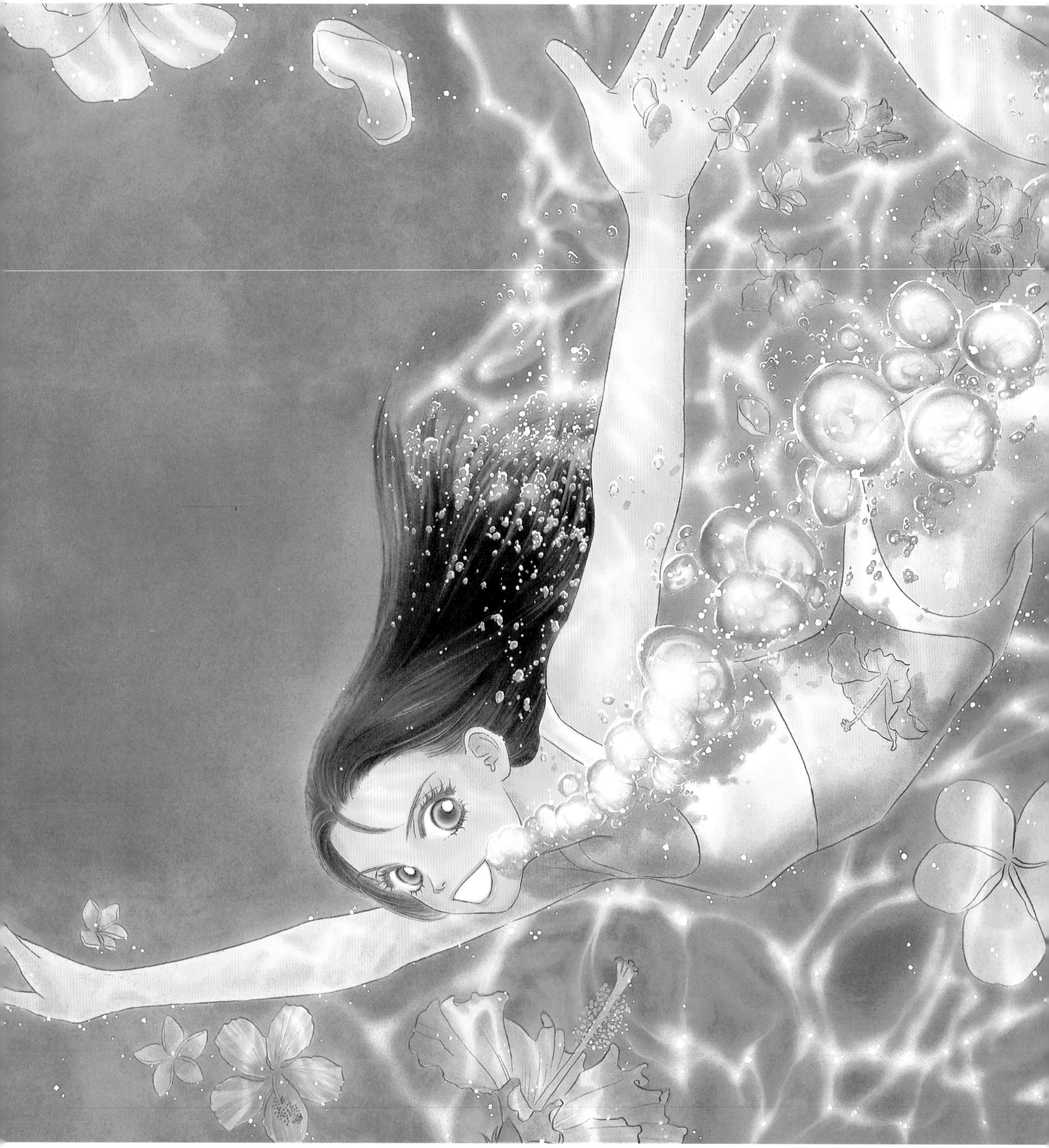

別冊フレンド1998年6月号「ピーチガール」見開き扉用イラスト［381×564mm］

別冊フレンド1997年9月号「ピーチガール」連載開始予告用イラスト[269×211mm]

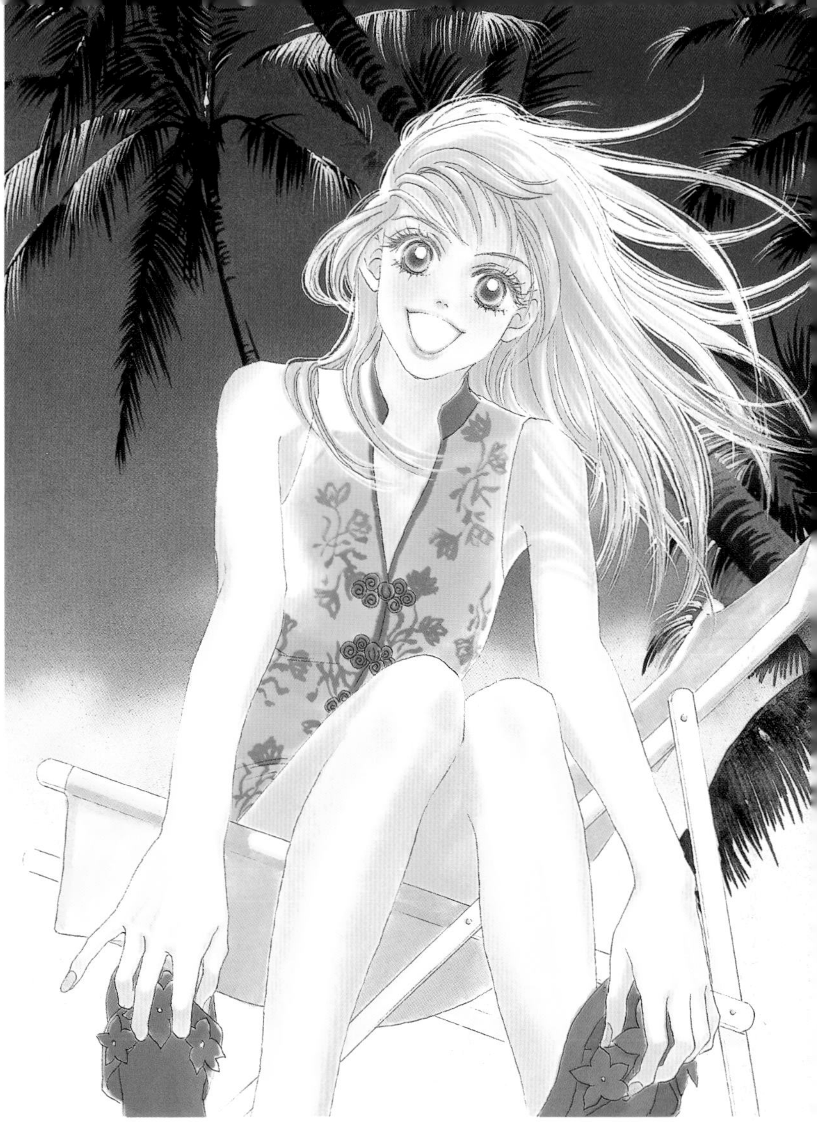

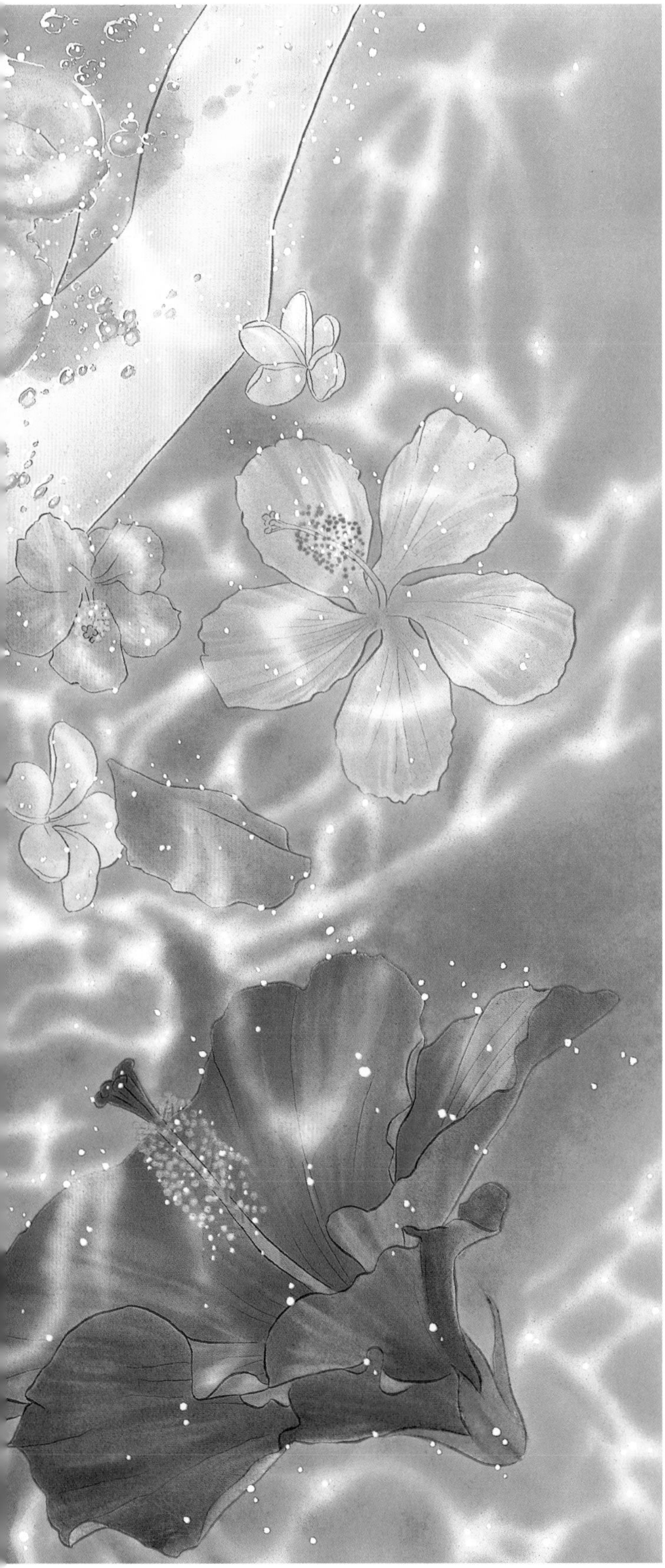

別冊フレンド1997年9月号「ピーチガール」BFオリジナルテレホンカードプレゼント用イラスト[213×168mm]

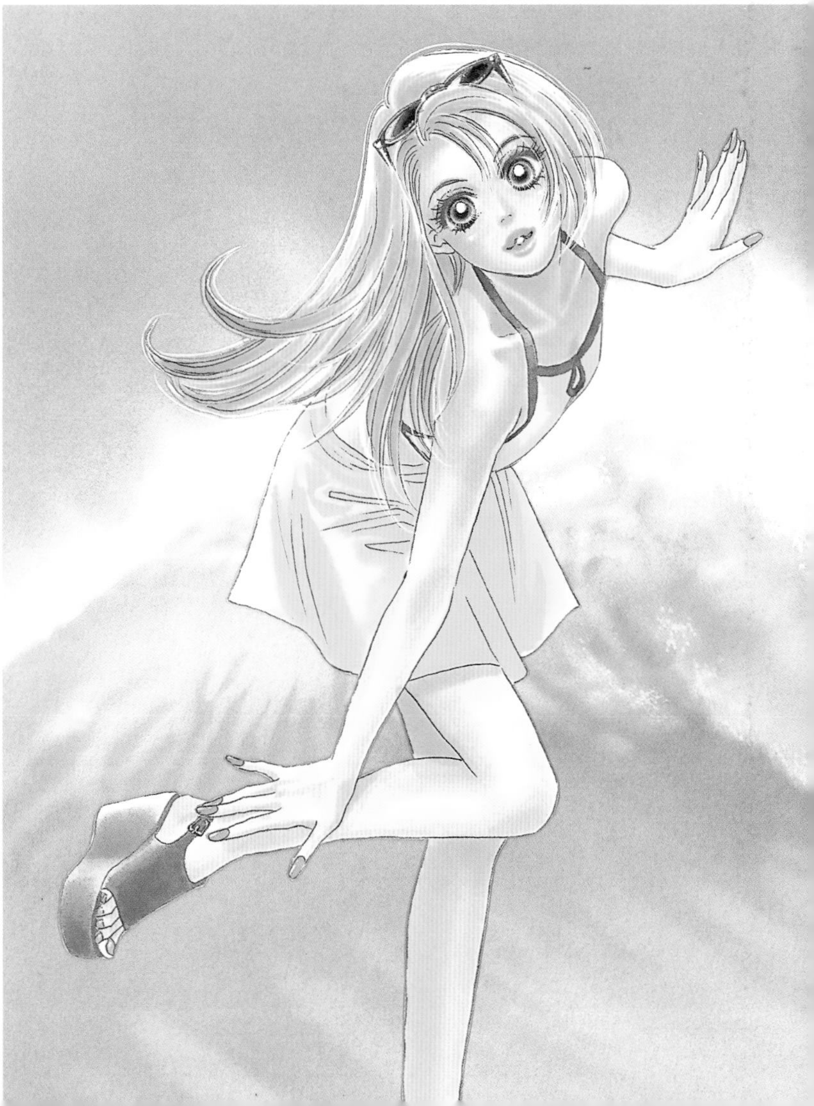

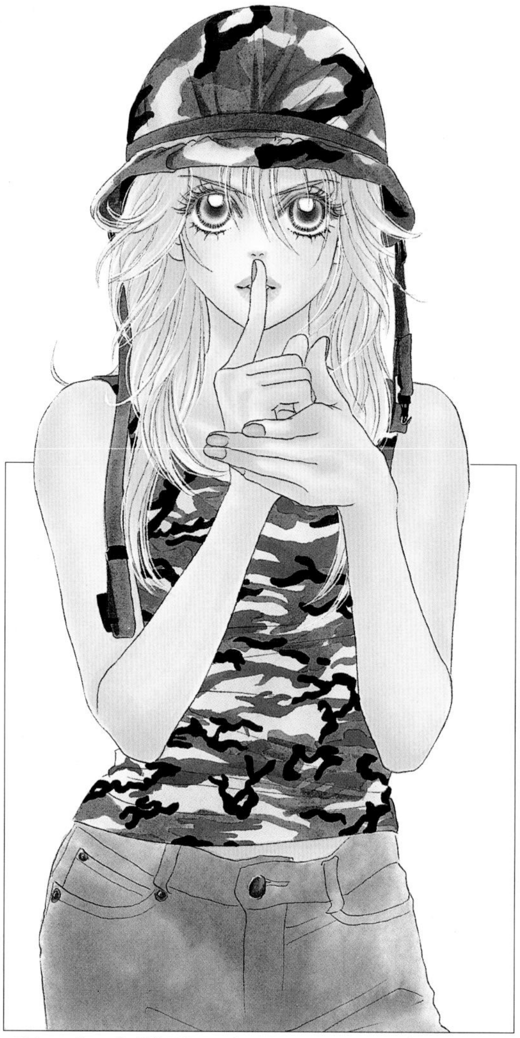

別冊フレンド1998年8月号 別冊フレンドロゴ変更告知カット用イラスト[257×112mm]

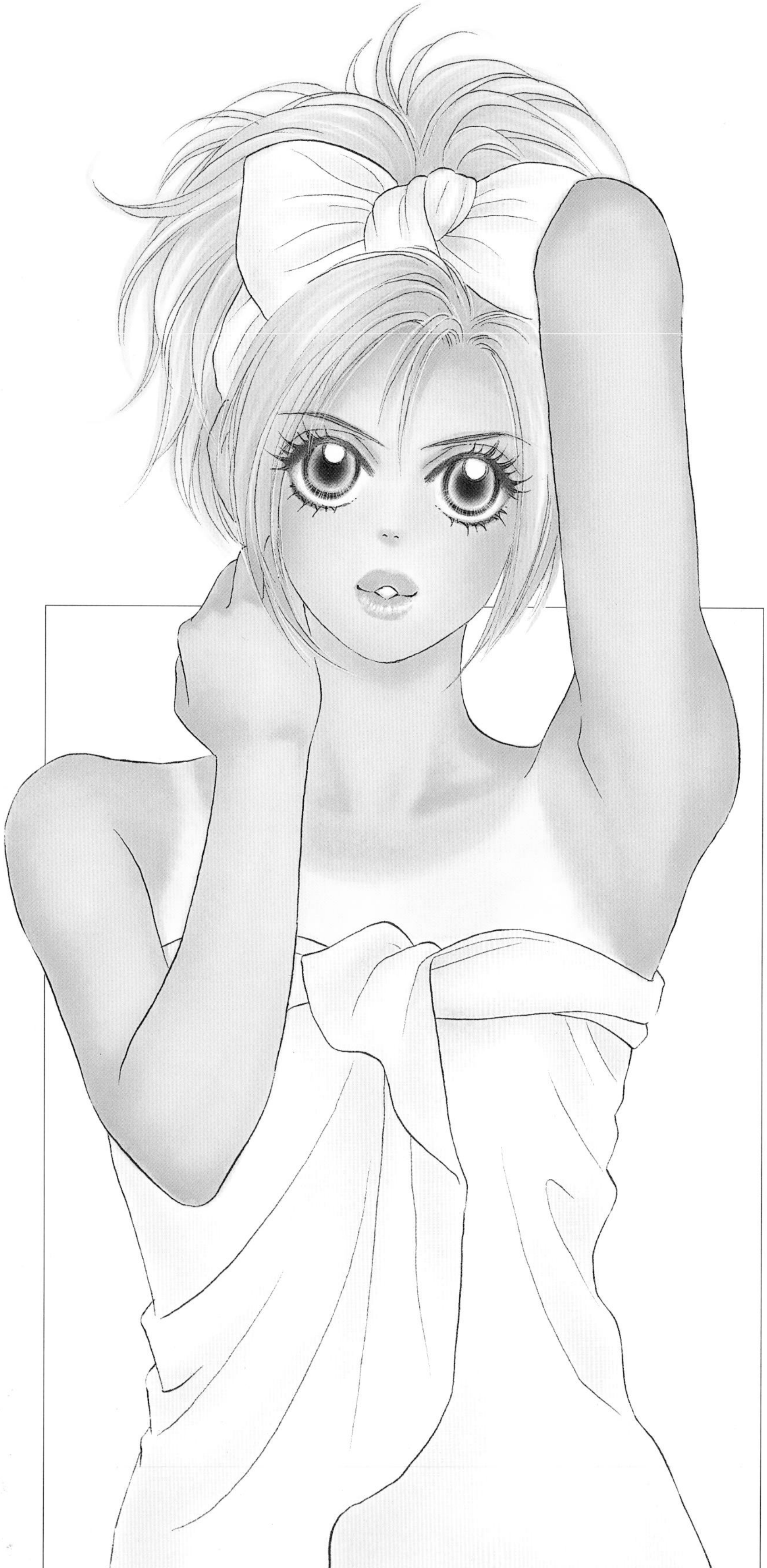

別冊フレンド1998年10月号「ピーチガール」表紙用イラスト[337×159mm]

Girl

# Peach

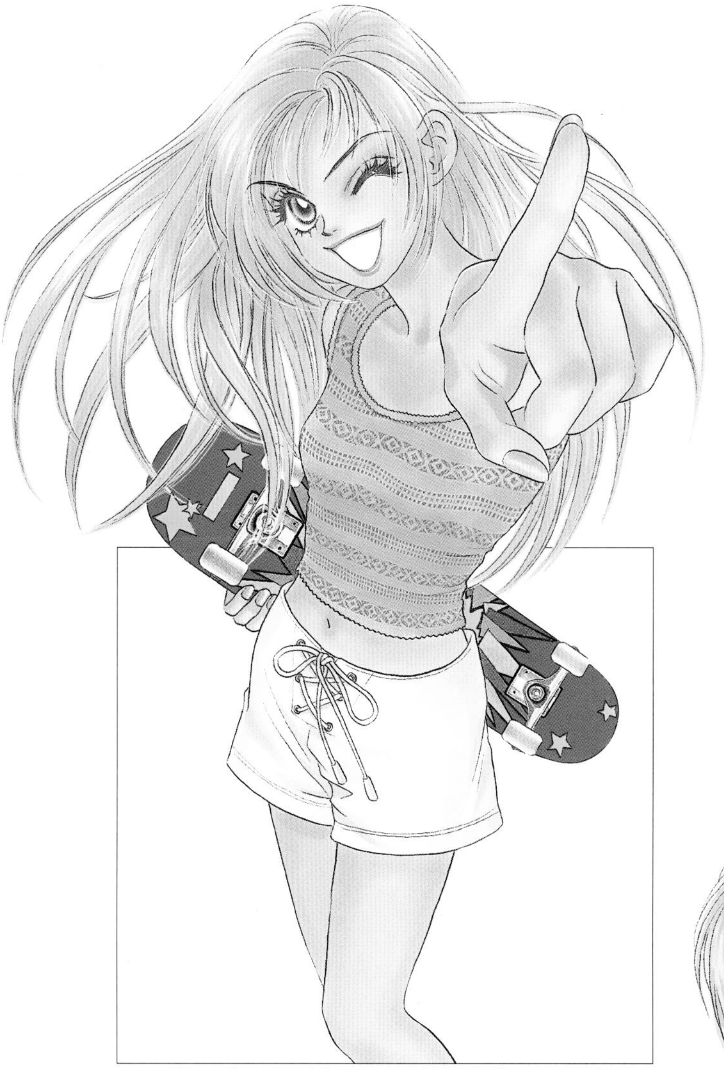

別冊フレンド1998年9月号「ピーチガール」表紙用イラスト［356×231mm］

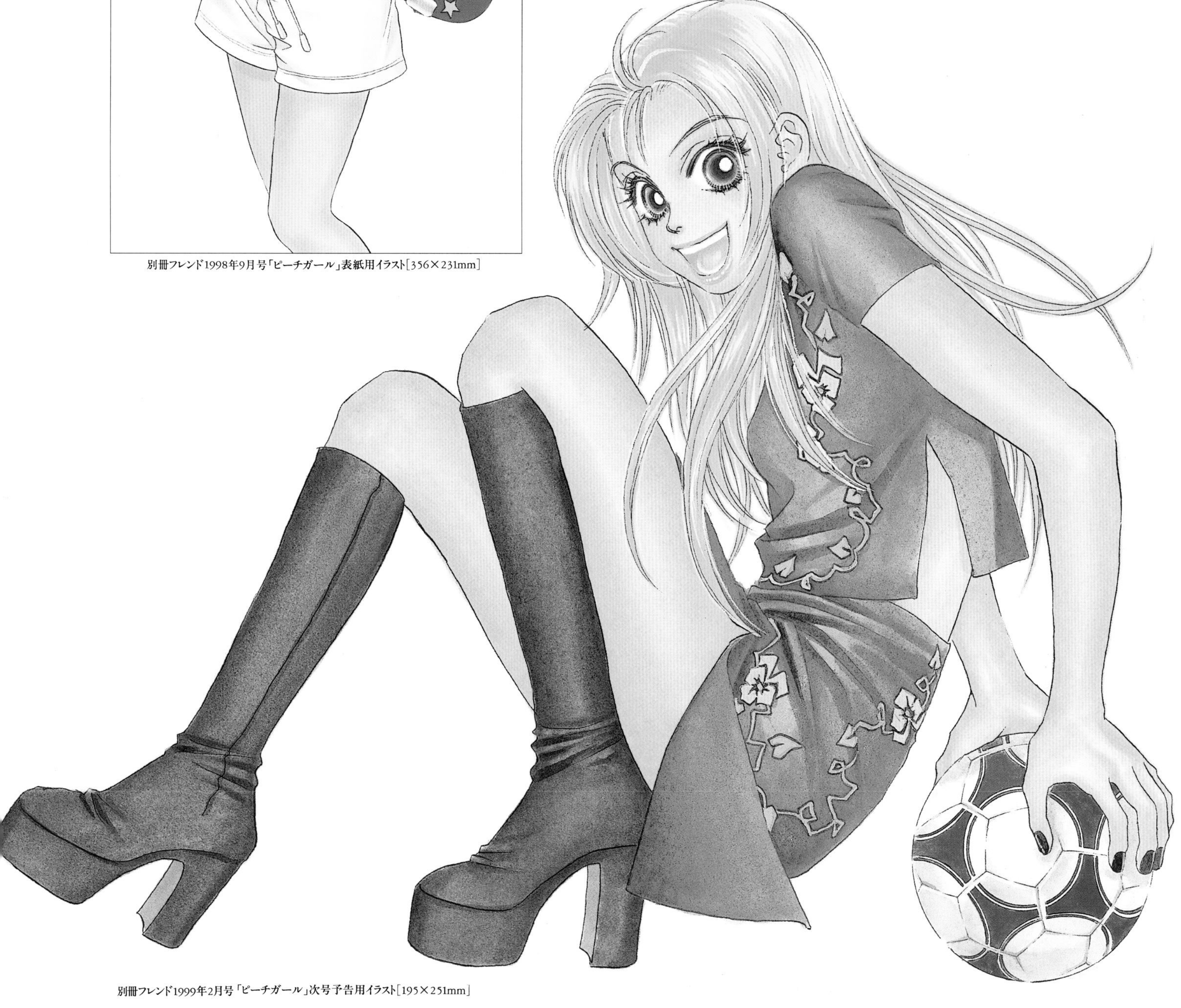

別冊フレンド1999年2月号「ピーチガール」次号予告用イラスト［195×251mm］

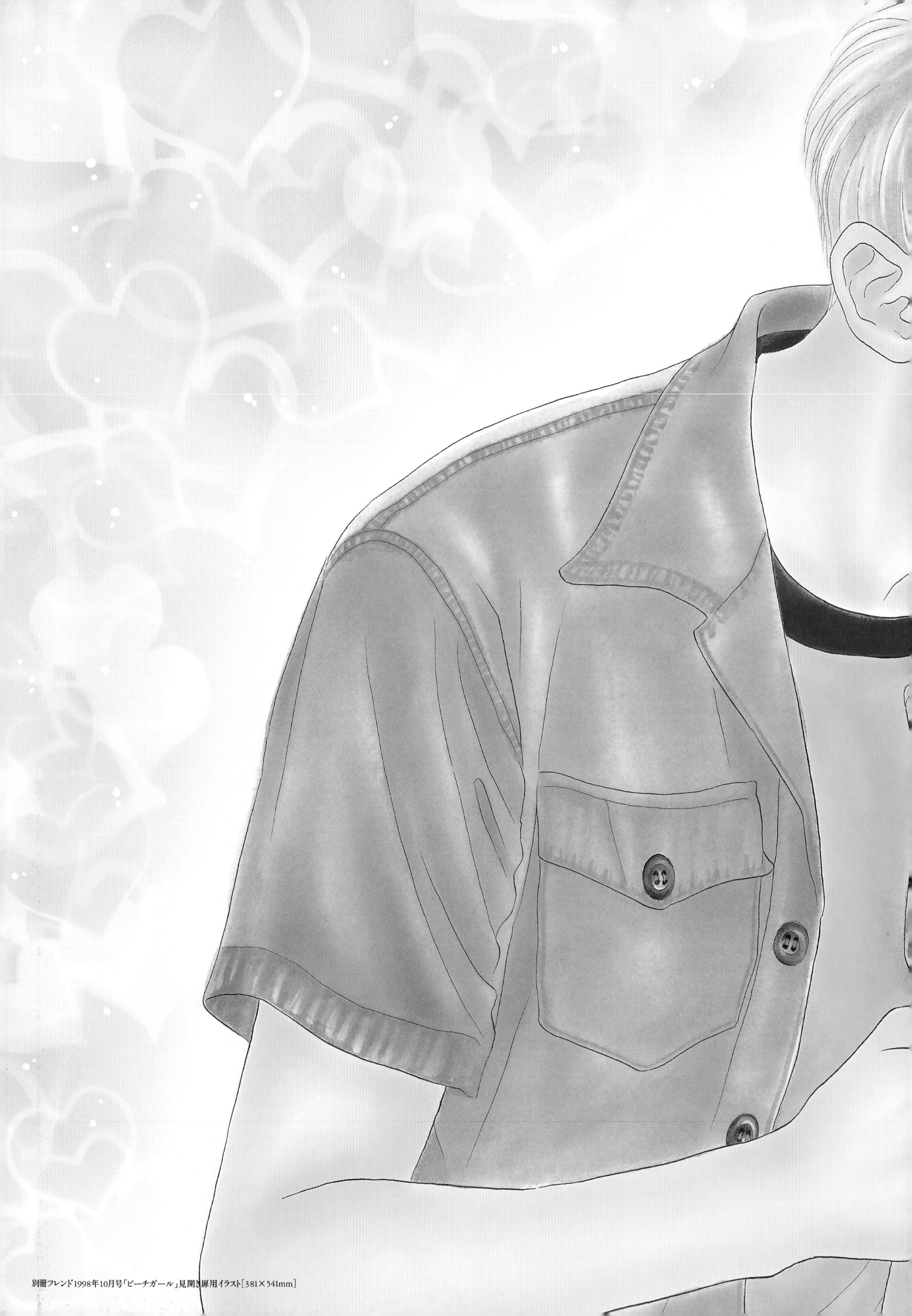

別冊フレンド1998年10月号「ピーチガール」見開き扉用イラスト［381×541mm］

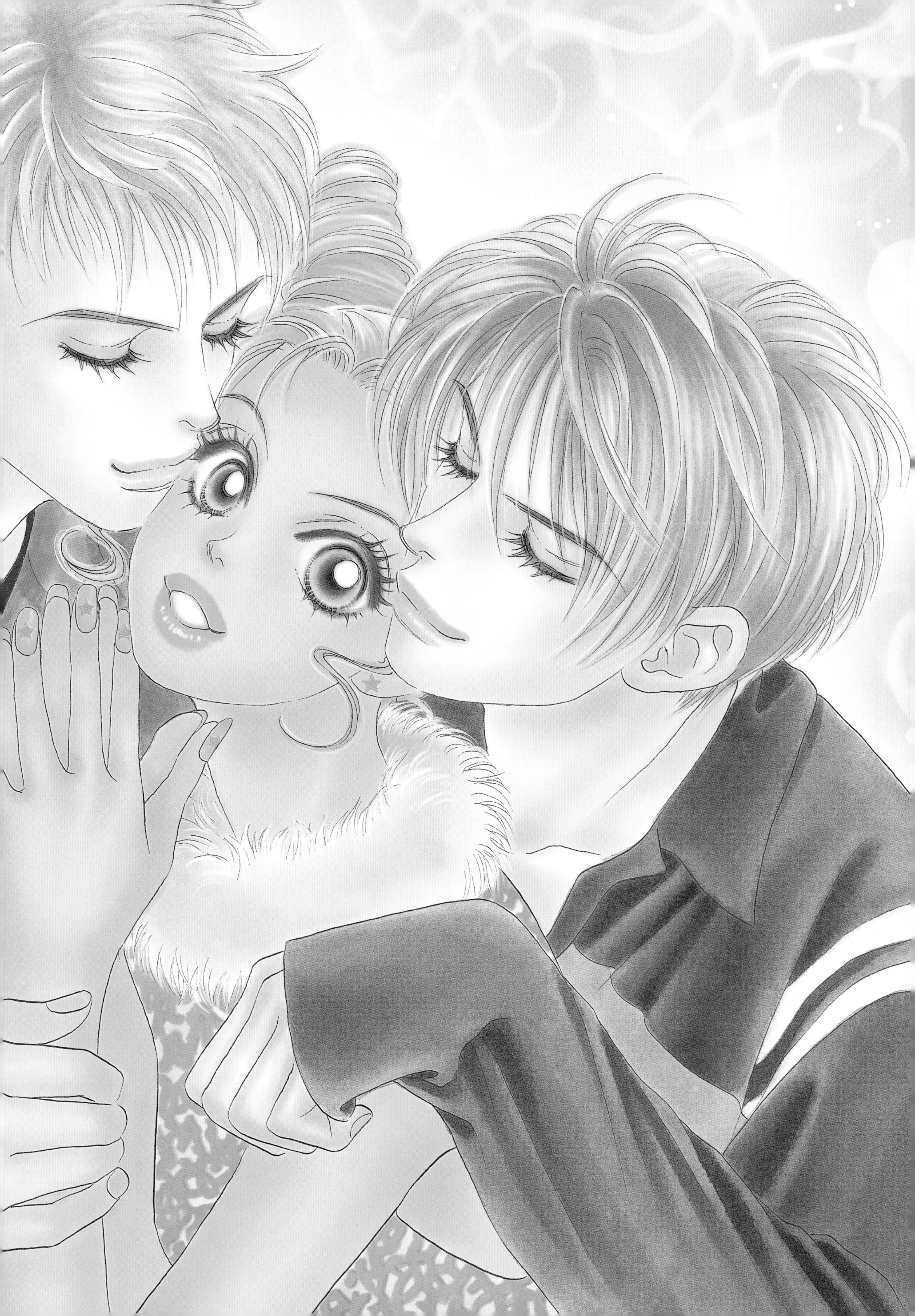

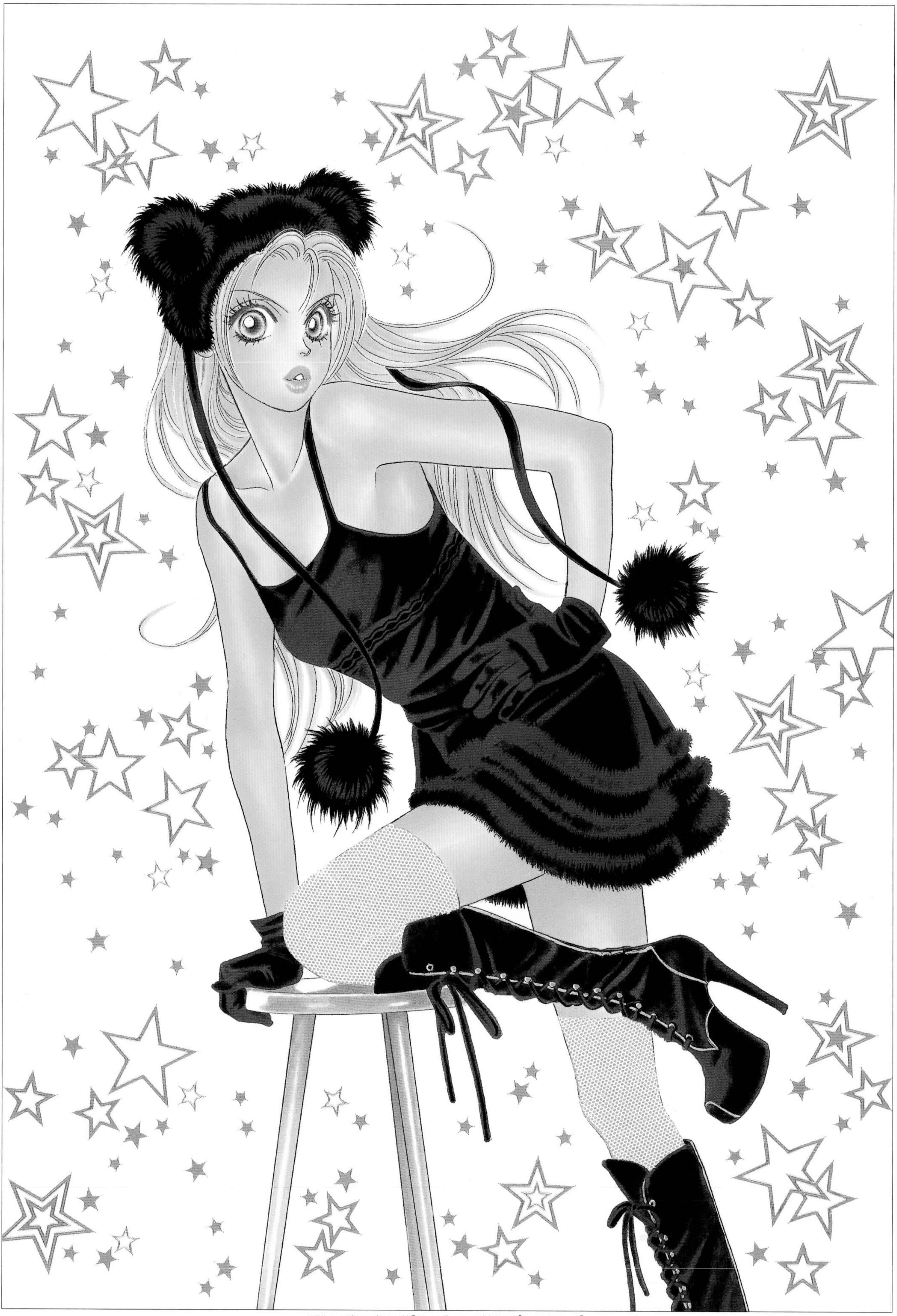

別冊フレンド1998年11月号「ピーチガール」扉用イラスト［375×272mm］



別冊フレンド1998年12月号「ピーチガール」表紙用イラスト［363×254mm］

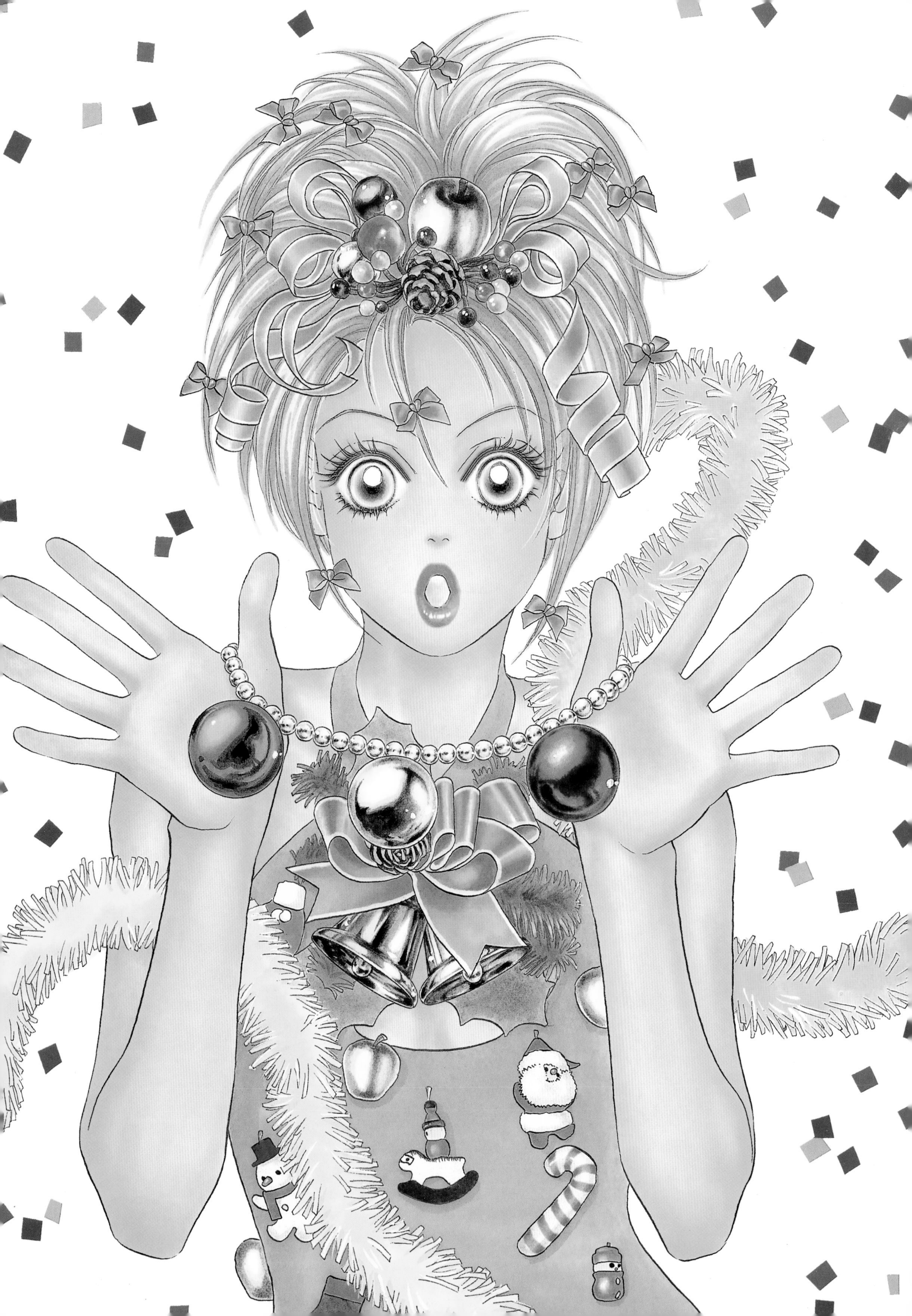

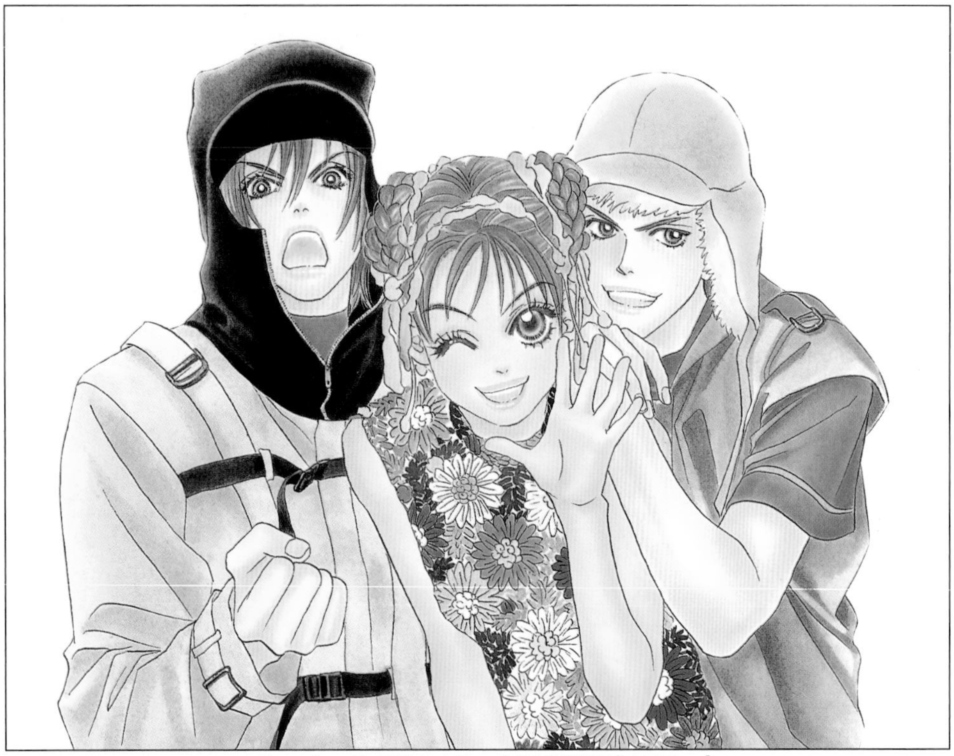

別冊フレンド1998年12月号「ピーチガール」次号予告用イラスト[153×180mm]

1999年4月「ピーチガール」ファンレター返信用ポストカード用イラスト[172×123mm]

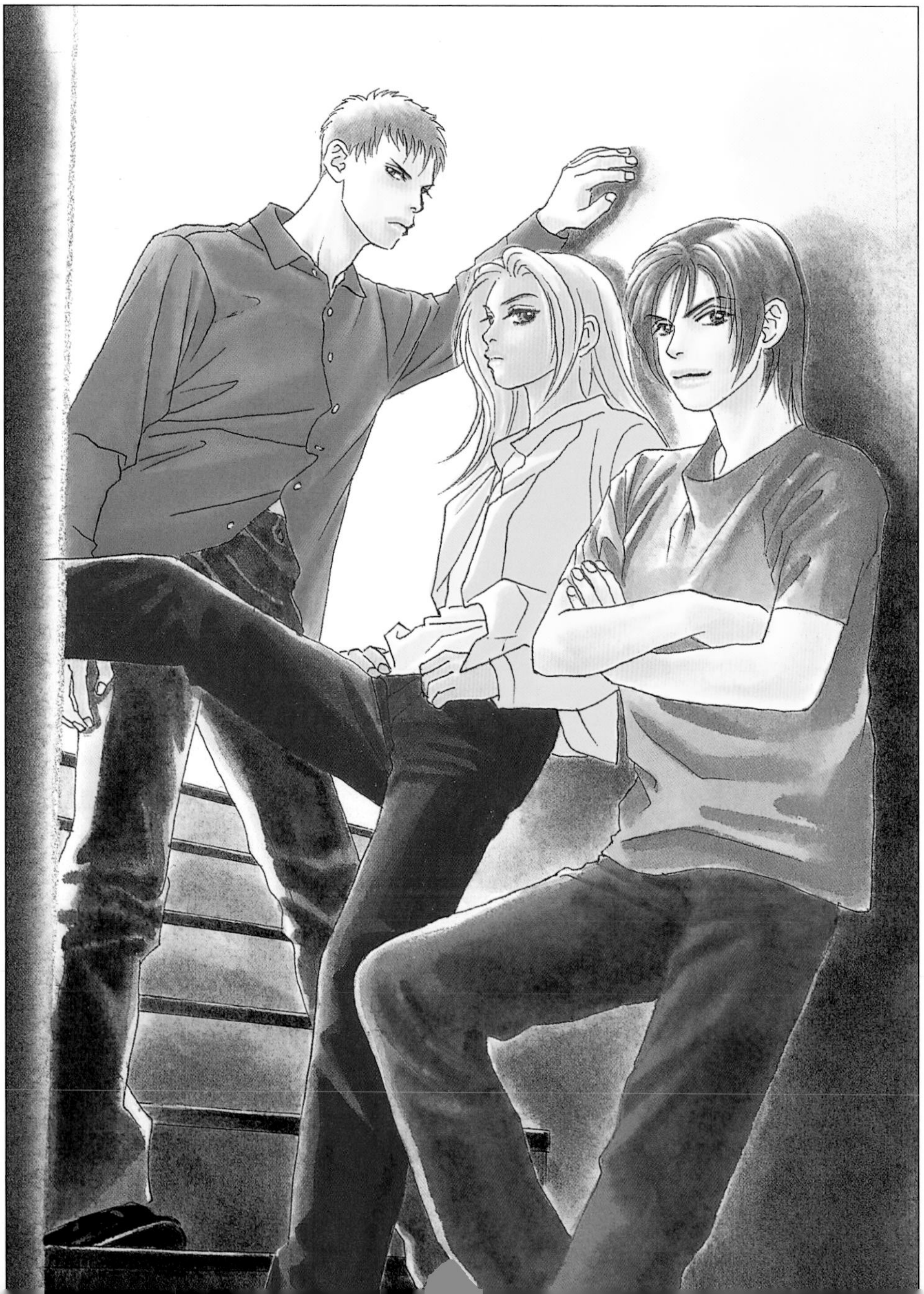

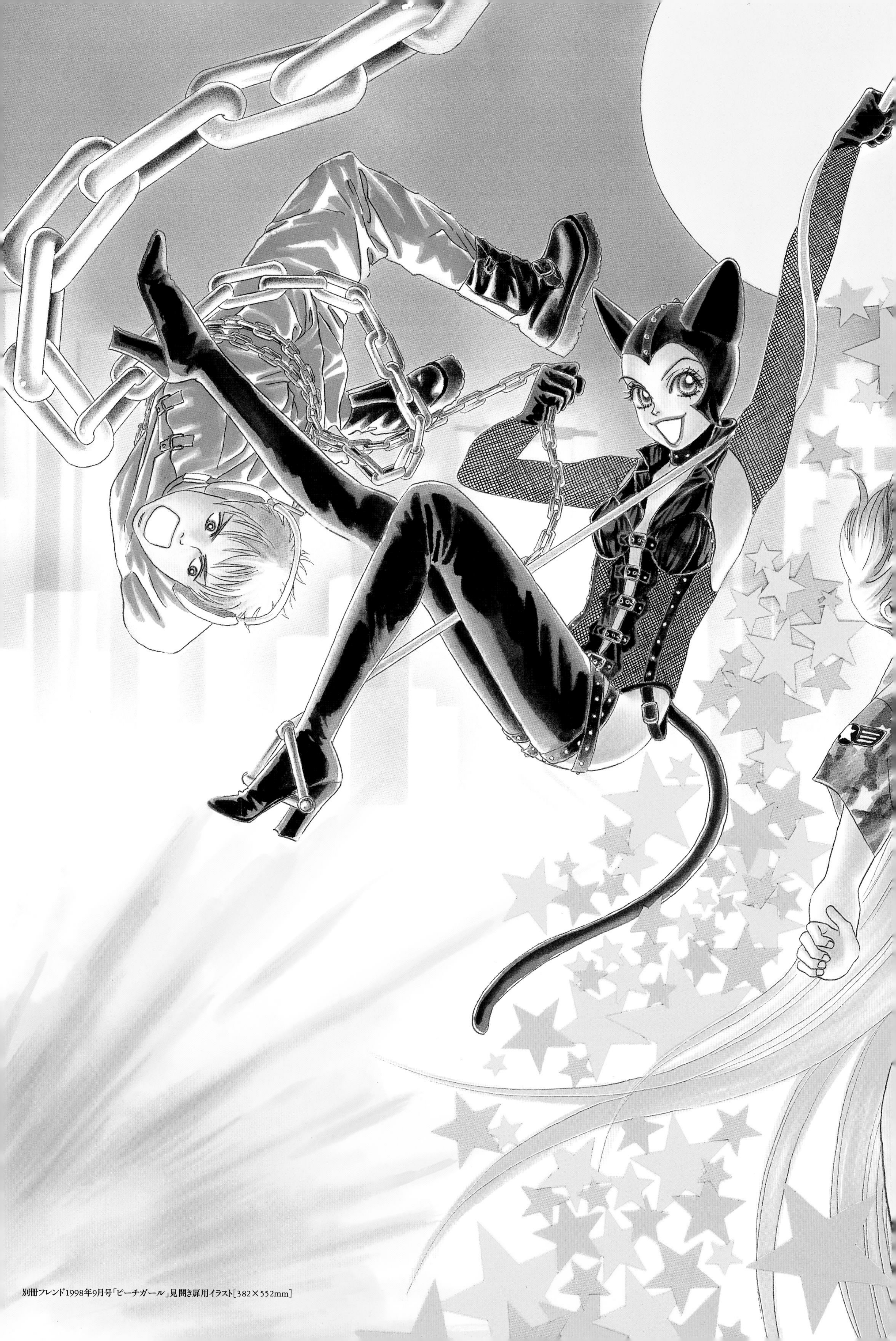

別冊フレンド1998年9月号「ピーチガール」見開き扉用イラスト[382×552mm]

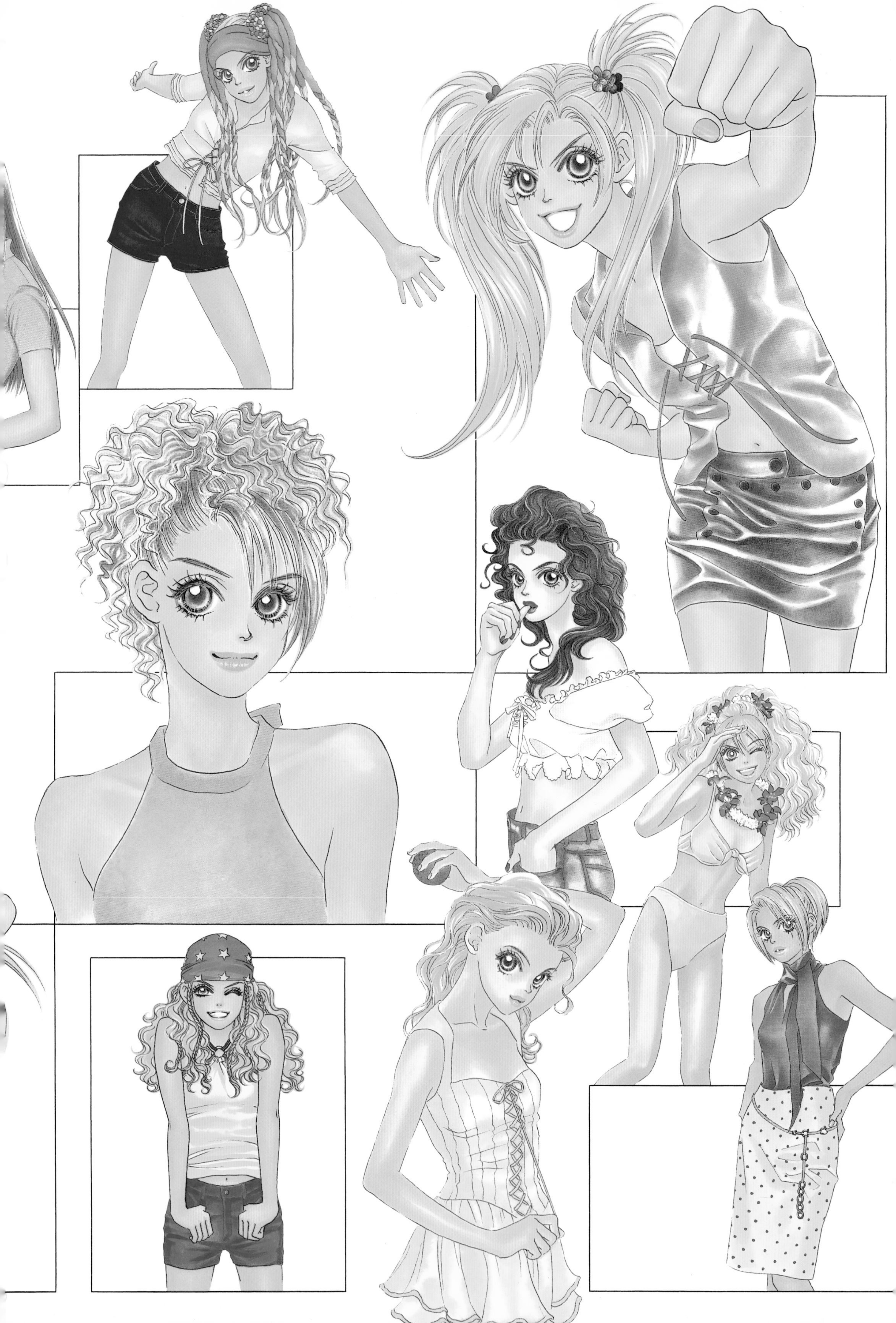

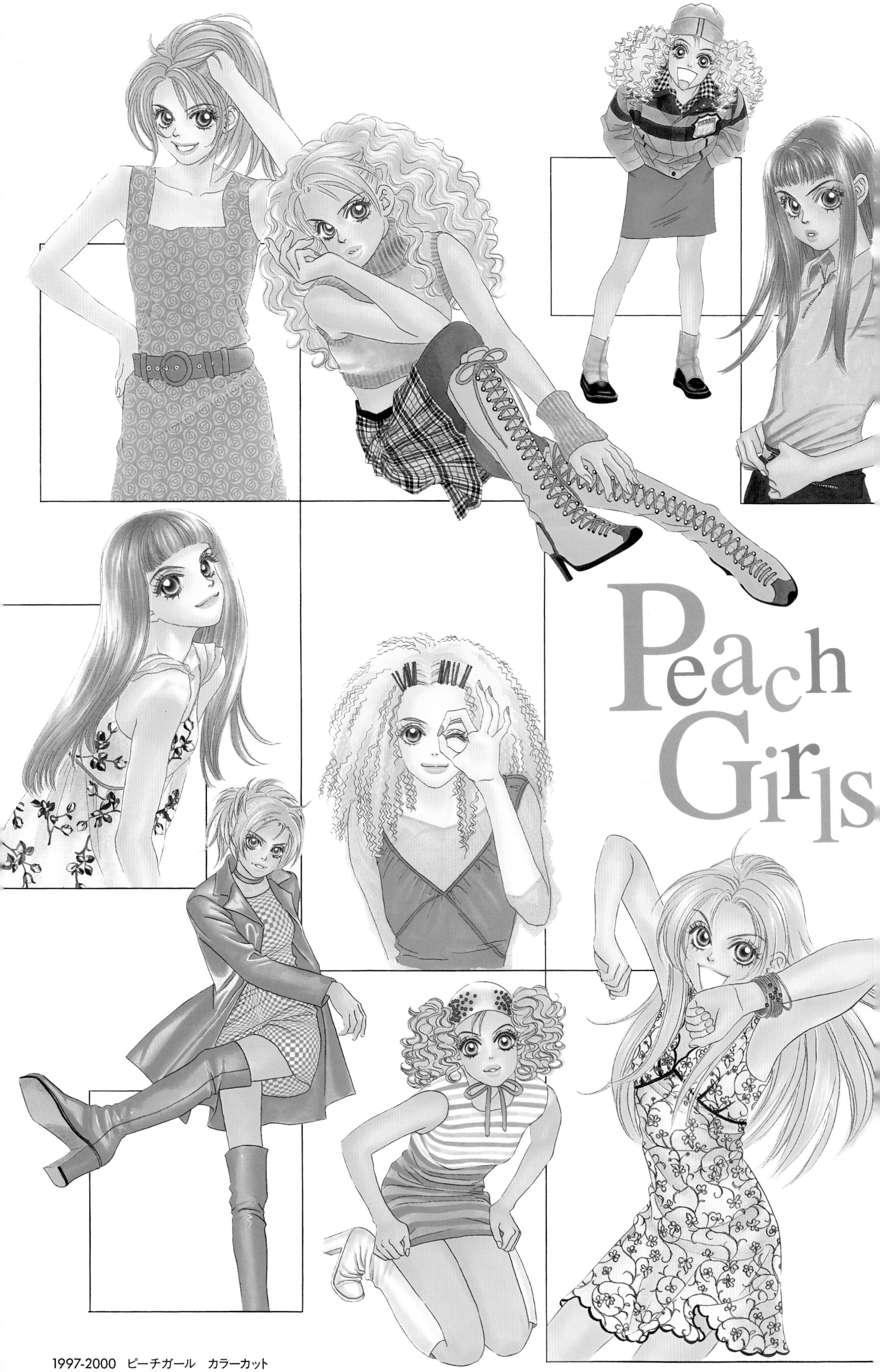
Peach Girls

1997-2000 ピーチガール カラーカット

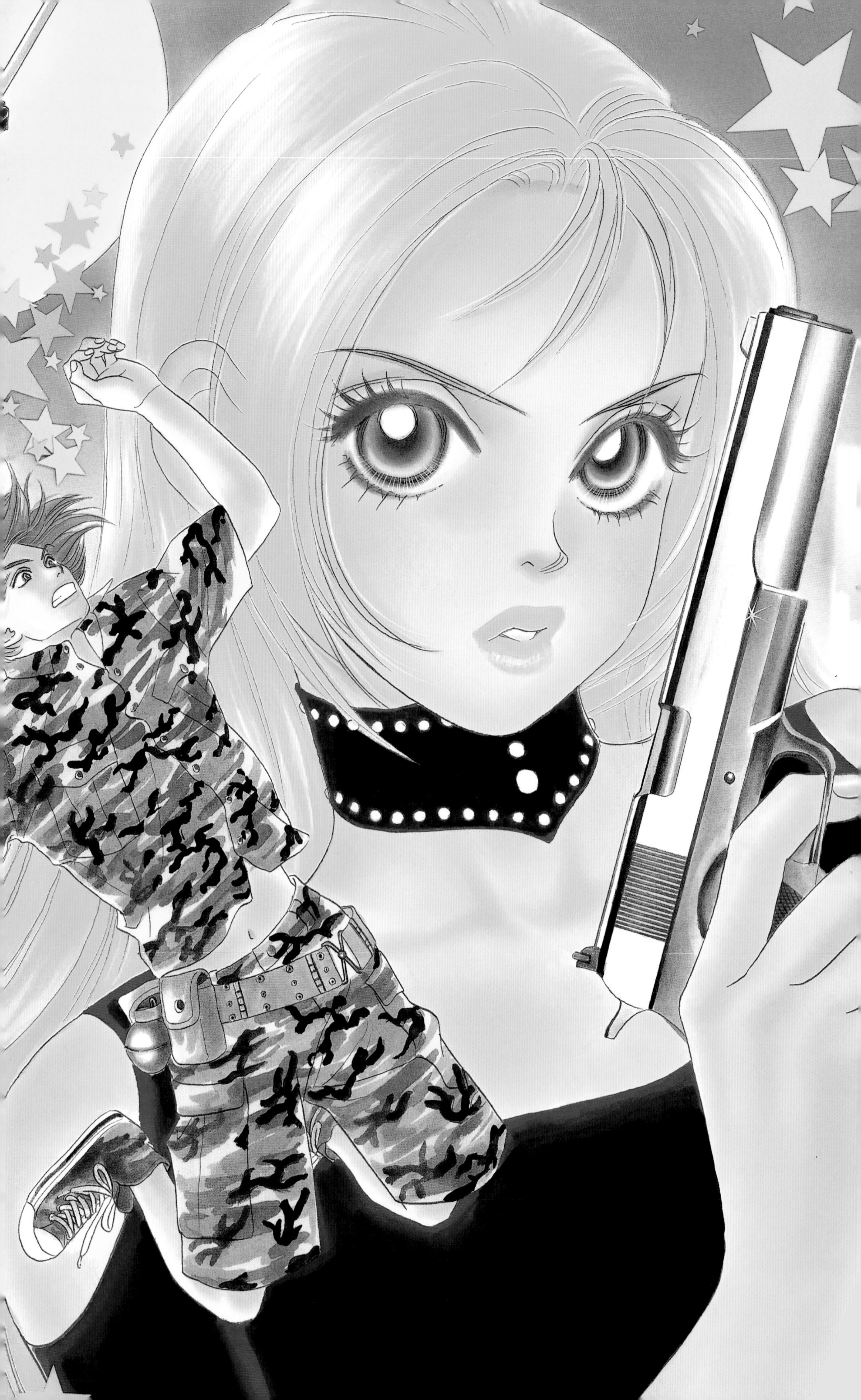

# PEACH GIRL
# 1999 works
## January～December

「ピーチガール」別冊フレンド'99年掲載のイラストを集めました。

別冊フレンド1998年8月号「ピーチガール」次号予告用イラスト[227×183mm]

♥ Everyone knows Momo and Toji are together,
but Sae tries to break them up while they fall head
over heels for each other. With Kiley and model Gigolo
in the picture, the love triangle never ends!

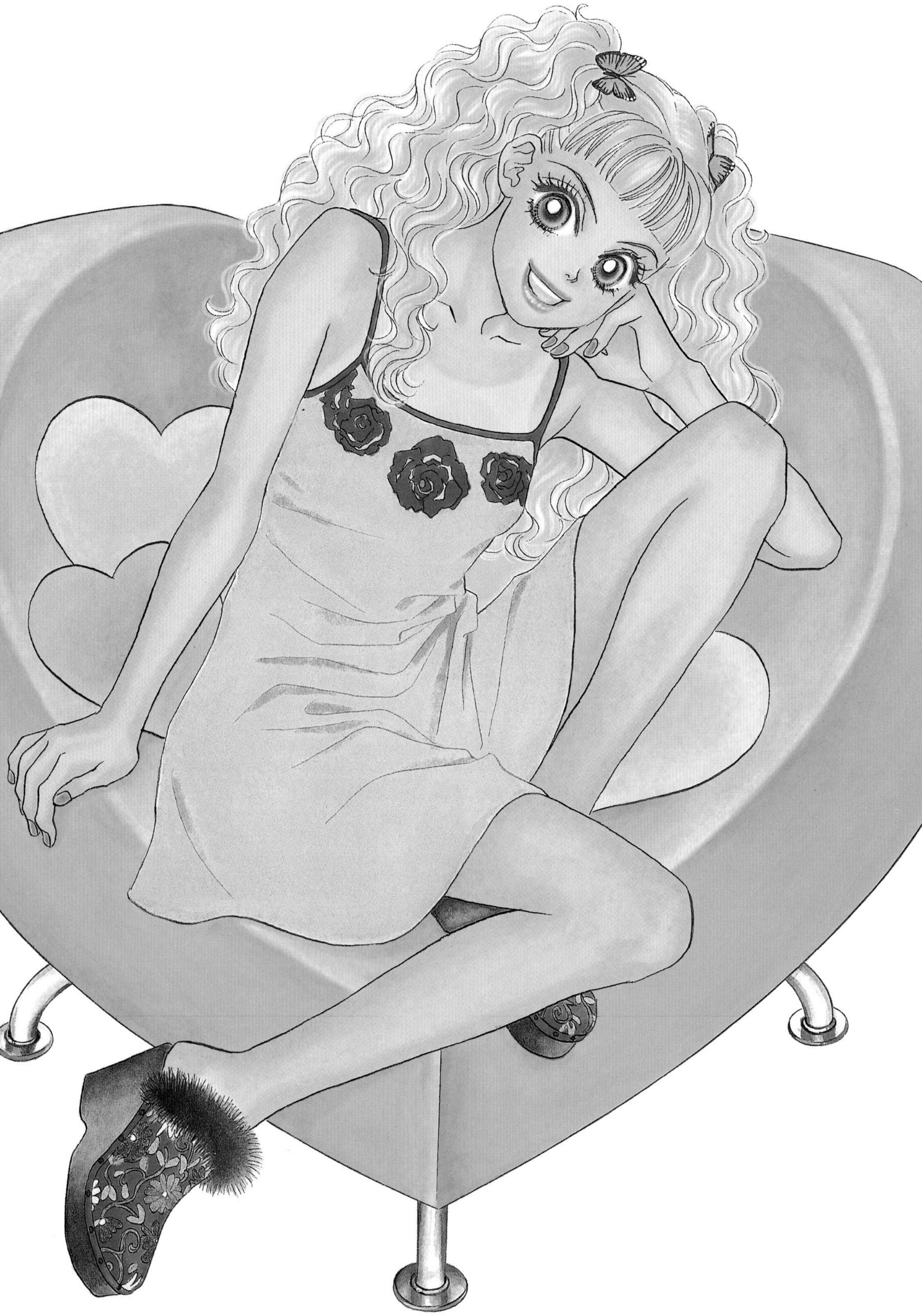

別冊フレンド1999年2月号「ピーチガール」表紙用イラスト［257×241mm］

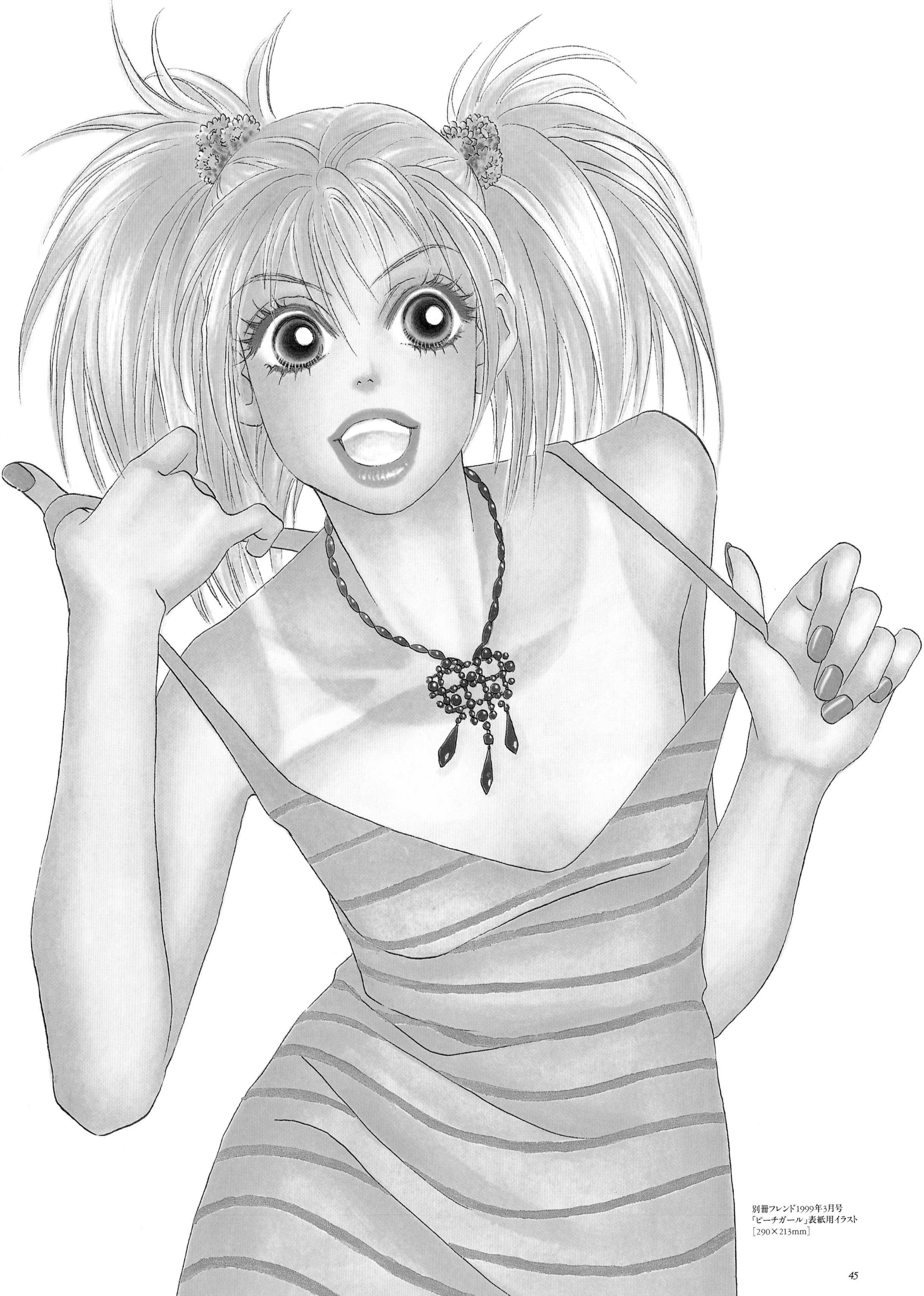

別冊フレンド1999年3月号
「ピーチガール」表紙用イラスト
［290×213mm］

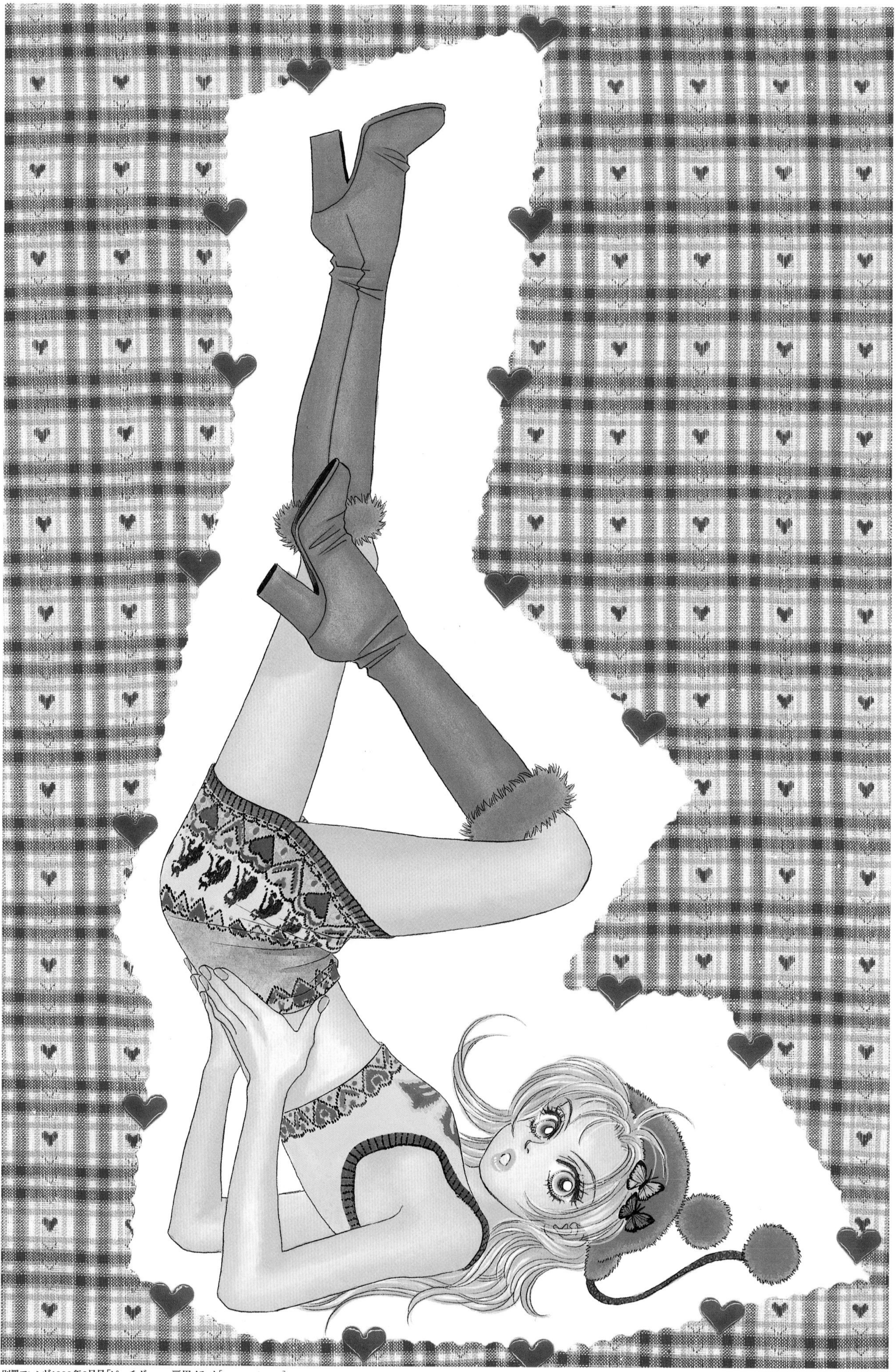

別冊フレンド1999年2月号「ピーチガール」扉用イラスト[380×265mm]



別冊フレンド1999年7月号「ピーチガール」表紙用イラスト[327×233mm]

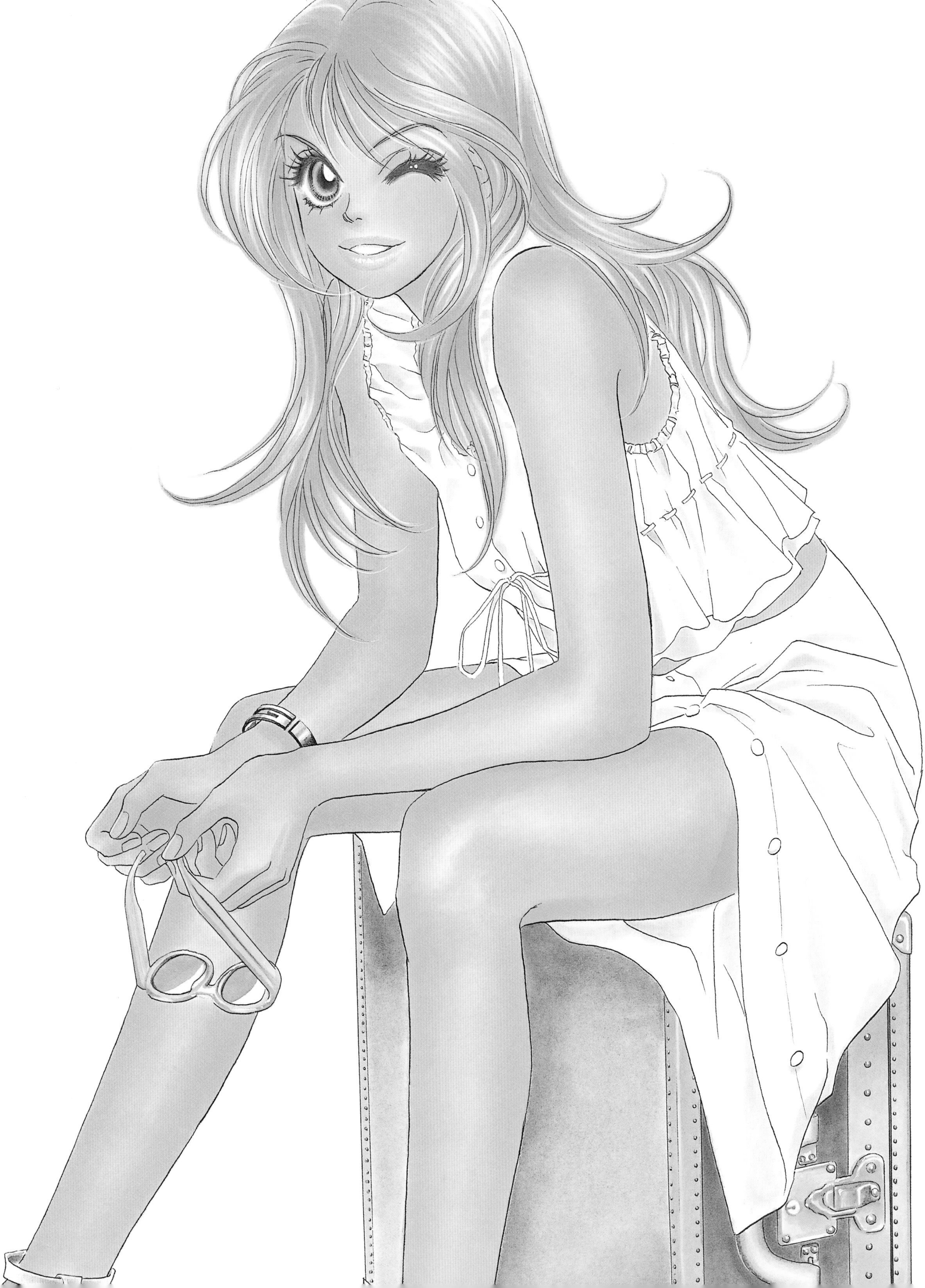

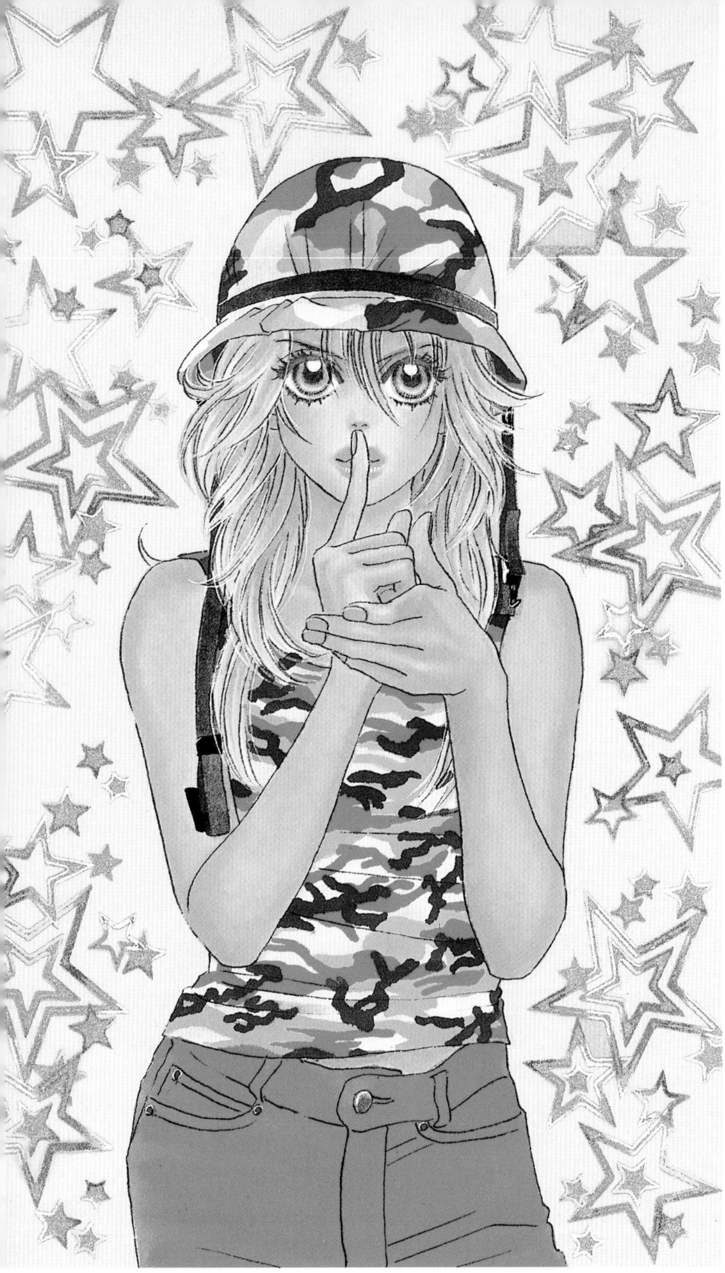

1999年4月「ピーチガール」ファンレター返信用ポストカード用イラスト［181×117mm］

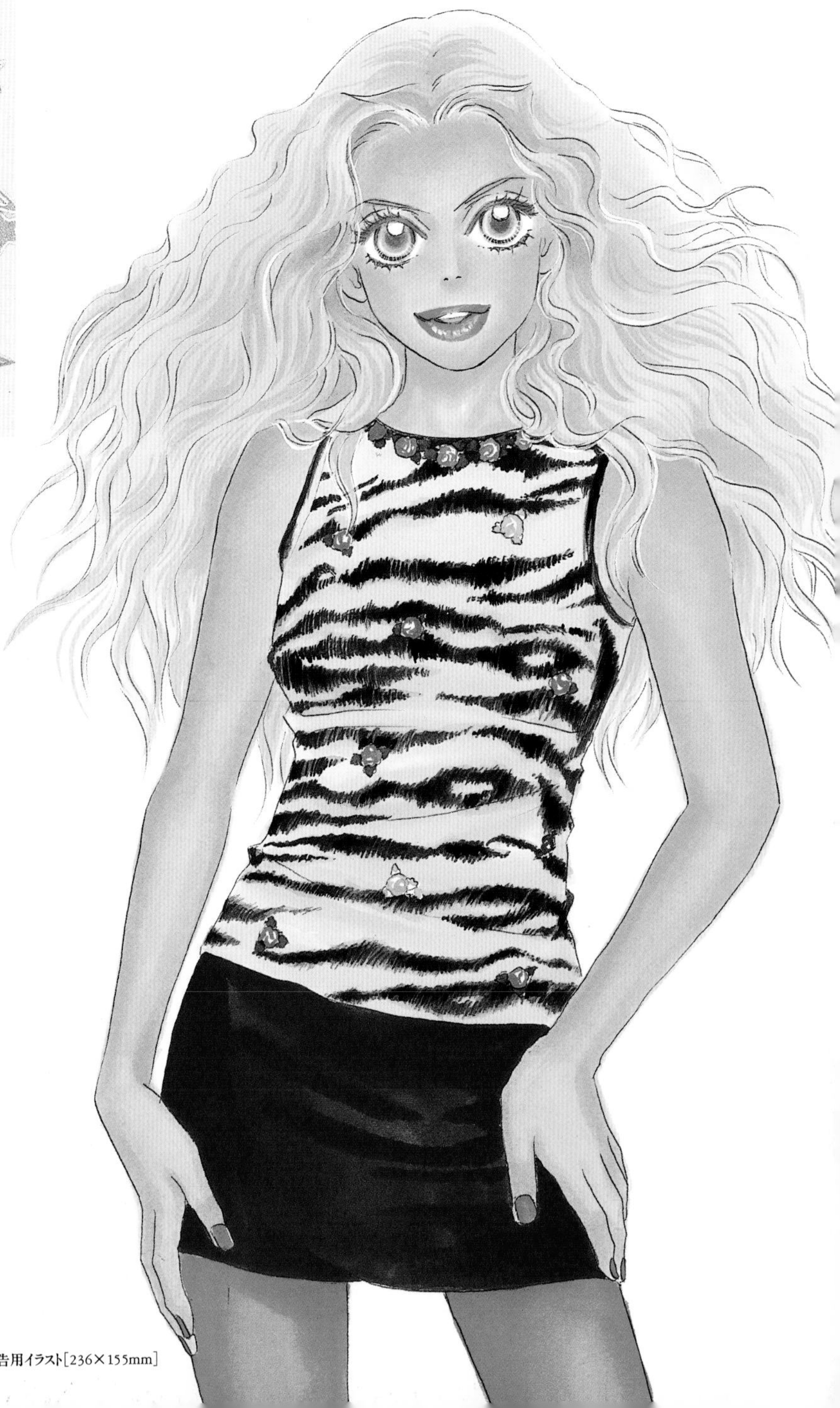

別冊フレンド2000年1月号「ピーチガール」次号予告用イラスト［236×155mm］

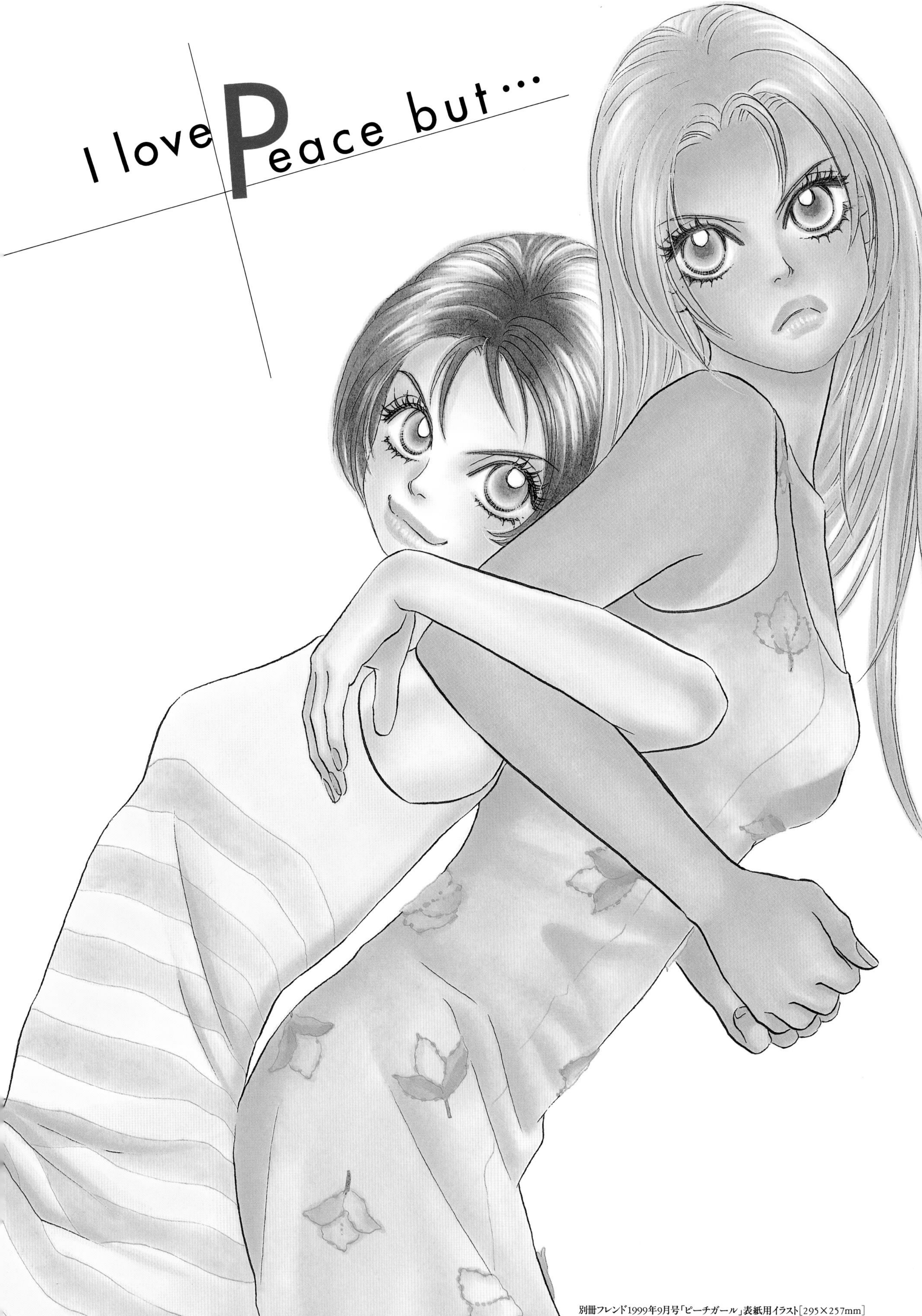
I love Peace but…

別冊フレンド1999年9月号「ピーチガール」表紙用イラスト［295×257mm］

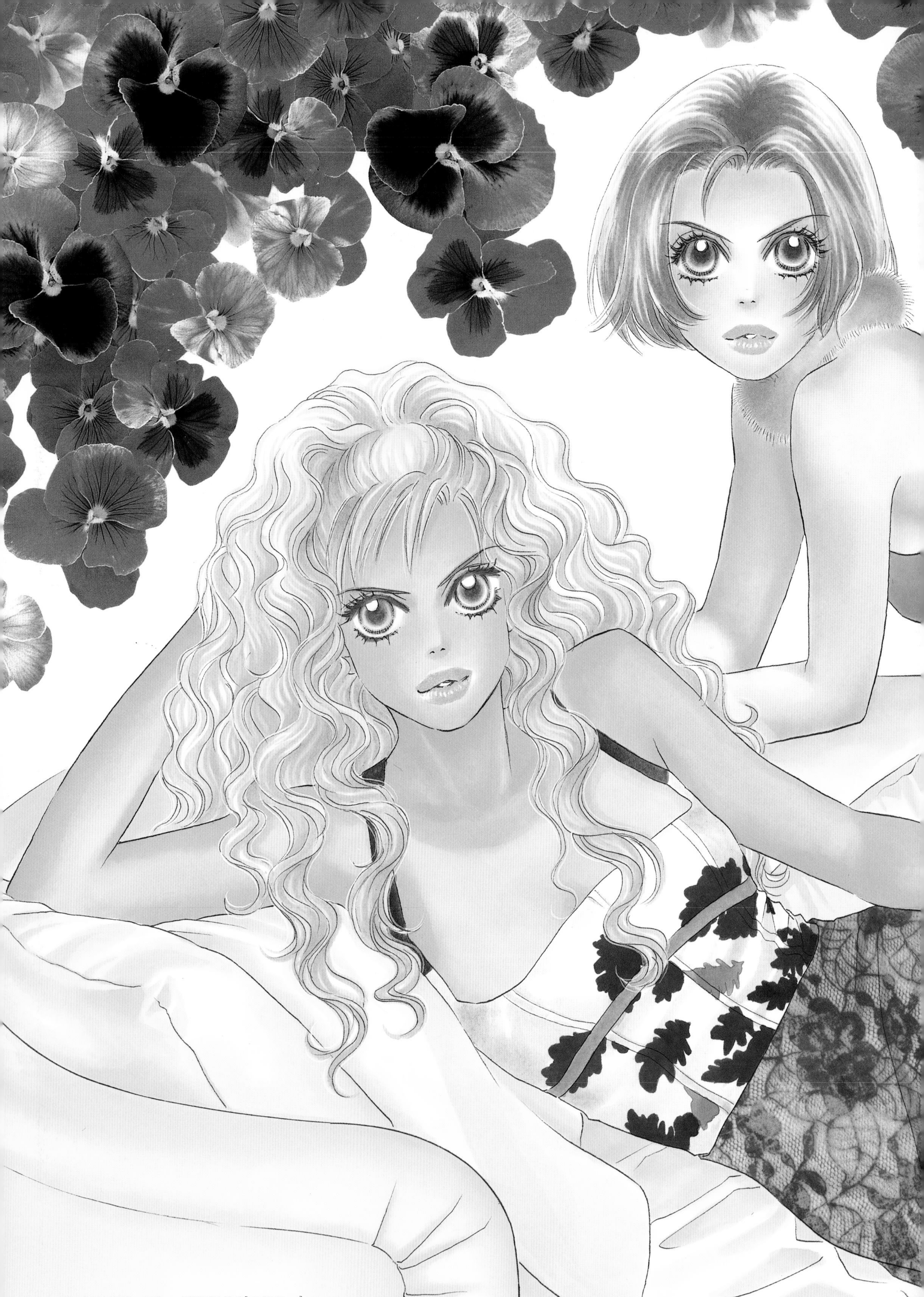

別冊フレンド1999年11月号「ピーチガール」見開き扉用イラスト[370×545mm]

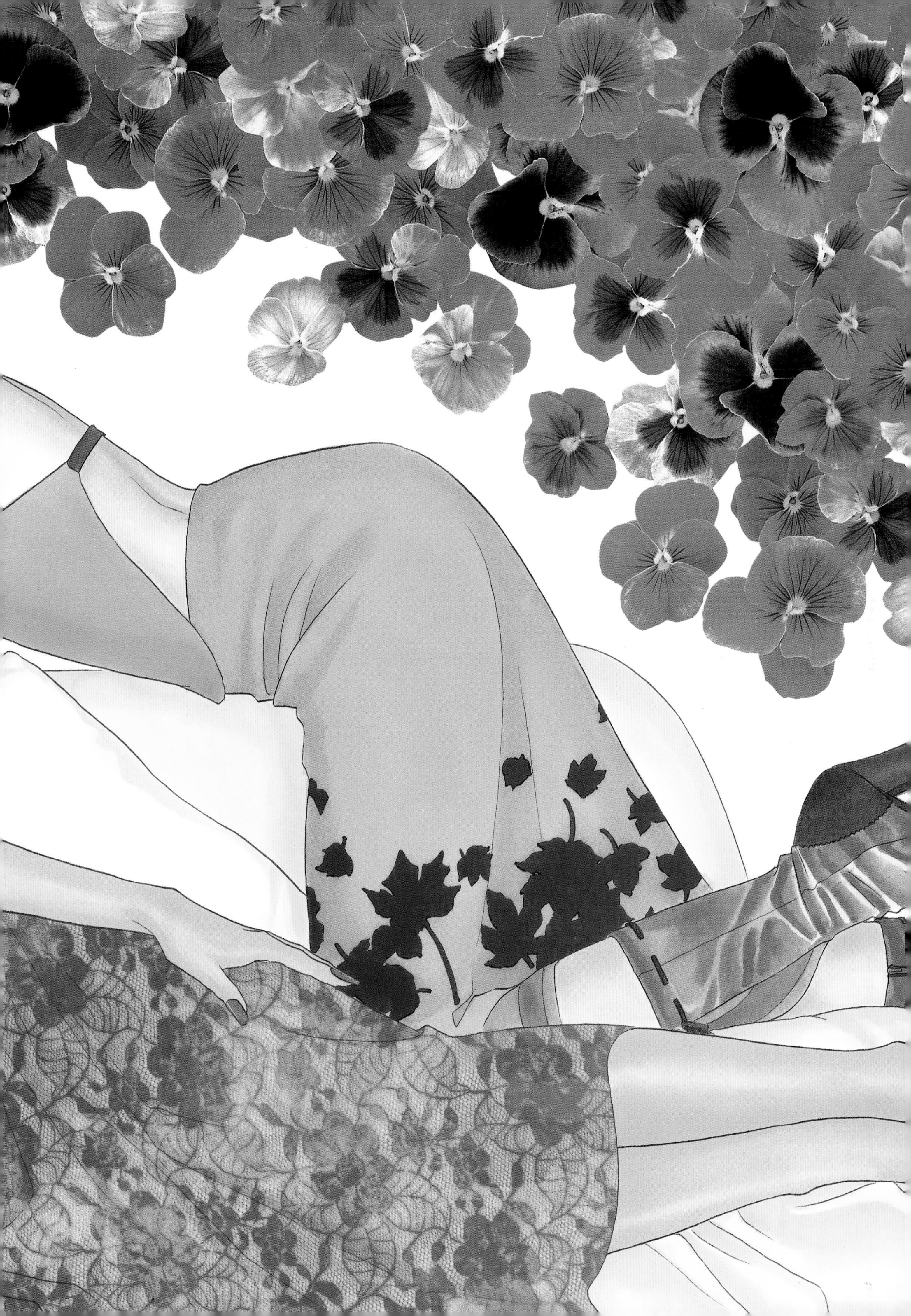

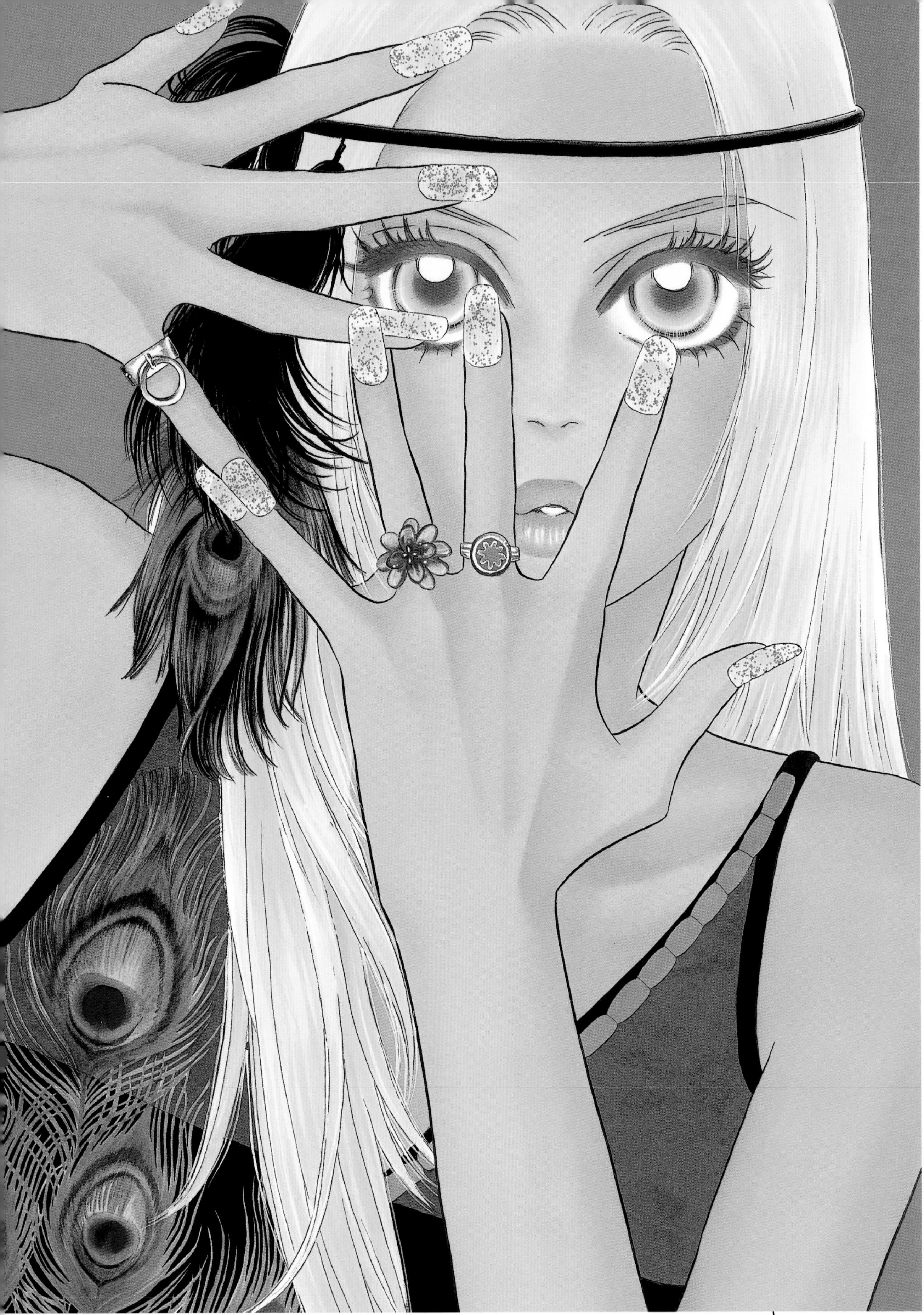

別冊フレンド1999年10月号「ピーチガール」扉用イラスト［365×263mm］

# POISON

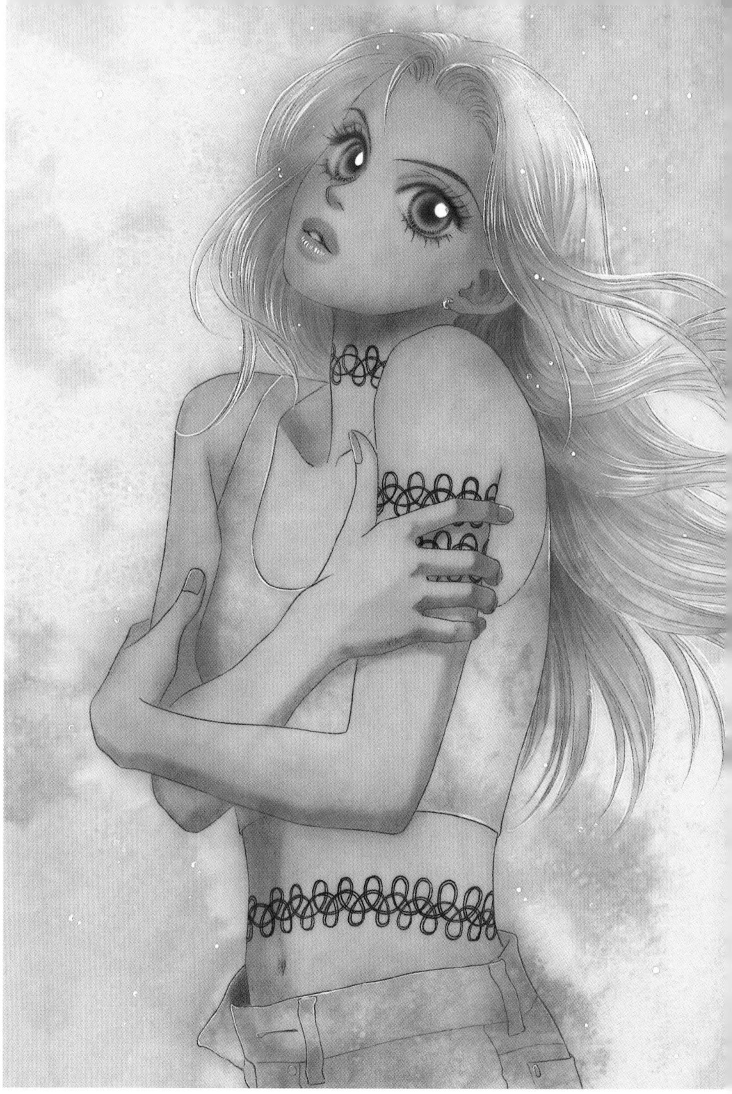

別冊フレンド1999年6月号「ピーチガール」扉用イラスト［367×276mm］

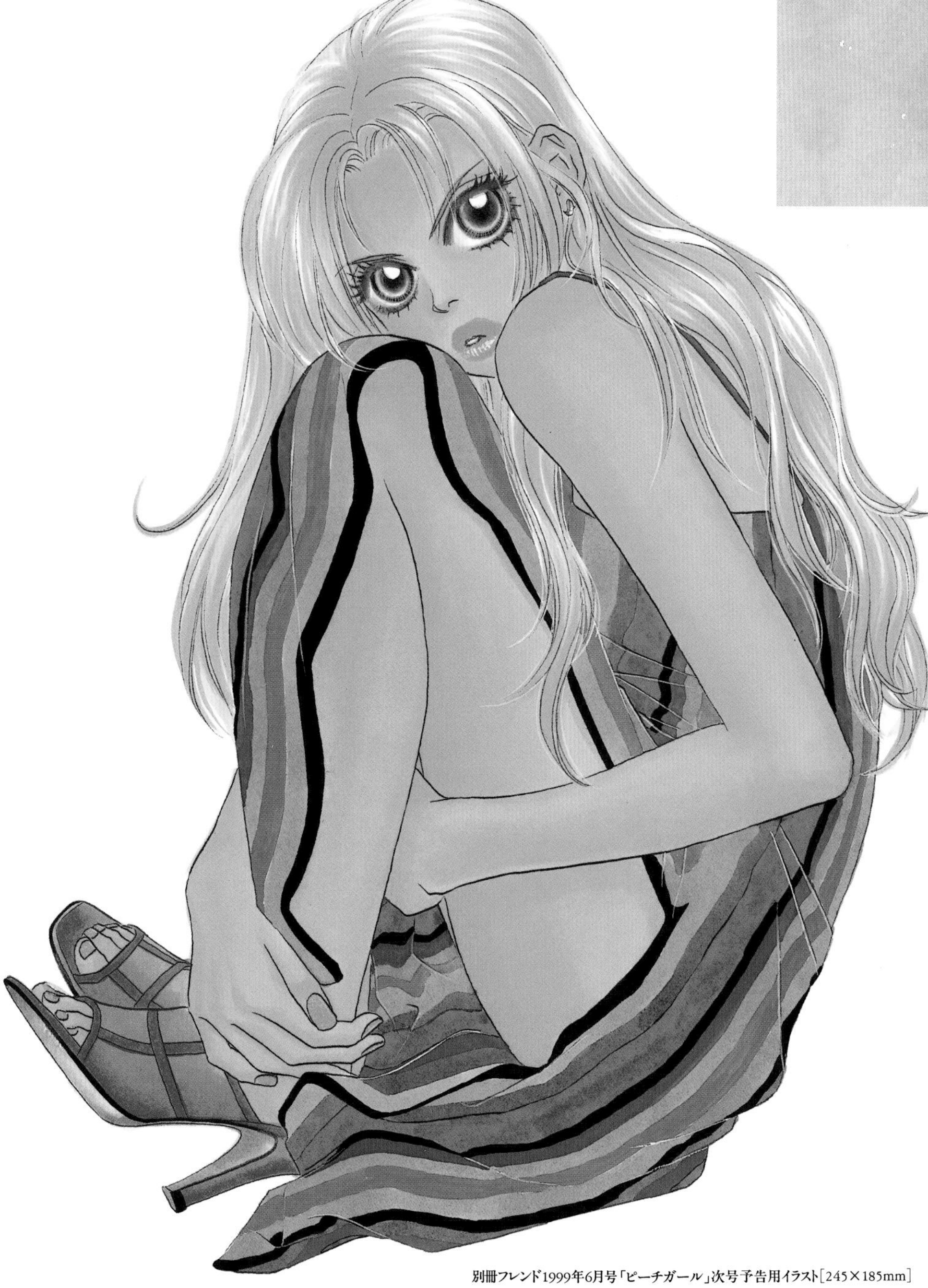

別冊フレンド1999年6月号「ピーチガール」次号予告用イラスト［245×185mm］

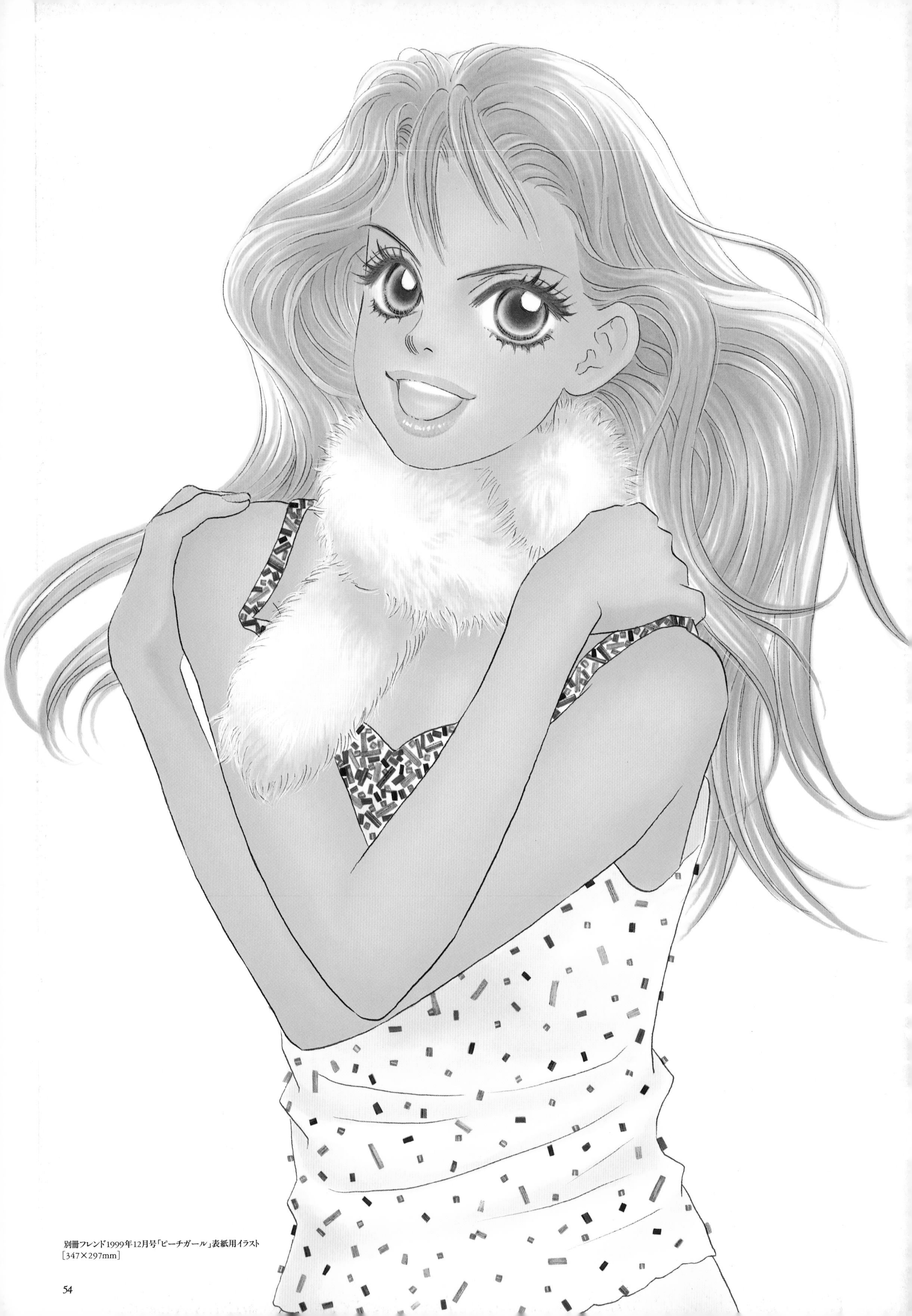

別冊フレンド1999年12月号「ピーチガール」表紙用イラスト
［347×297mm］

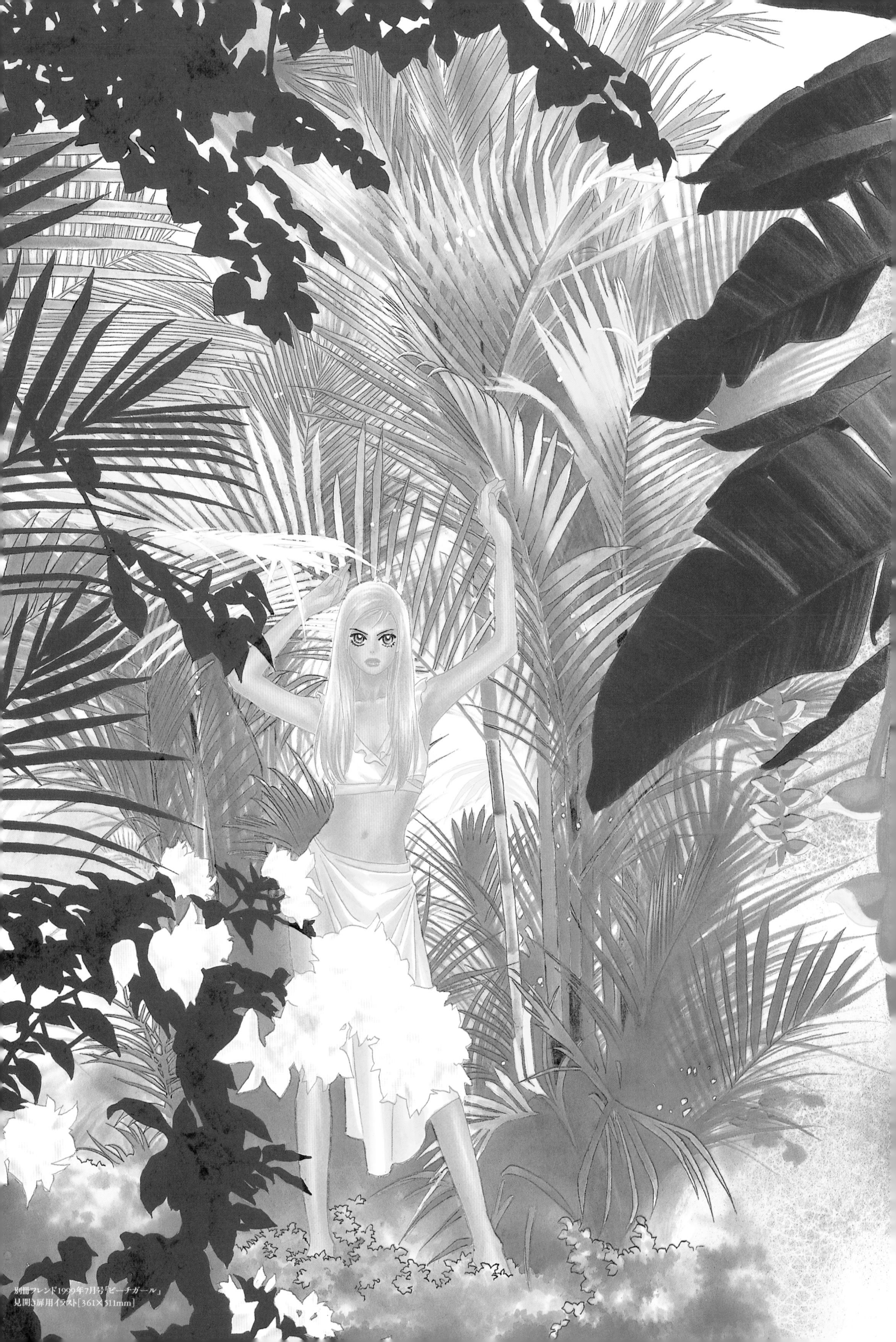

別冊フレンド1999年7月号「ピーチガール」
見開き扉用イラスト［361×511mm］

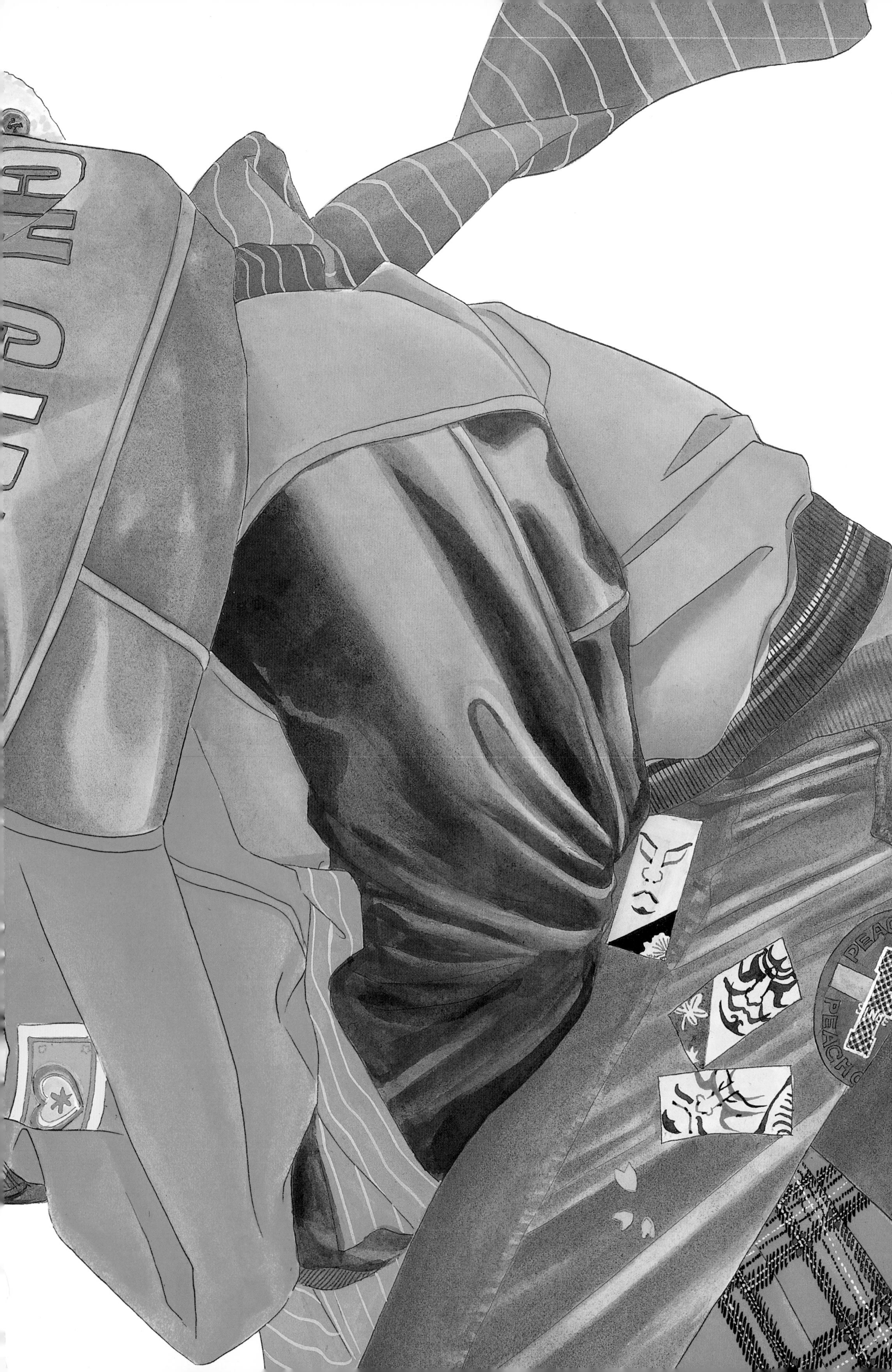
PEACH
PEACH

別冊フレンド1999年3月号「ピーチガール」見開き扉用イラスト[368×505mm]

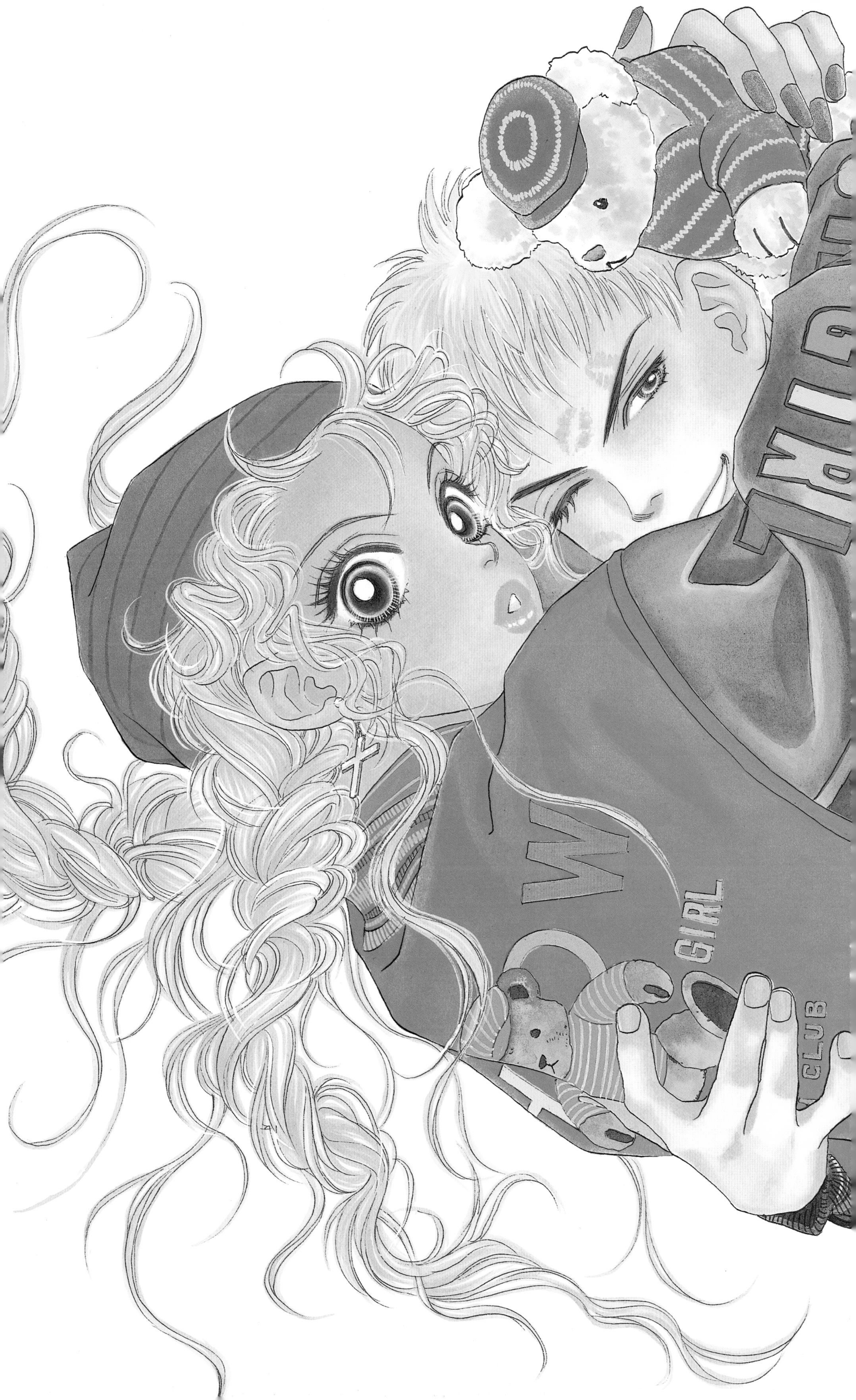
GIRL
CLUB

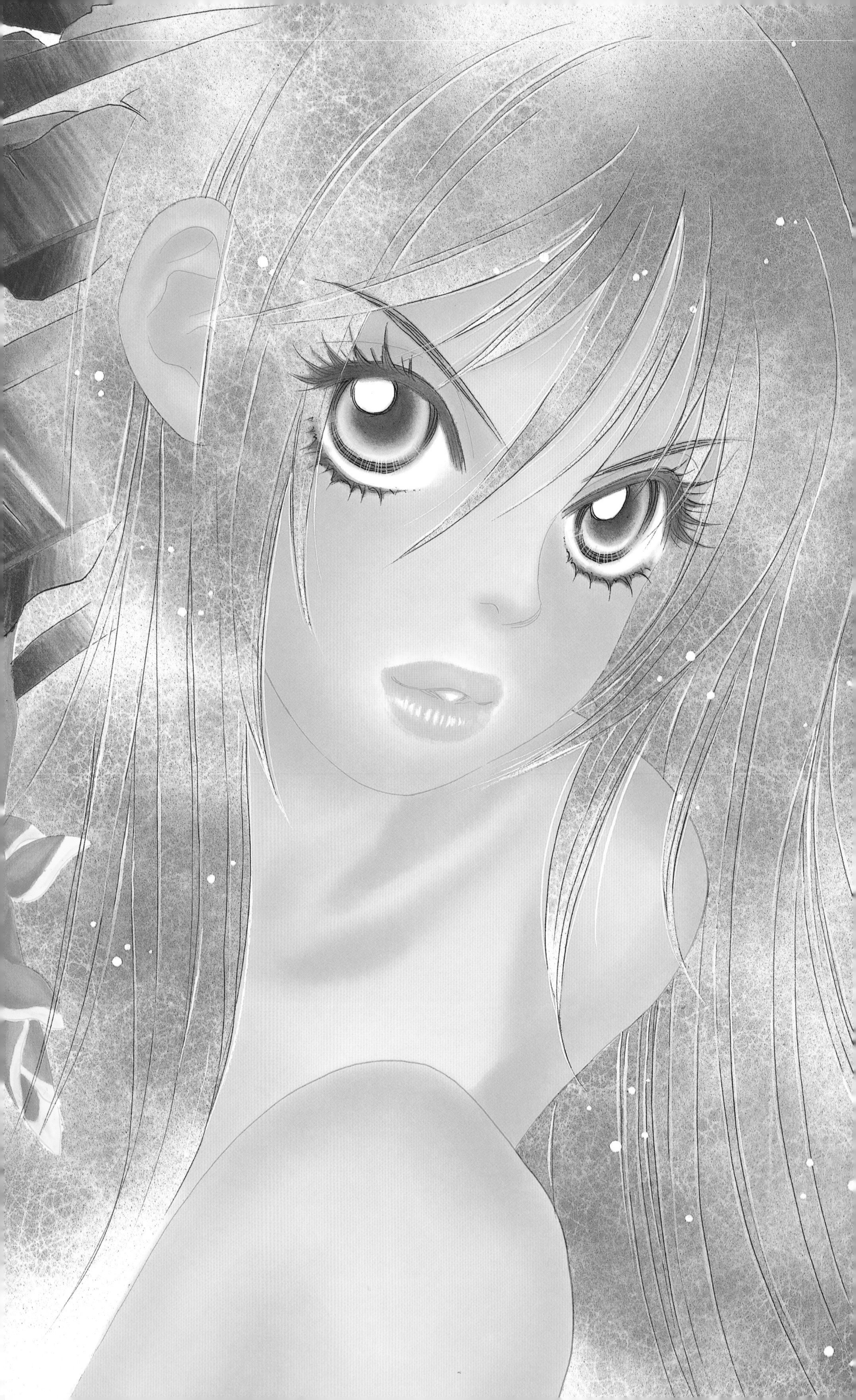

# PEACH GIRL
# 2000 works
### January～September
「ピーチガール」別冊フレンド2000年9月号掲載までのイラストを集めました。

別冊フレンド1999年9月号「ピーチガール」次号予告用イラスト［124×169mm］

Trap → Counterattack → Counterattack → the end of love…?
The war between Momo and Sae is so brutal; will Toji's sudden change
of heart bring it to an end…? Will Momo's new love blossom into
something beautiful or will it just wither away…?

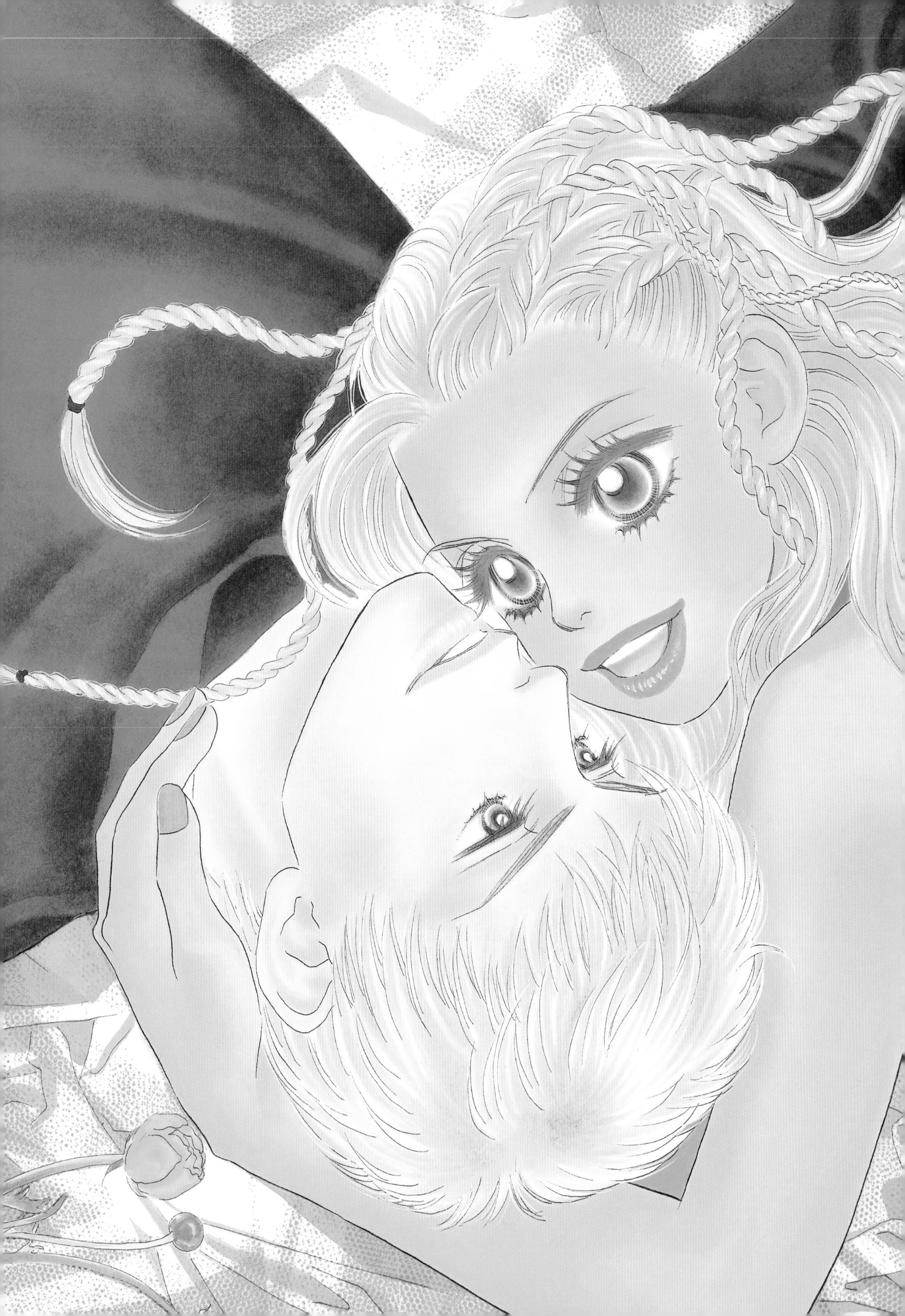

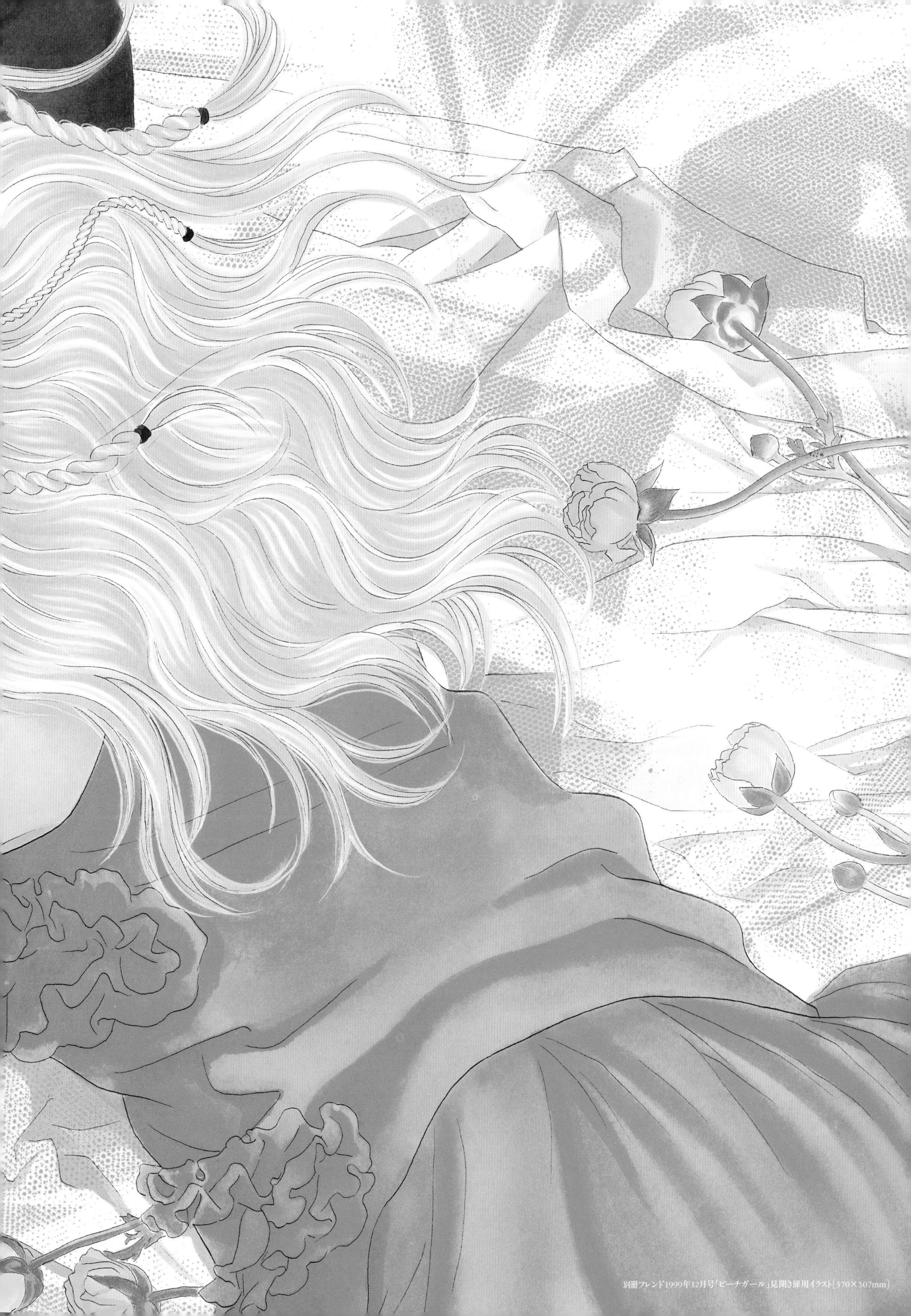
別冊フレンド1999年12月号「ピーチガール」見開き扉用イラスト[370×507mm]

# PLEASURE

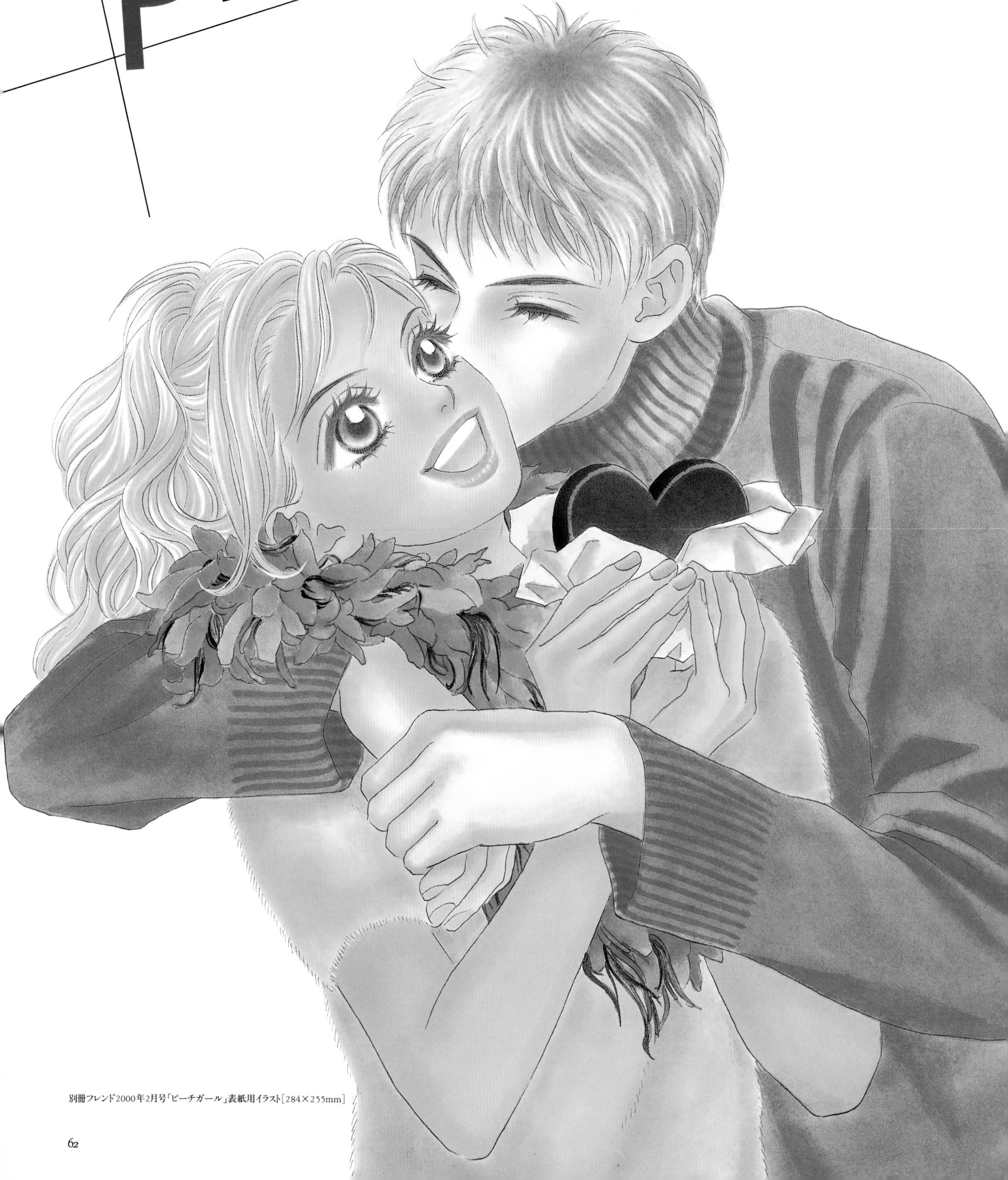

別冊フレンド2000年2月号「ピーチガール」表紙用イラスト［284×255mm］

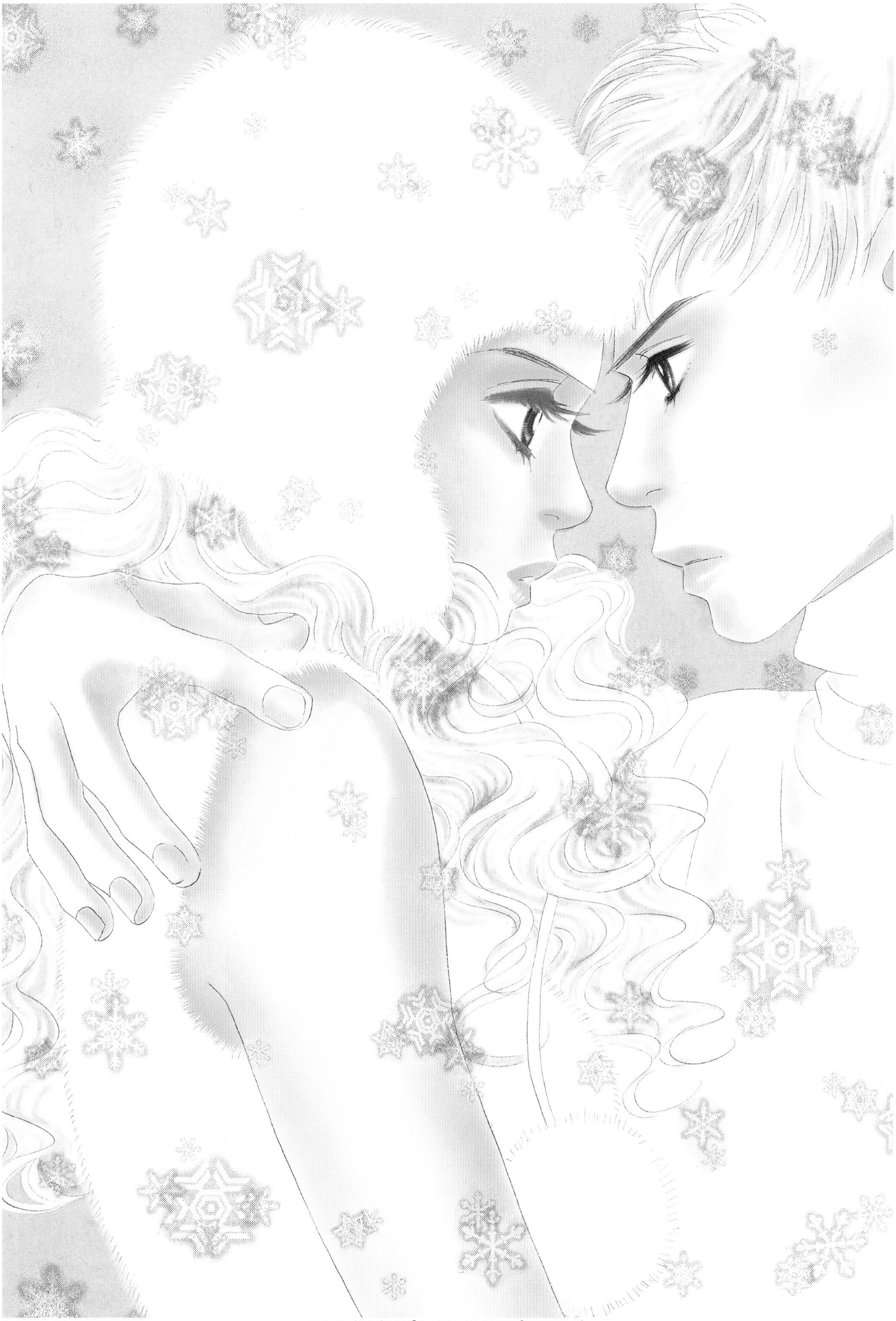

別冊フレンド2000年2月号「ピーチガール」扉用イラスト[369×279mm]

# Powerful

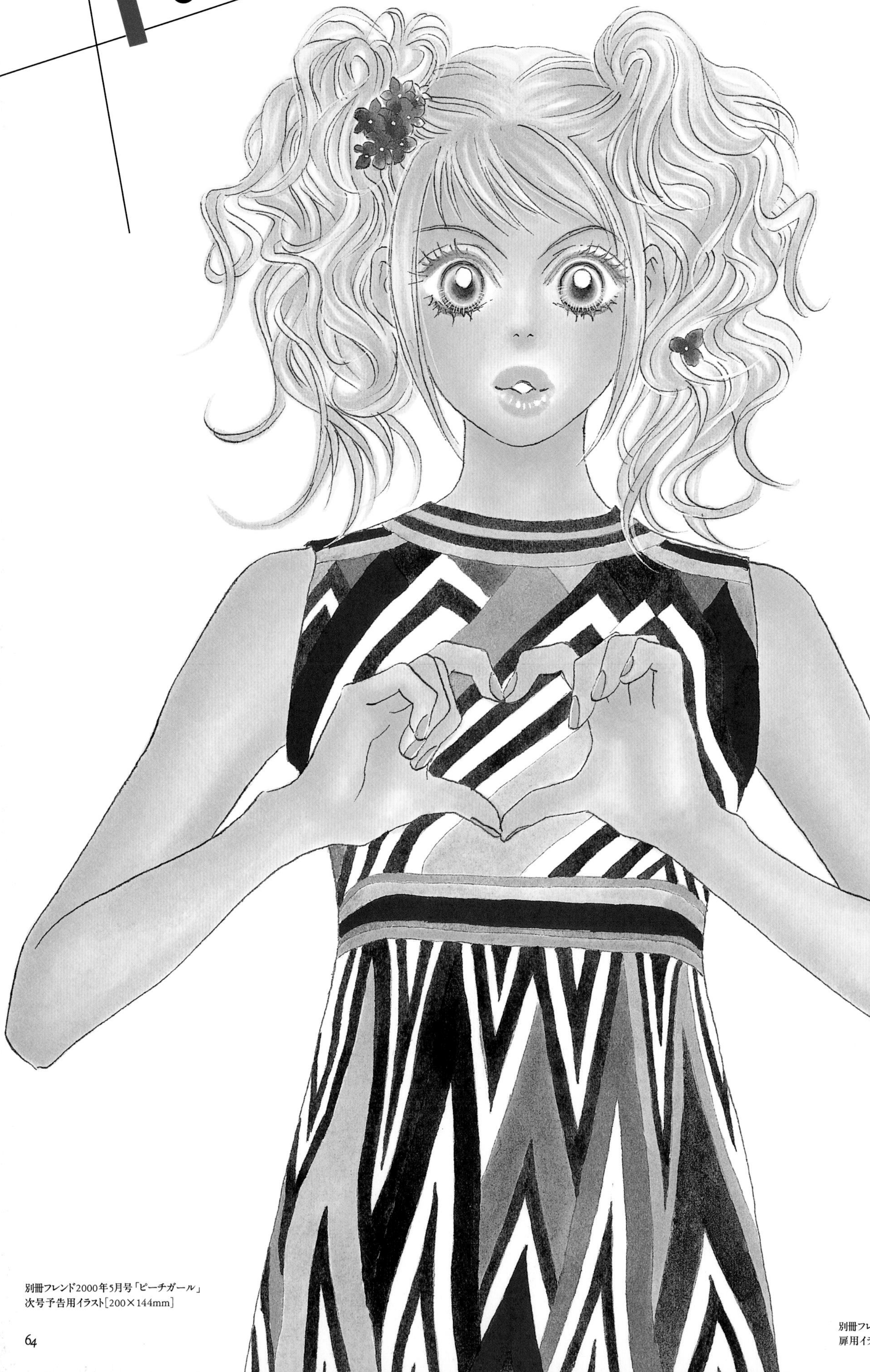

別冊フレンド2000年5月号「ピーチガール」
次号予告用イラスト［200×144mm］

別冊フレンド2000年5月号「ピーチガール」
扉用イラスト［345×260mm］

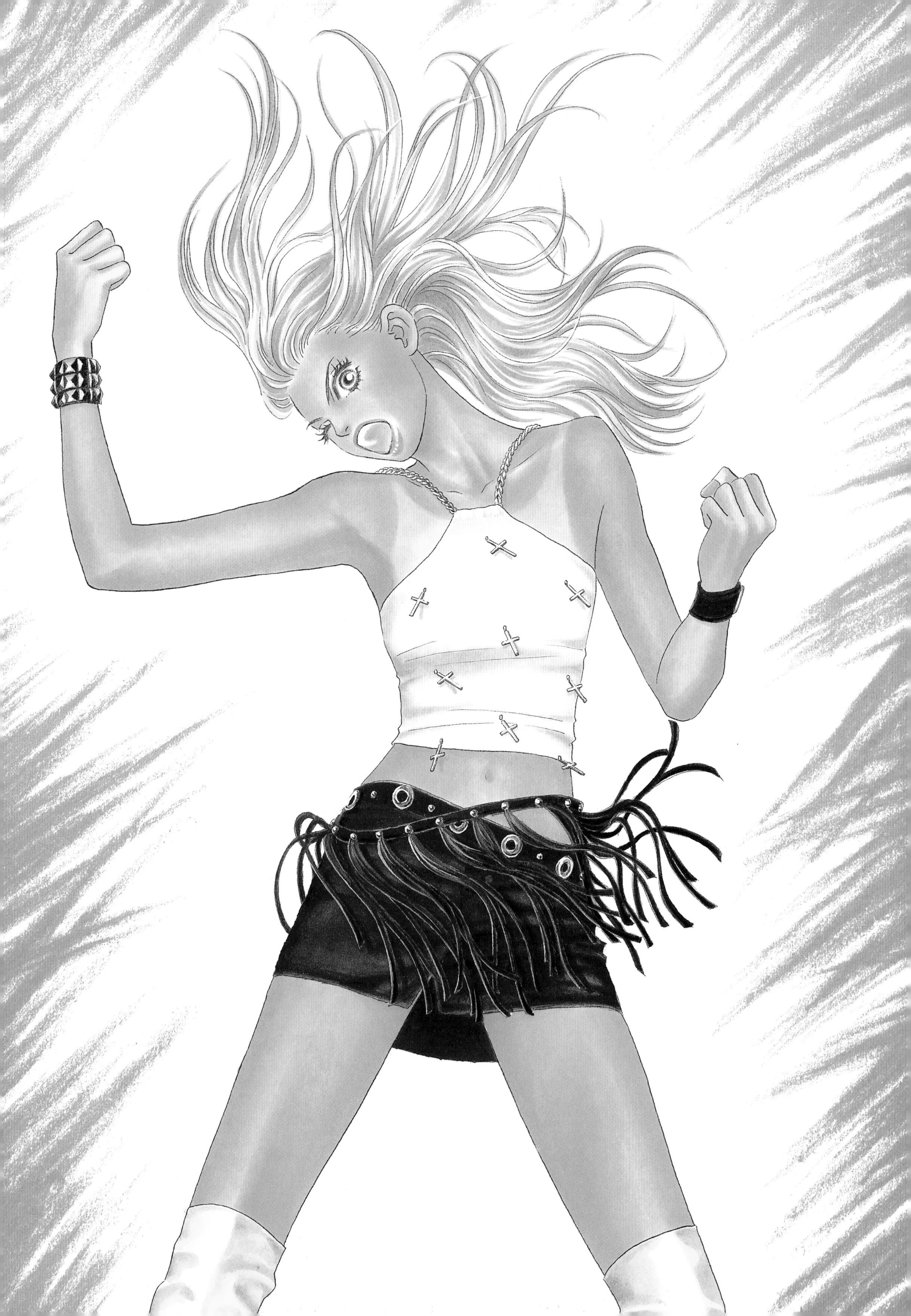

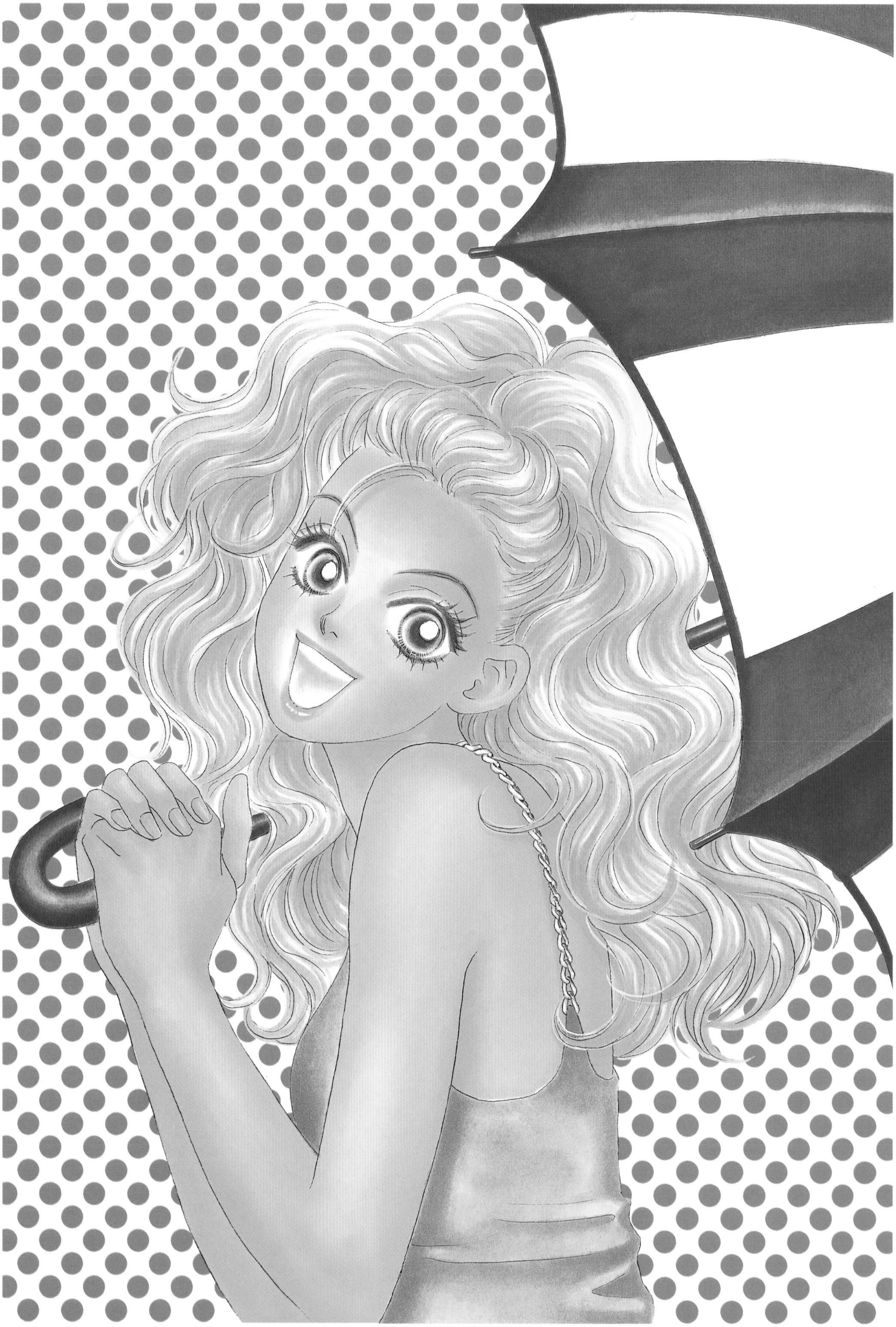

別冊フレンド2000年6月号「ピーチガール」表紙用イラスト［339×239mm］

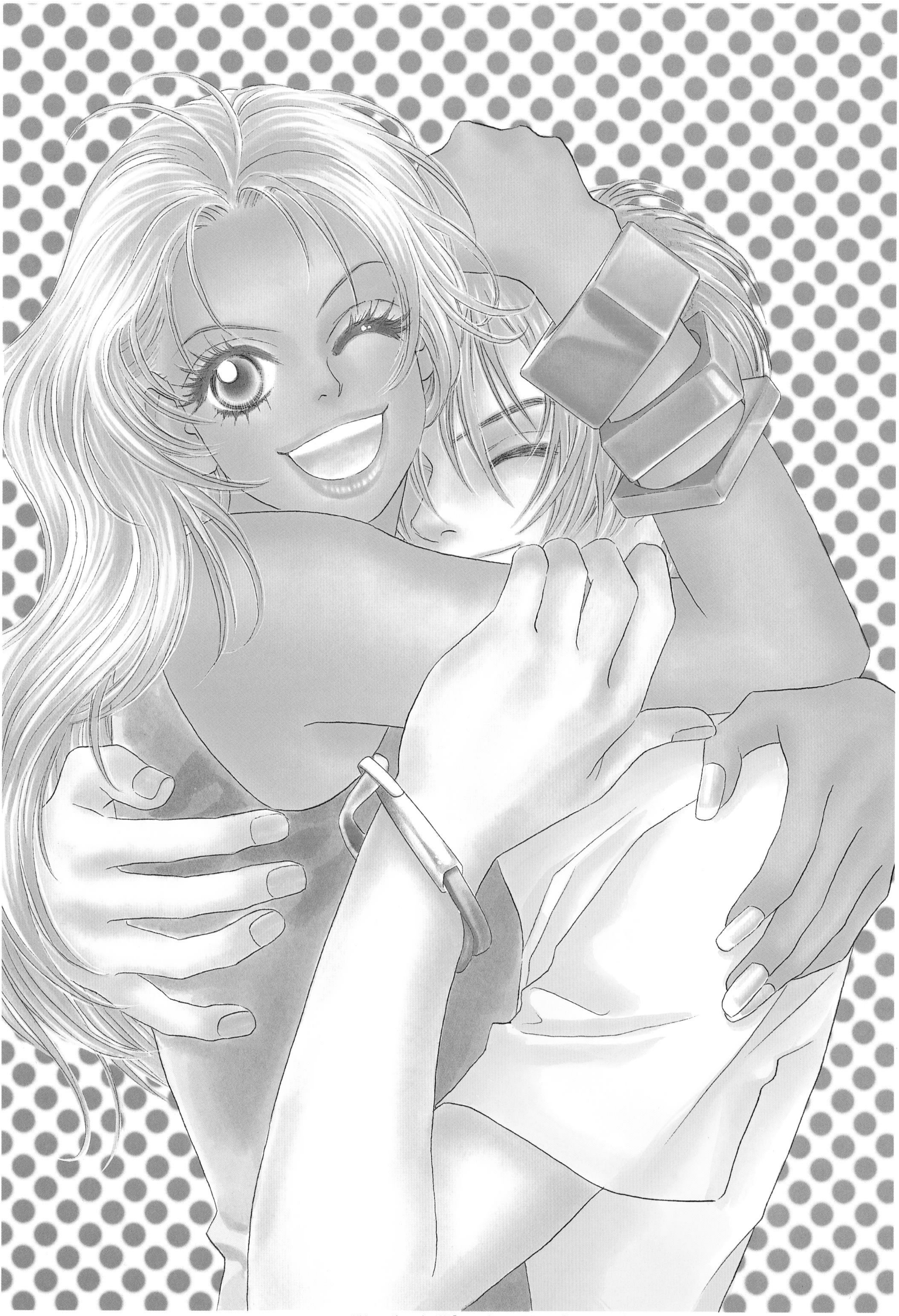

別冊フレンド2000年7月号「ピーチガール」扉用イラスト［348×245mm］

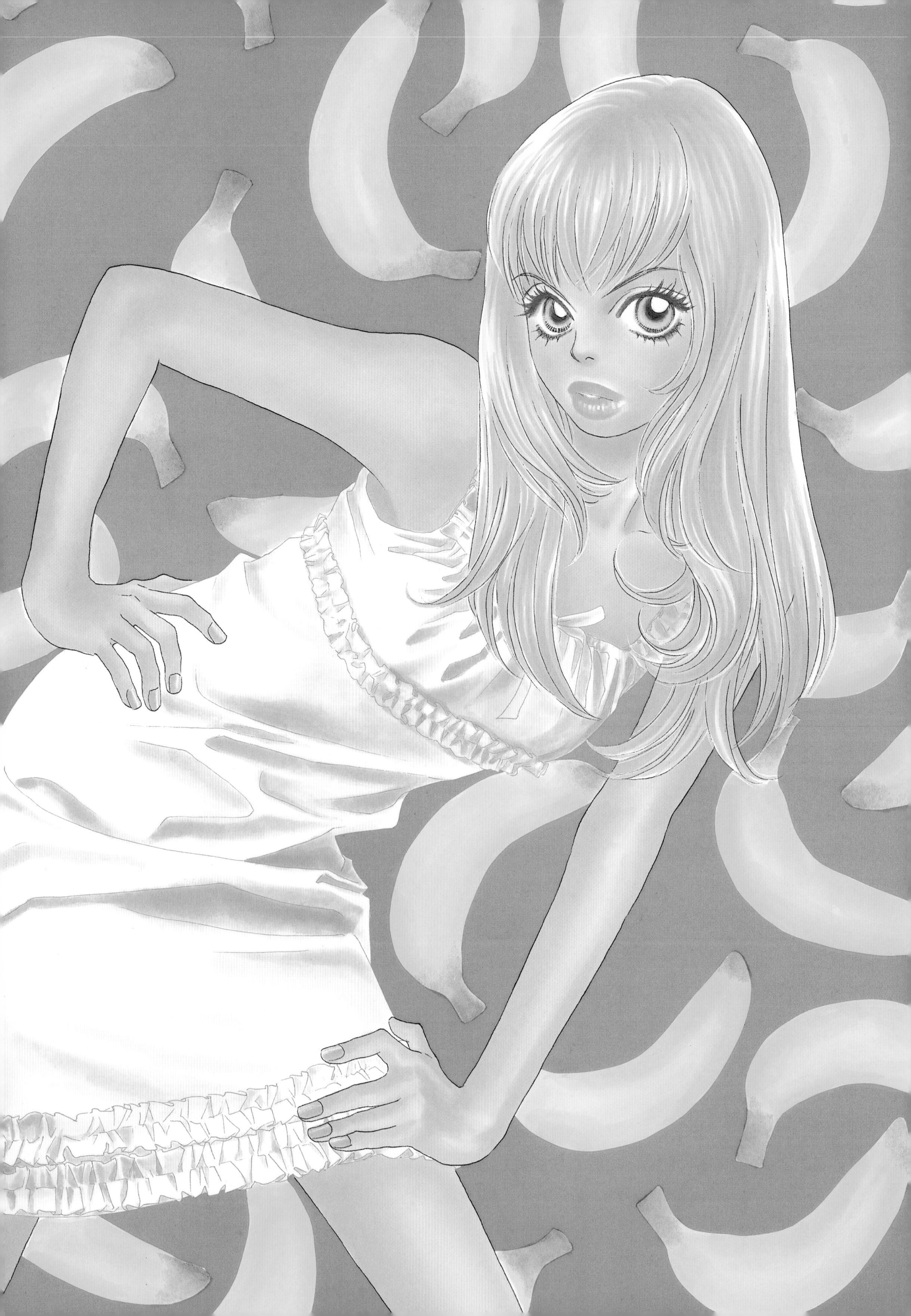

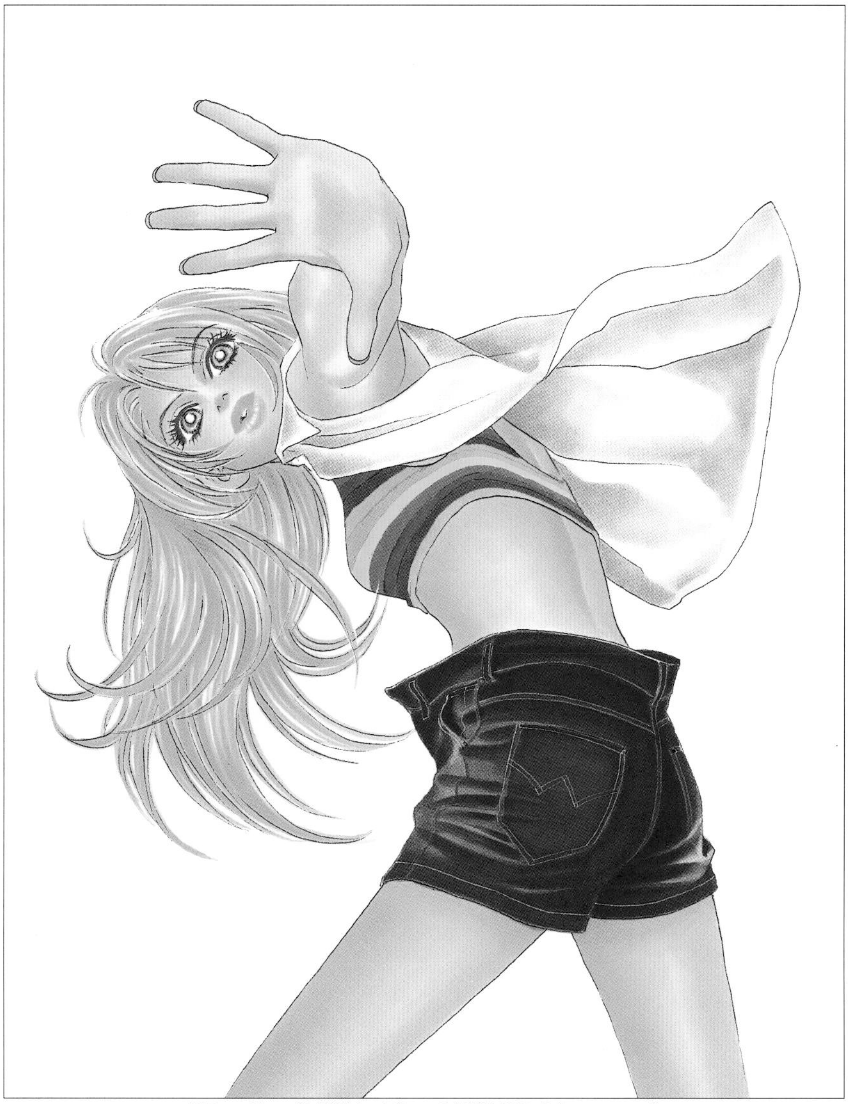

別冊フレンド2000年9月号「ピーチガール」次号予告用イラスト［245×193mm］

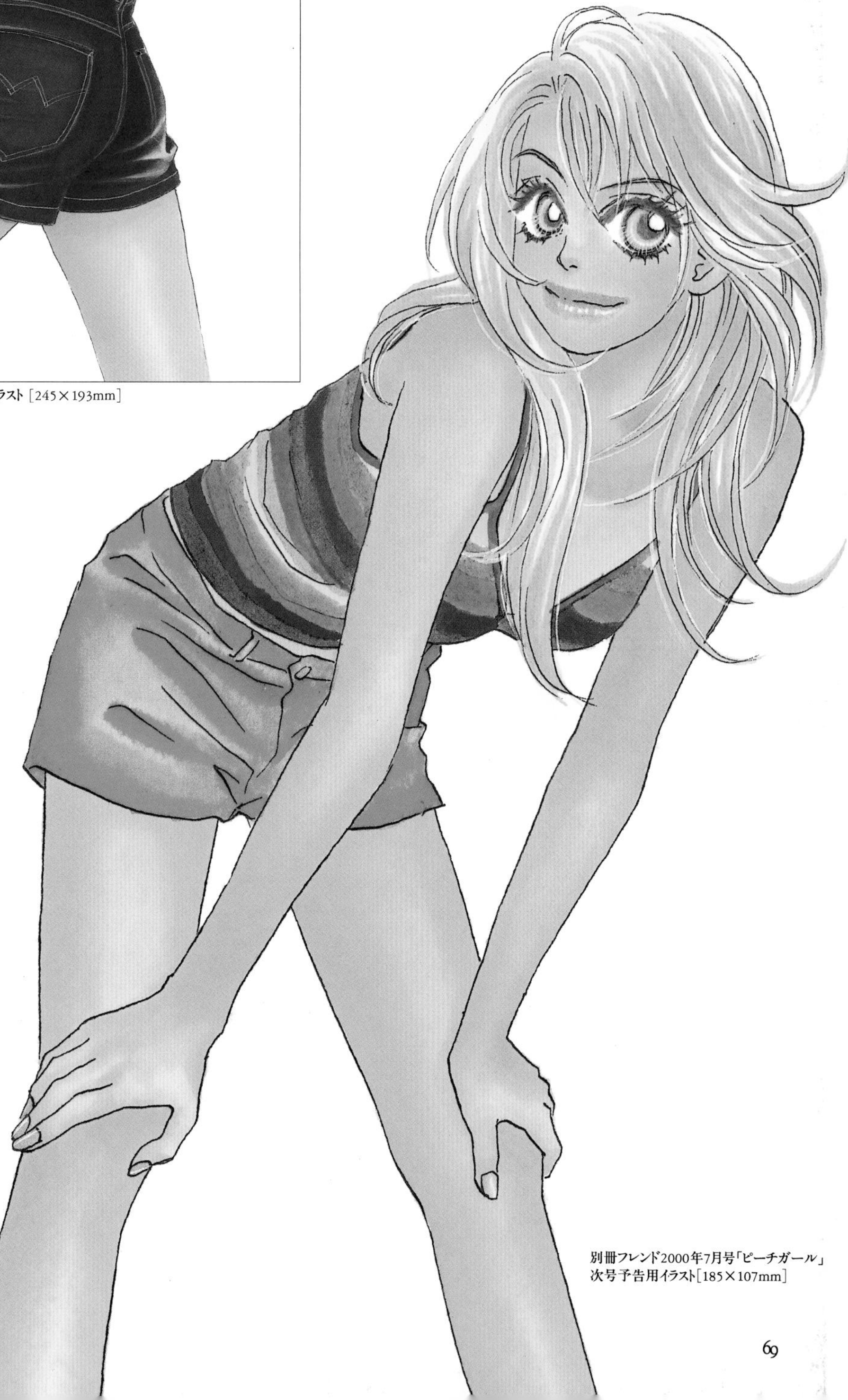

別冊フレンド2000年7月号「ピーチガール」
次号予告用イラスト［185×107mm］

別冊フレンド2000年9月号「ピーチガール」扉用イラスト［350×248mm］

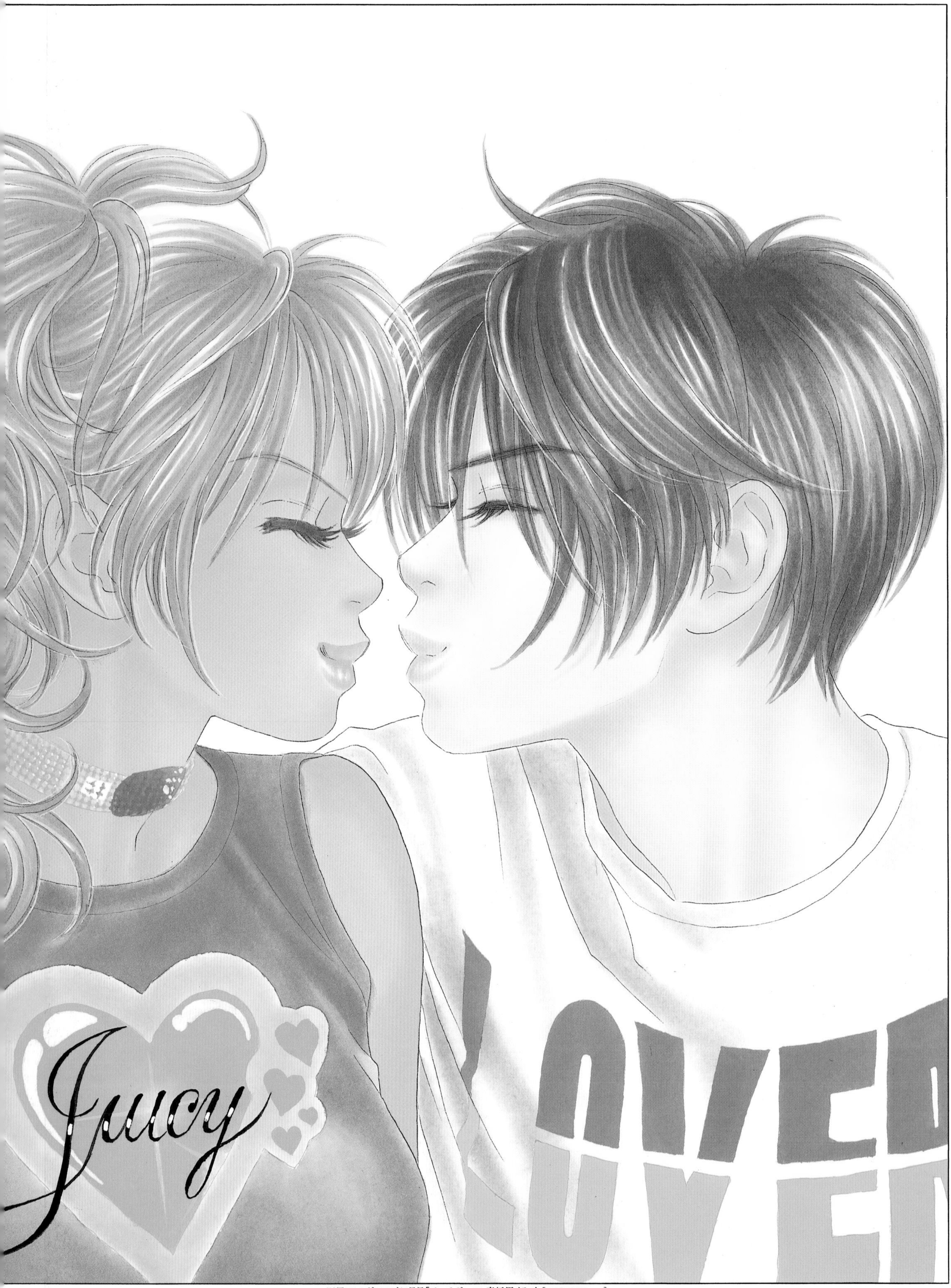
Juicy
LOVER
LOVER
別冊フレンド2000年9月号「ピーチガール」表紙用イラスト［286×252mm］

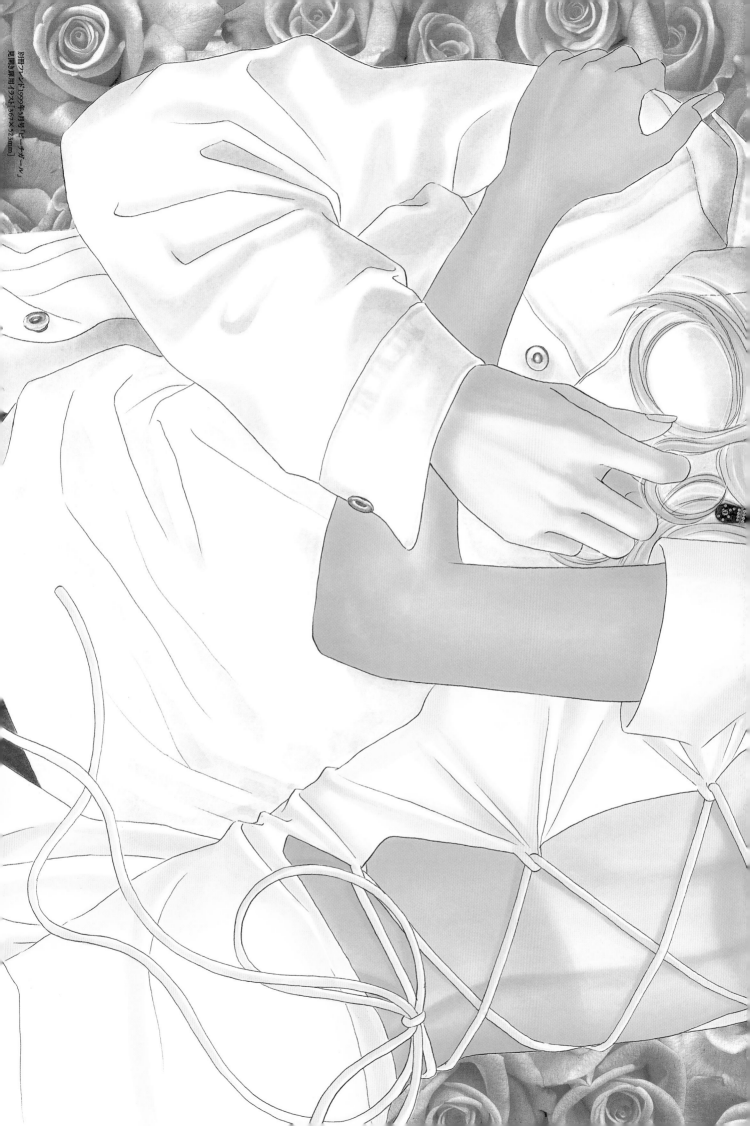
別冊フレンド「1999年3月号「ピーターガール」
見開き用イラスト[367×253mm]

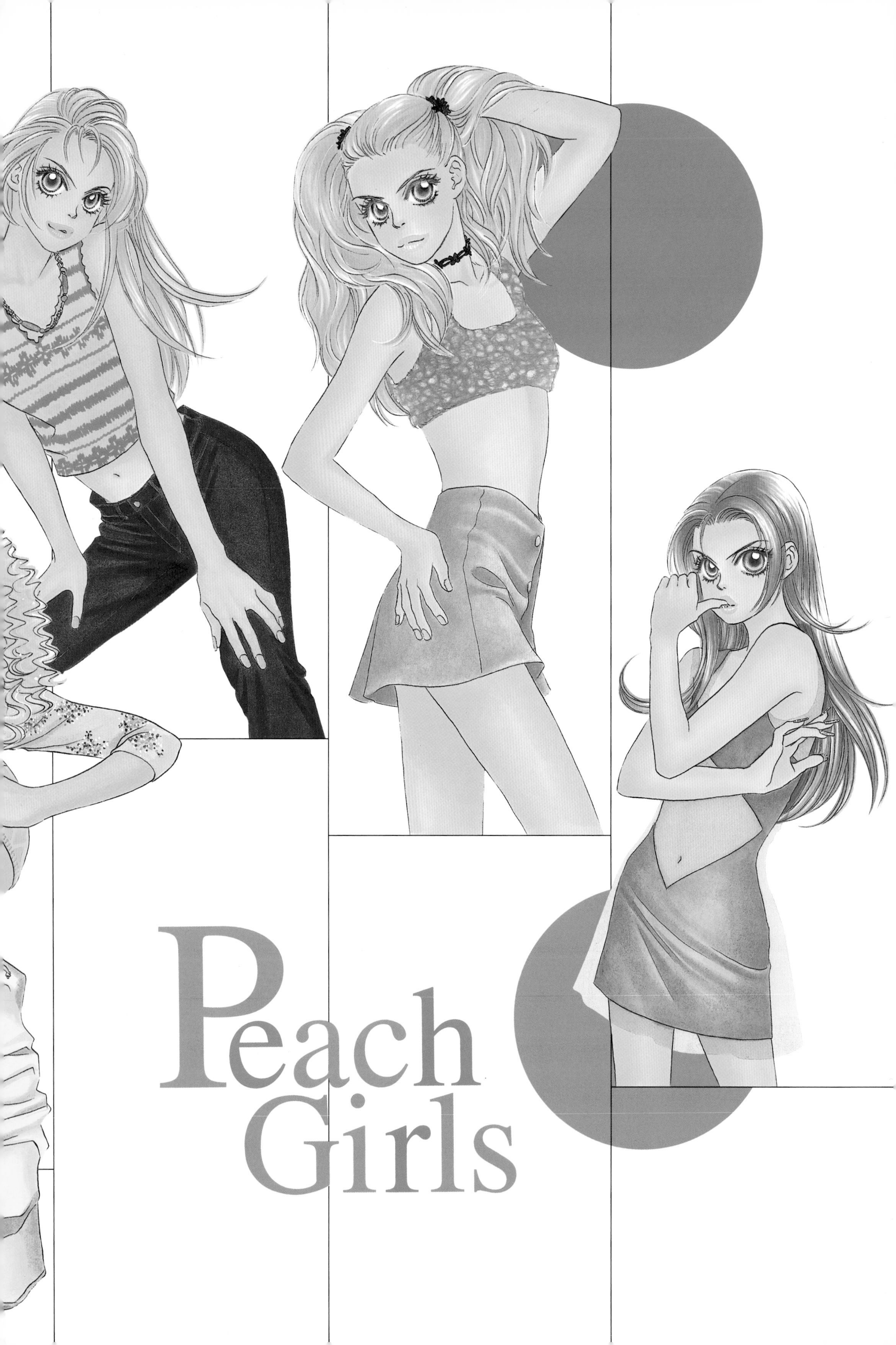
Peach
Girls

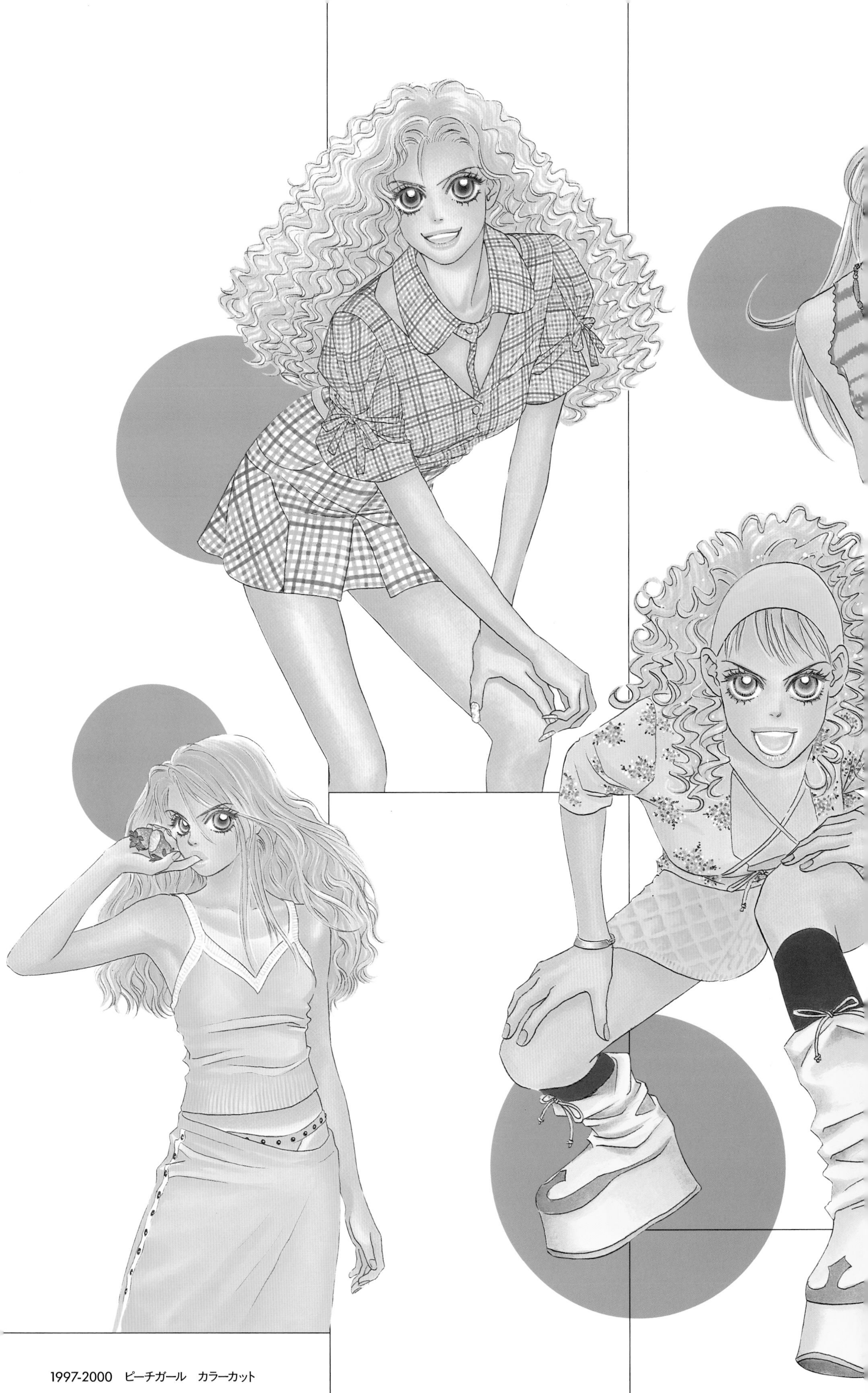

1997-2000　ピーチガール　カラーカット

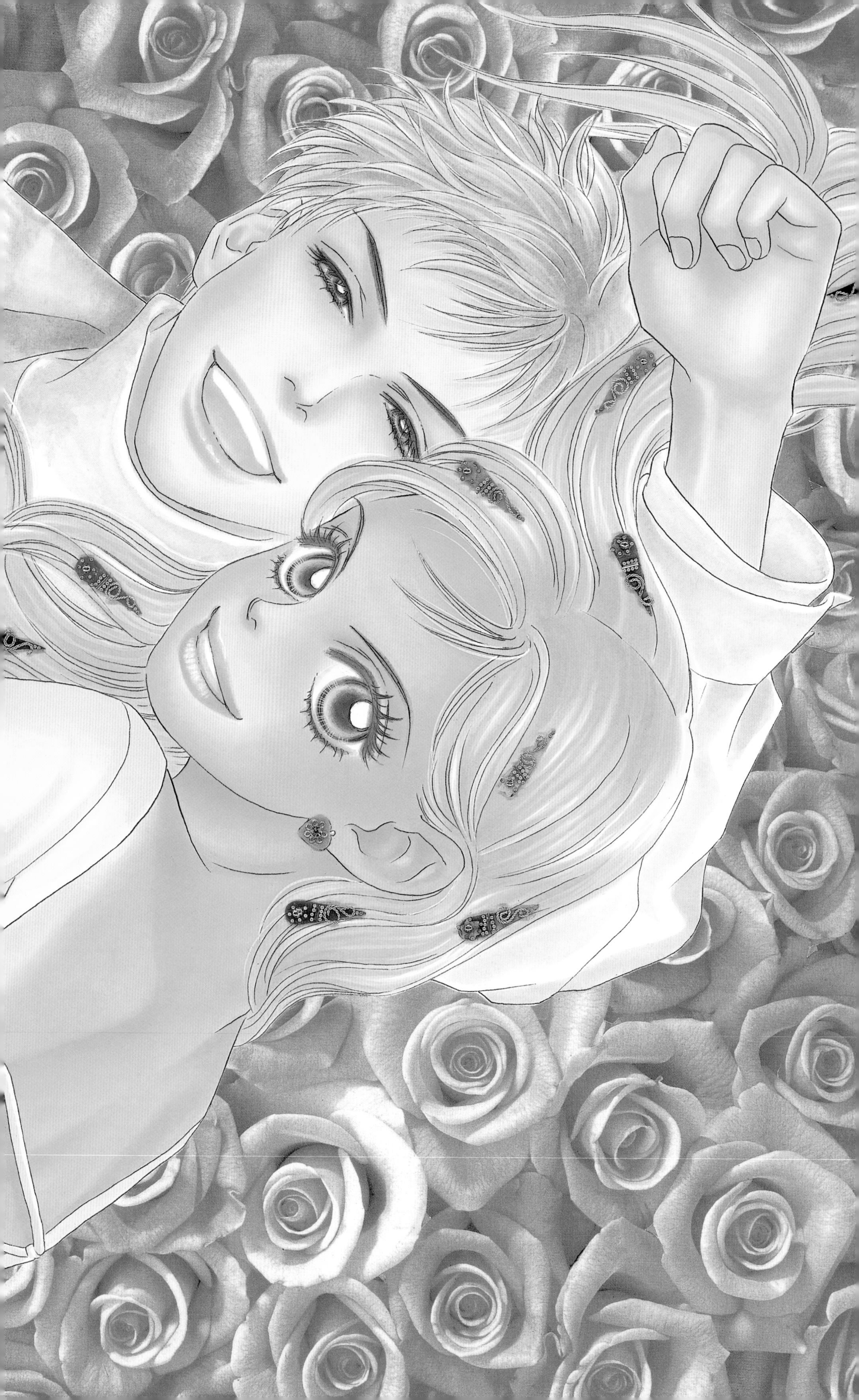

Pre-PEACH works
# Glass Hearts

1996-1997年　別冊フレンドで連載した「ガラスの鼓動」のイラストを集めました。

別冊フレンド1996年3月号「ガラスの鼓動」表紙用イラスト[366×258mm]

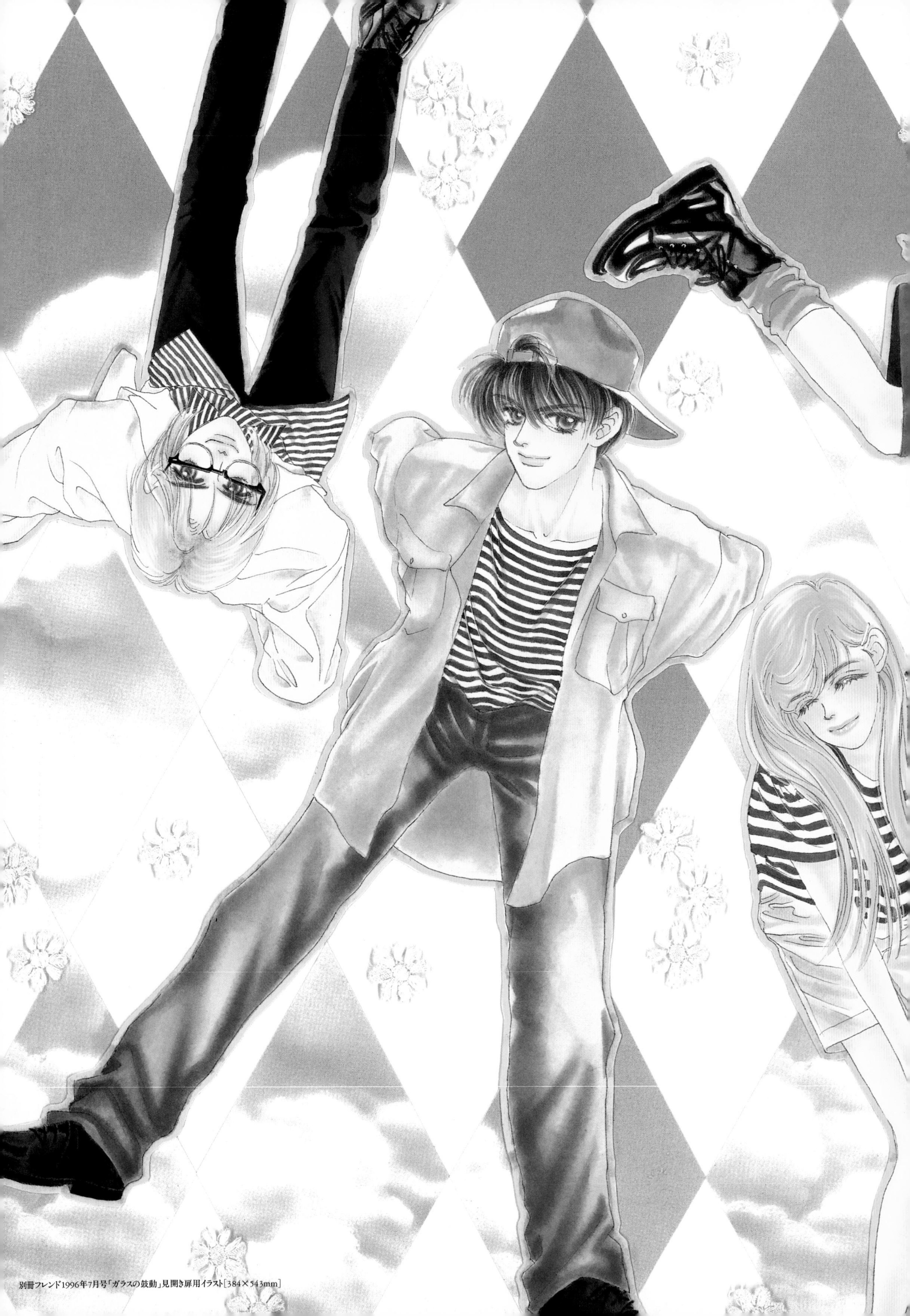

別冊フレンド1996年7月号「ガラスの鼓動」見開き扉用イラスト［384×543mm］

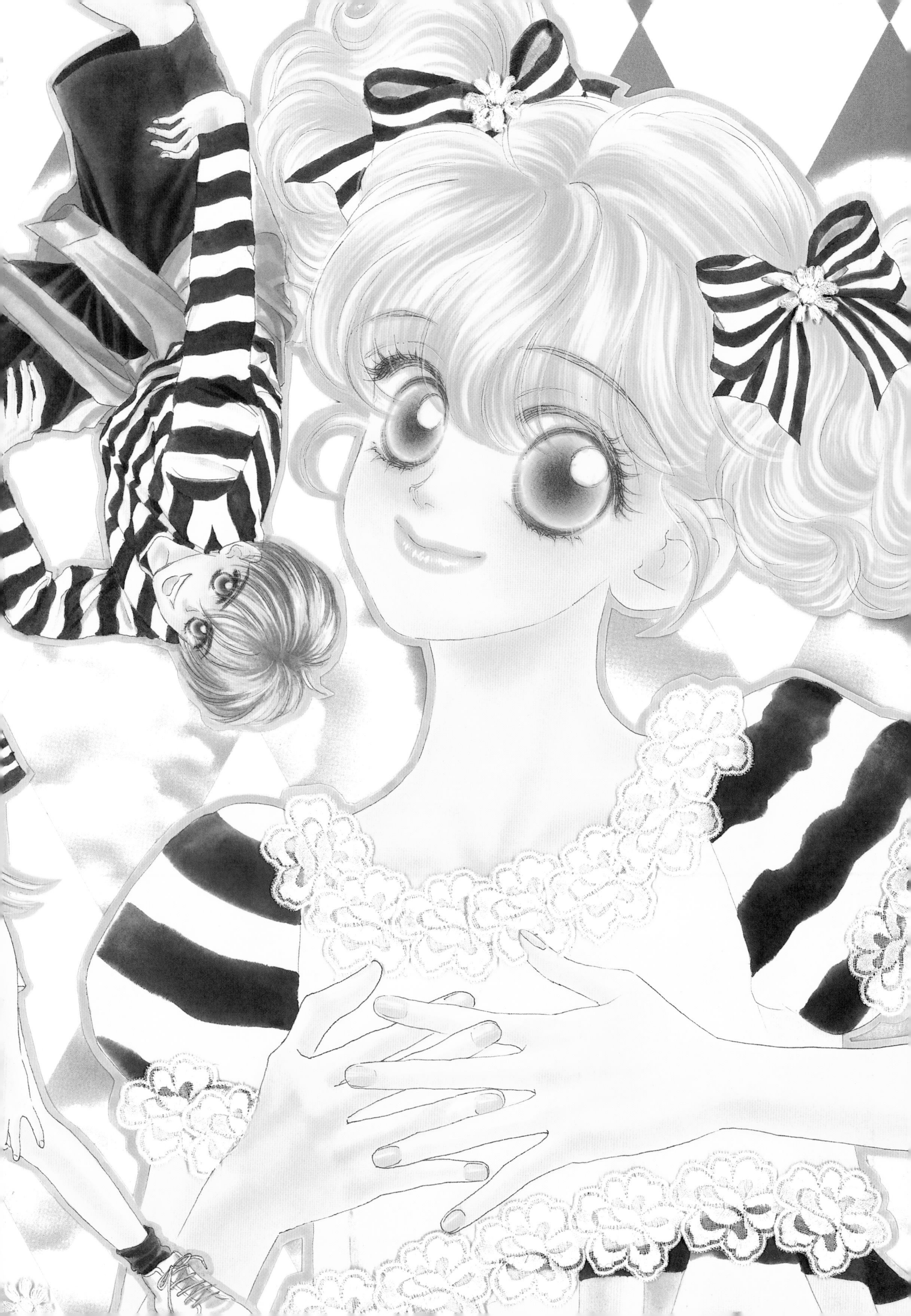

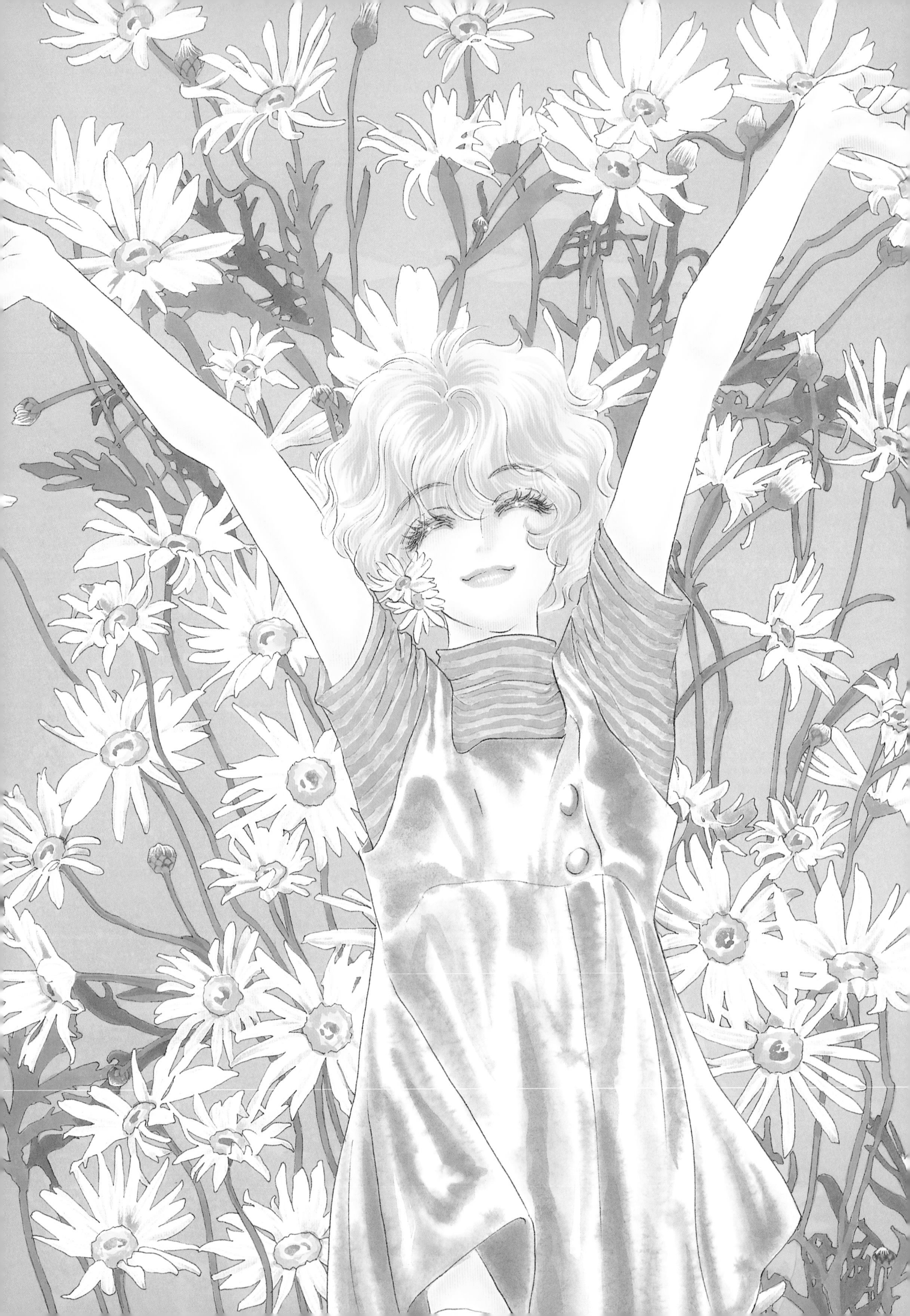

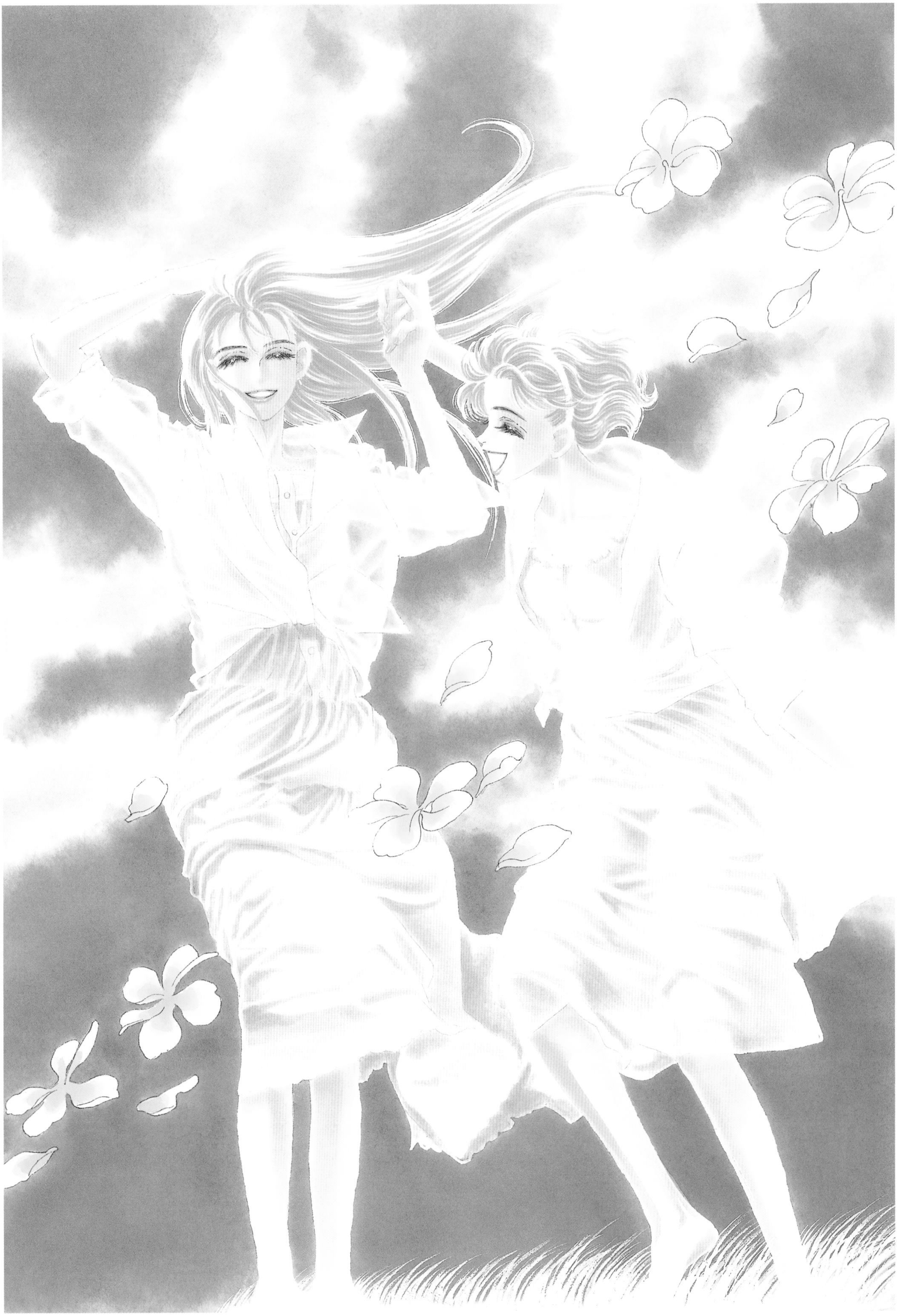
別冊フレンド1996年9月号「ガラスの鼓動」扉用イラスト［387×283mm］

別冊フレンド1996年5月号「ガラスの鼓動」扉用イラスト［383×278mm］

別冊フレンド1996年12月号「ガラスの鼓動」扉用イラスト[370×262mm]

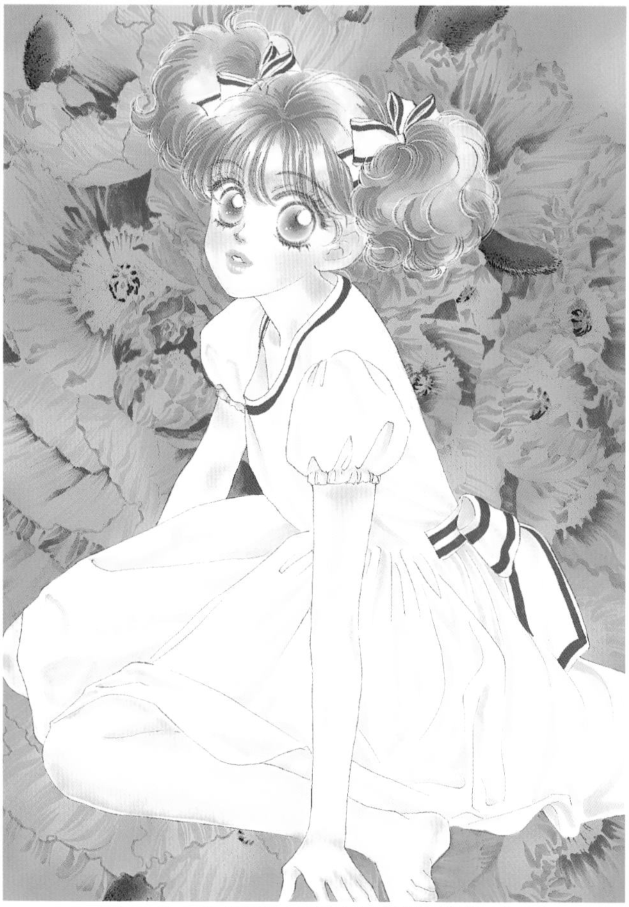

別冊フレンド1996年8月号「ガラスの鼓動」扉用イラスト[387×283mm]

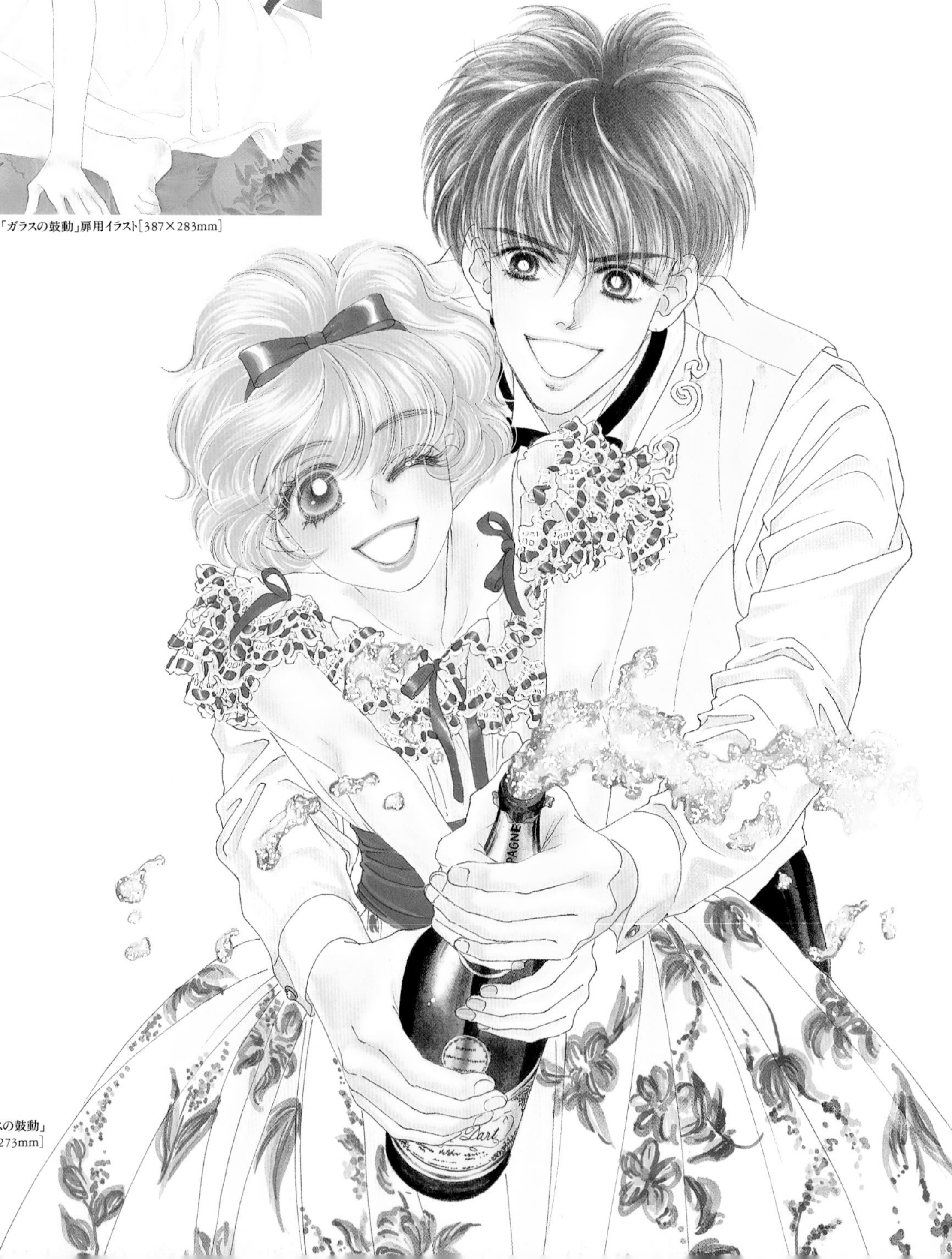

別冊フレンド1996年12月号「ガラスの鼓動」
表紙用イラスト[312×273mm]

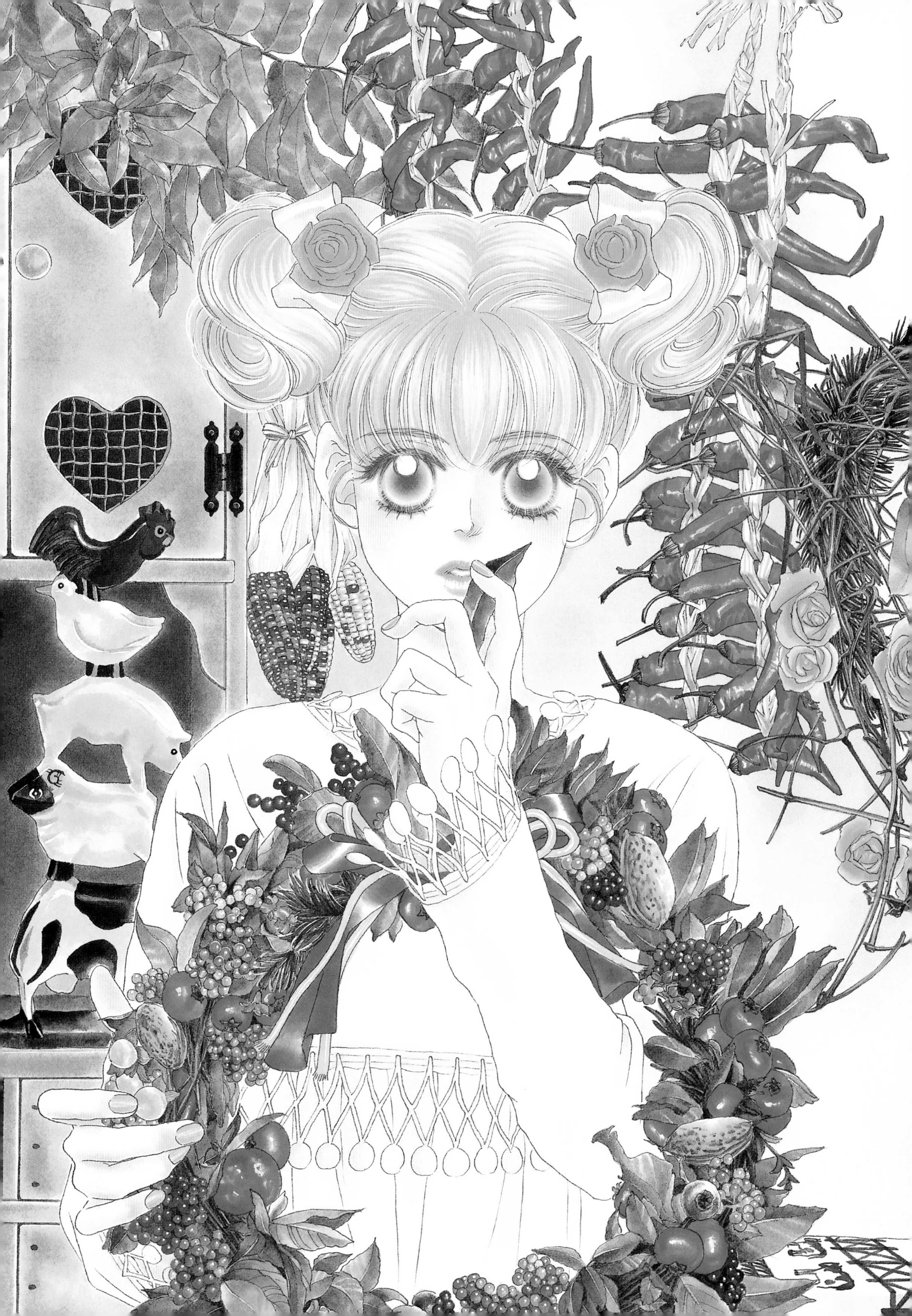

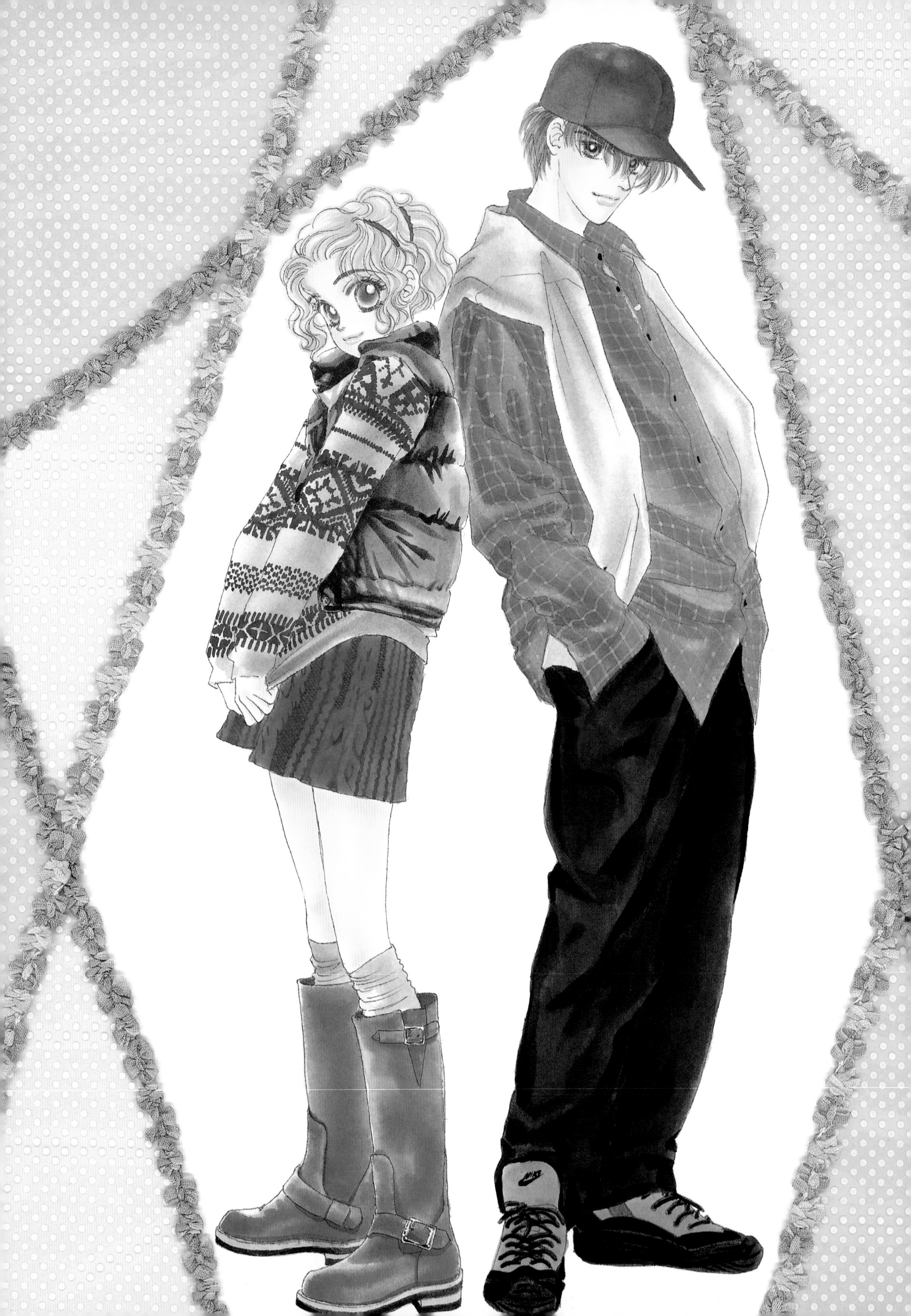

1996年6月発売「ガラスの鼓動」第1巻KCカバー用イラスト［281×195mm］

別冊フレンド1997年3月号「ガラスの鼓動」扉用イラスト［386×267mm］

別冊フレンド1996年10月号「ガラスの鼓動」
扉用イラスト［387×285mm］

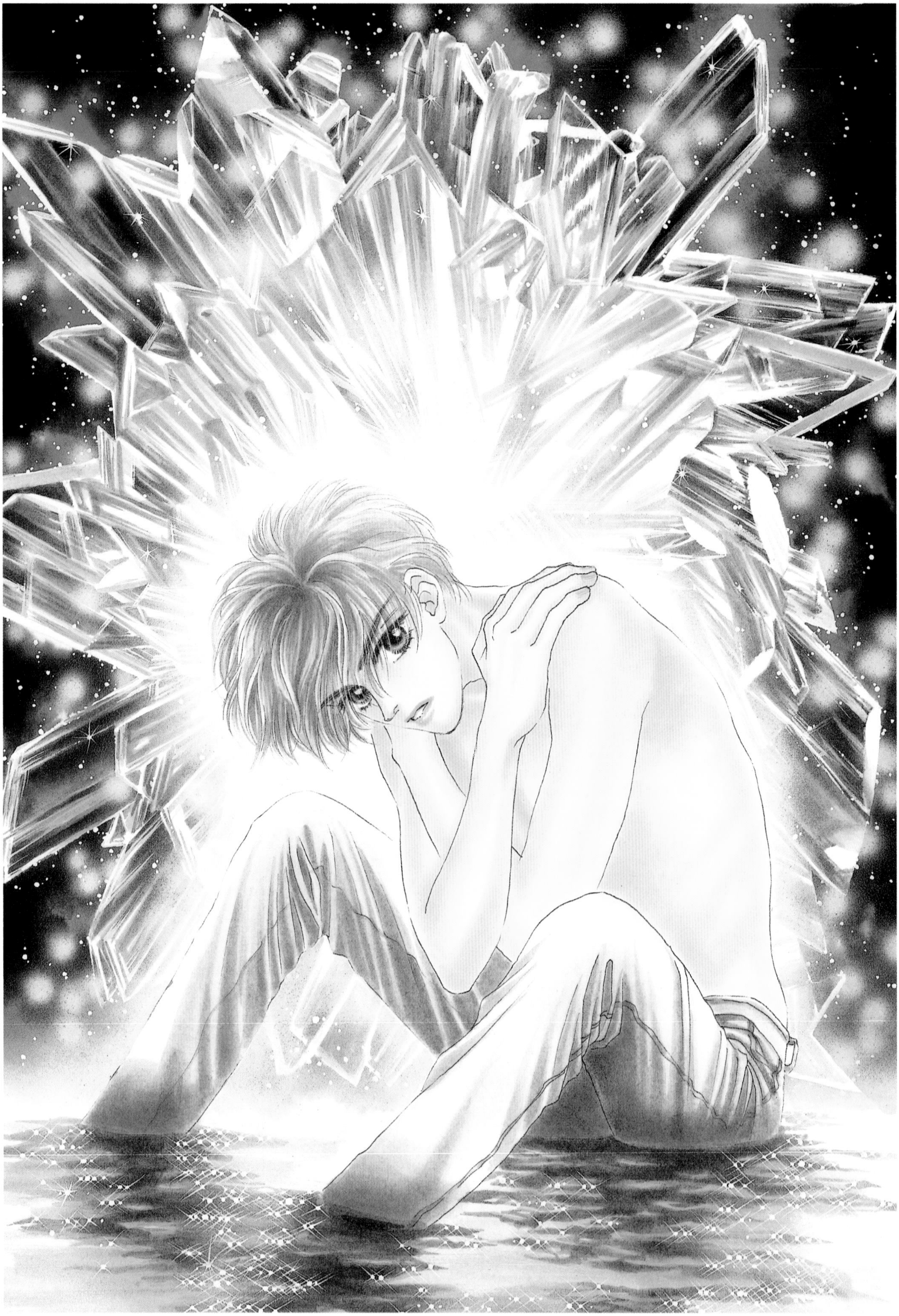

1996年10月発売「ガラスの鼓動」第2巻KCカバー用イラスト[310×220mm]



1997年2月発売「ガラスの鼓動」第3巻KCカバー用イラスト[284×192mm]

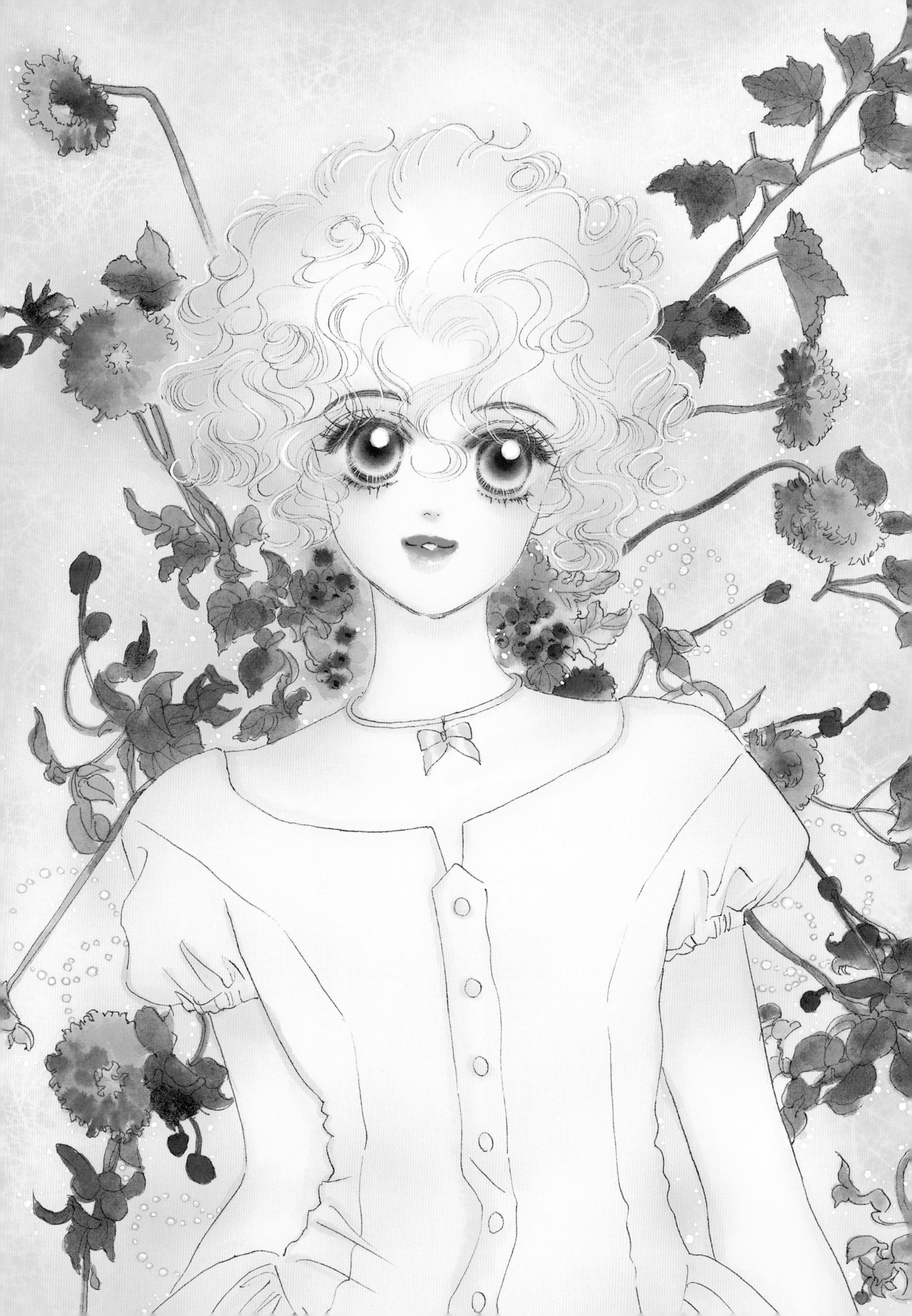

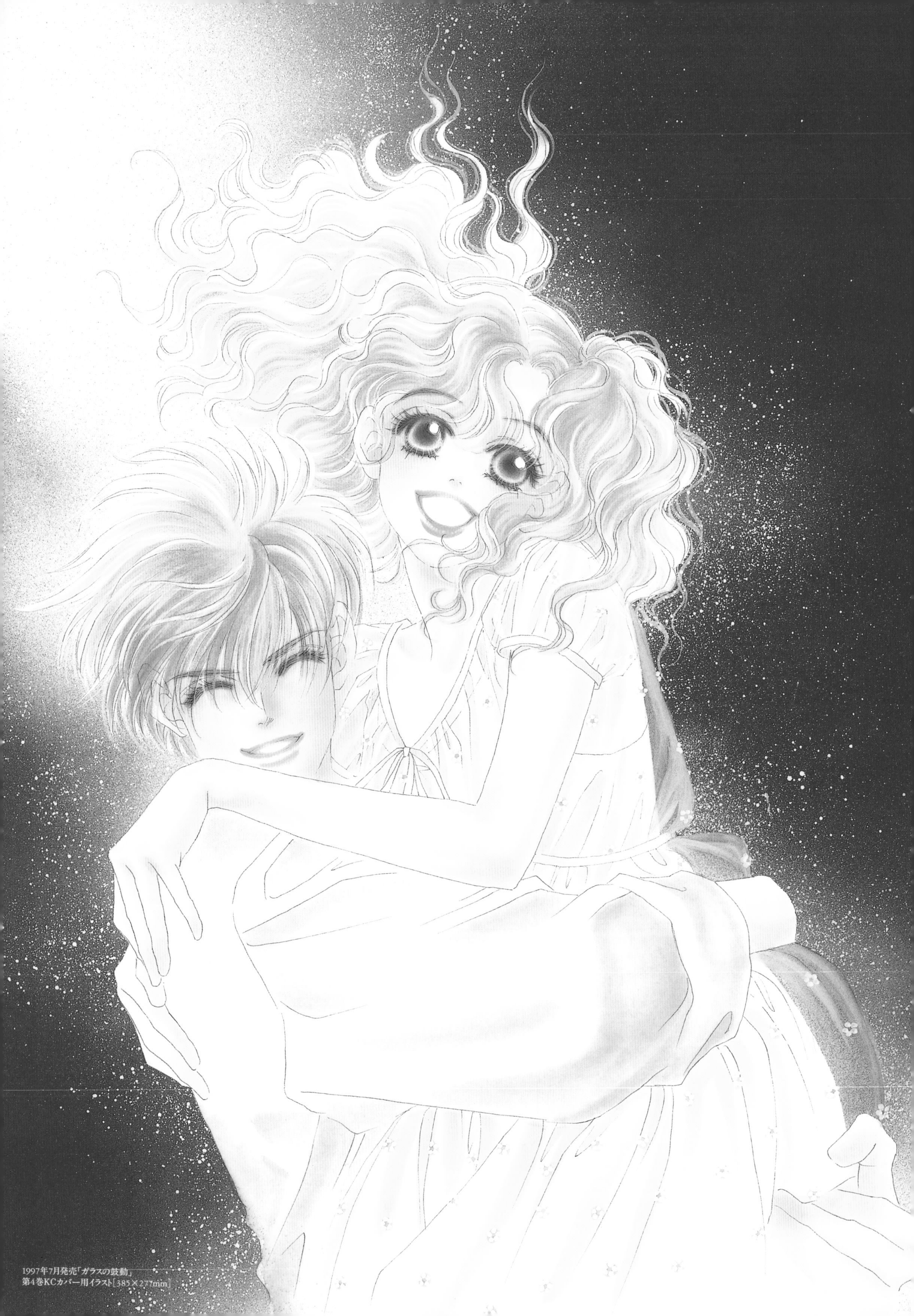

1997年7月発売「ガラスの鼓動」
第4巻KCカバー用イラスト［385×277mm］

Pre-PEACH works

# Angel Wars & Other works

1994-1995年　別冊フレンドで連載した「エンジェル★ウォーズ」と，長編読み切り2作，
そして別フレ，Julietの表紙を飾ったイラストを集めました。

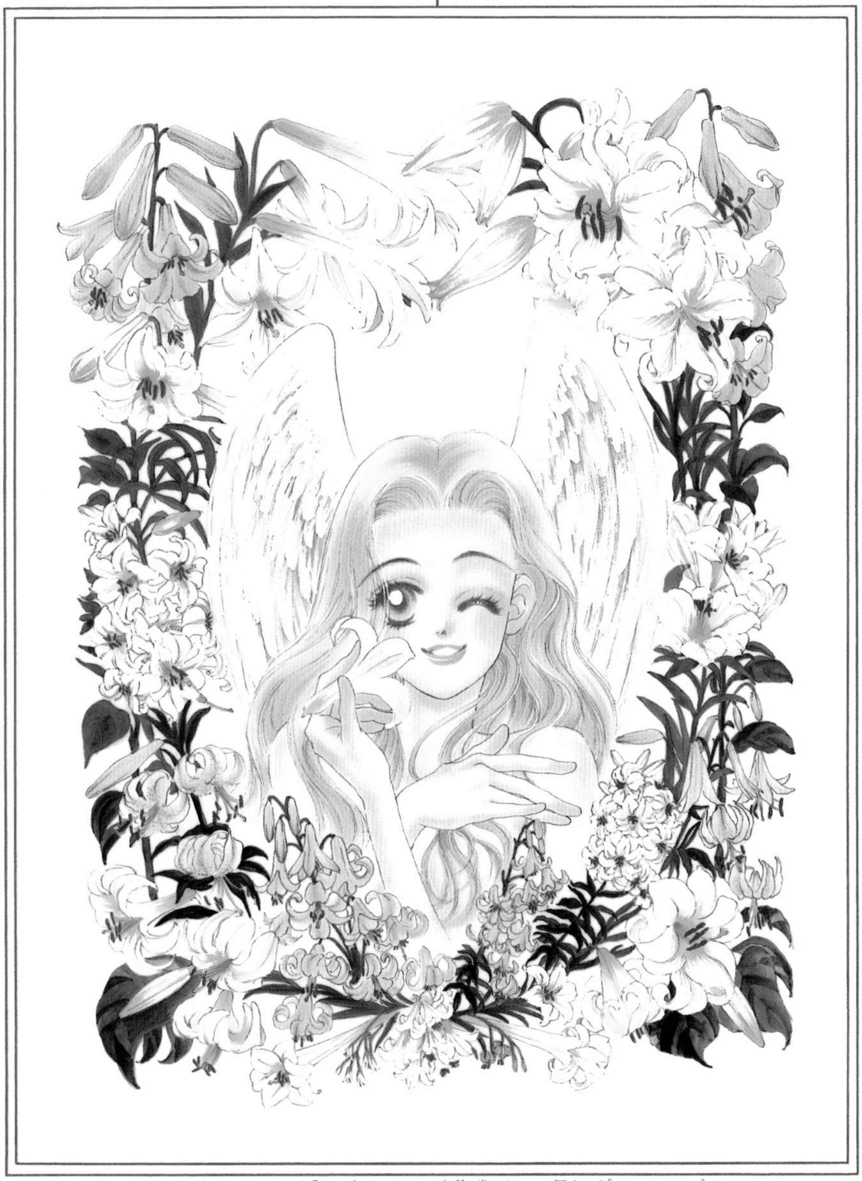

1995年2月発売「エンジェル★ウォーズ」第1巻KCカバー用イラスト[360×266mm]

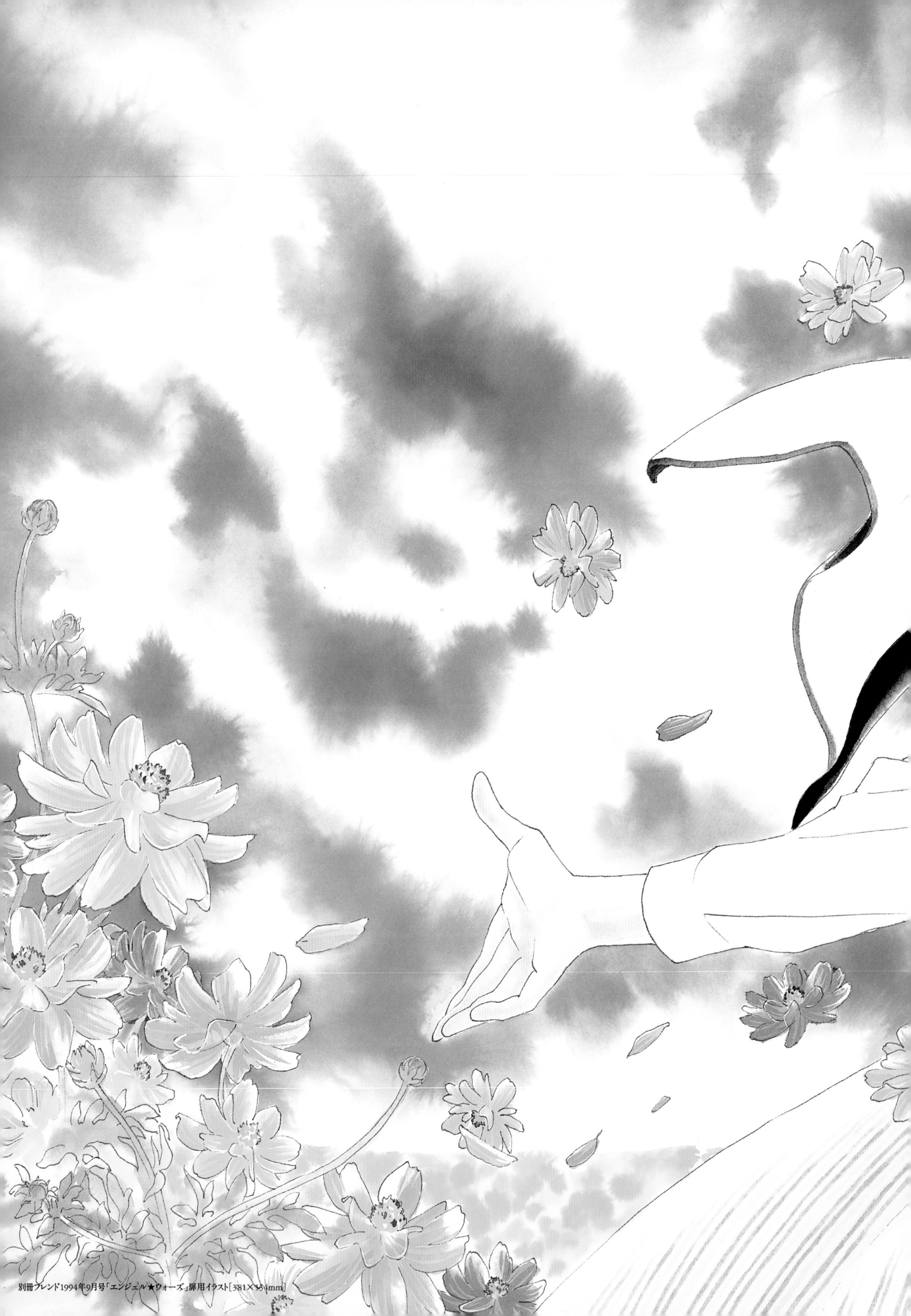

別冊フレンド1994年9月号「エンジェル★ウォーズ」扉用イラスト［381×534mm］

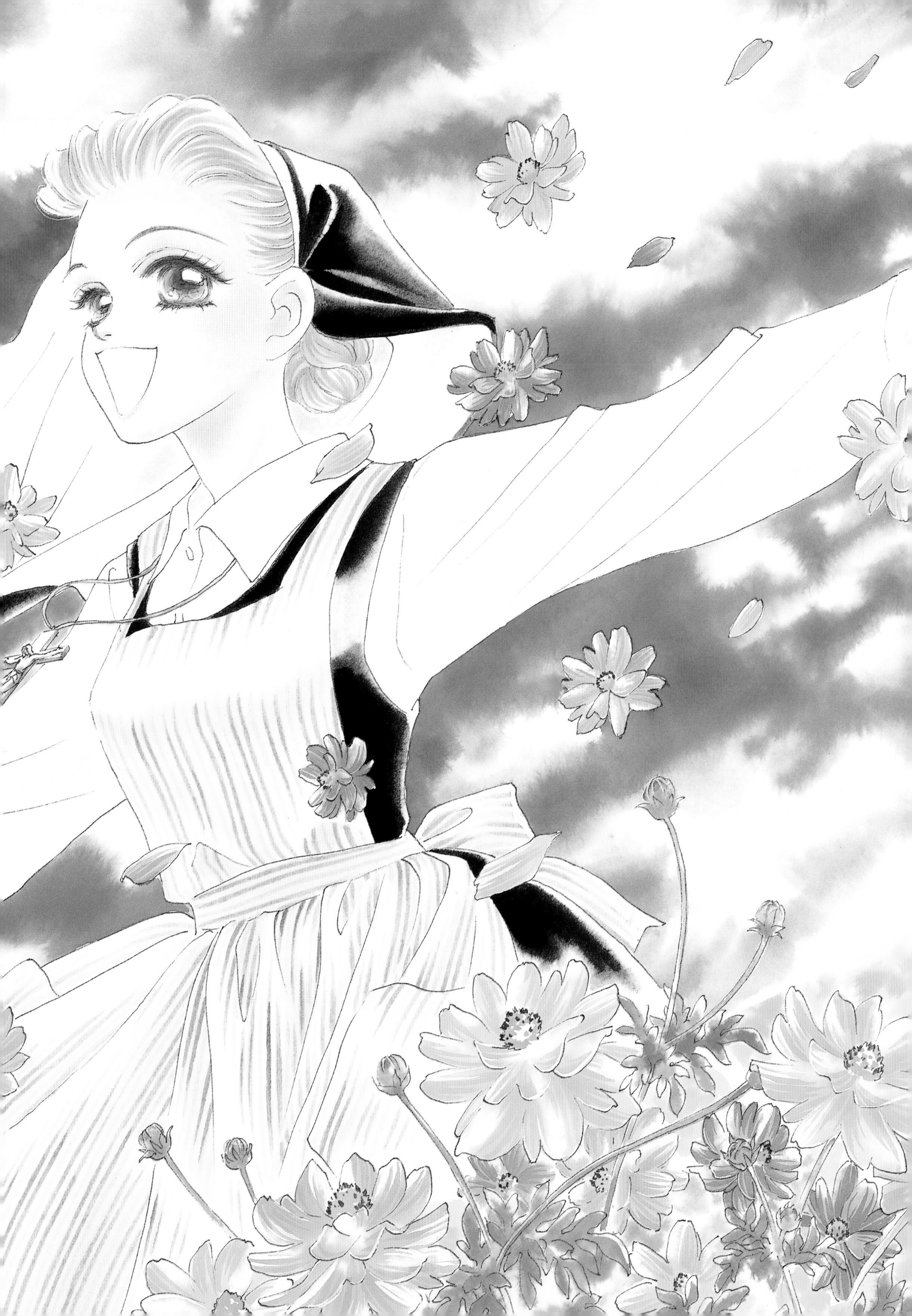

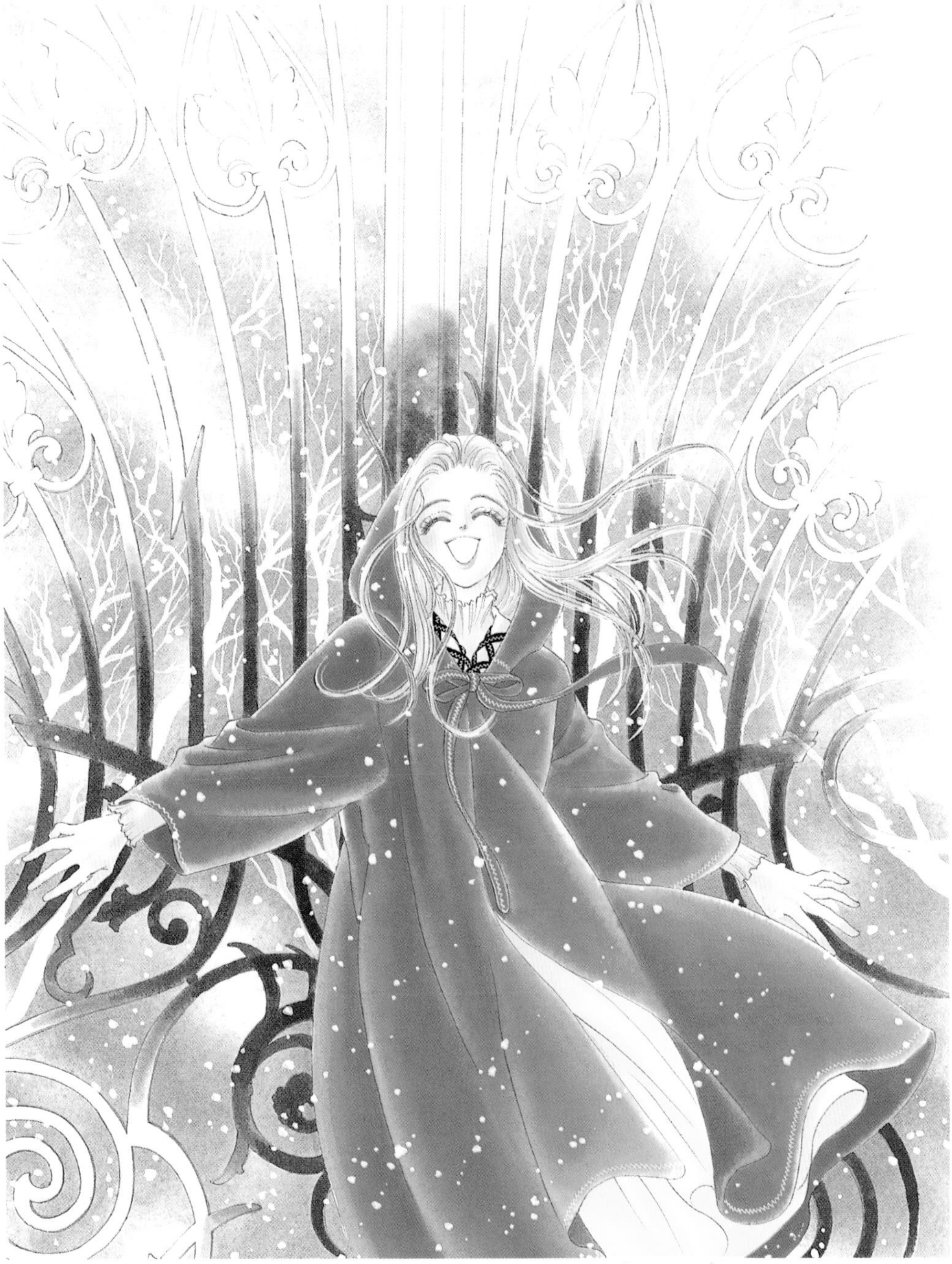

別冊フレンド1995年1月号「エンジェル★ウォーズ」扉用イラスト[371×266mm]

別冊フレンド1995年2月号「エンジェル★ウォーズ」扉用イラスト[355×251mm]

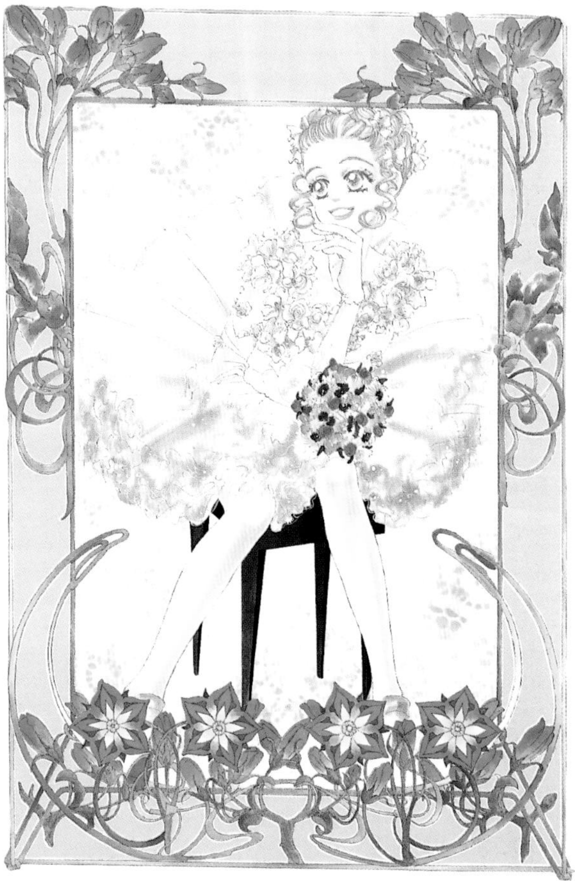

別冊フレンド1995年9月号「エンジェル★ウォーズ」扉用イラスト[371×254mm]

別冊フレンド1995年8月号「エンジェル★ウォーズ」扉用イラスト［385×537mm］

別冊フレンド1995年10月号「エンジェル★ウォーズ」扉用イラスト［383×281mm］

別冊フレンド1995年8月号テレホンカードプレゼント用イラスト［334×241mm］

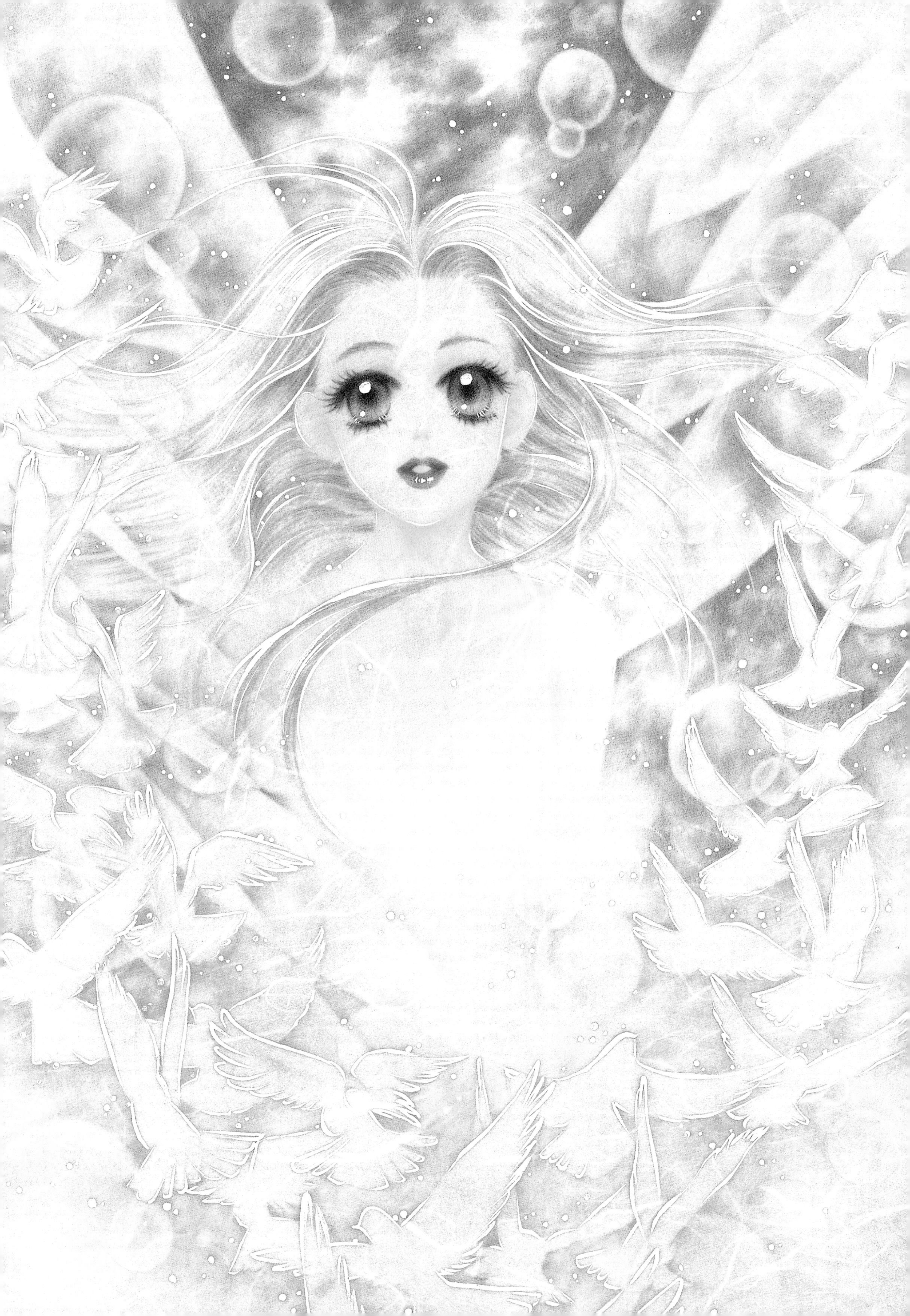

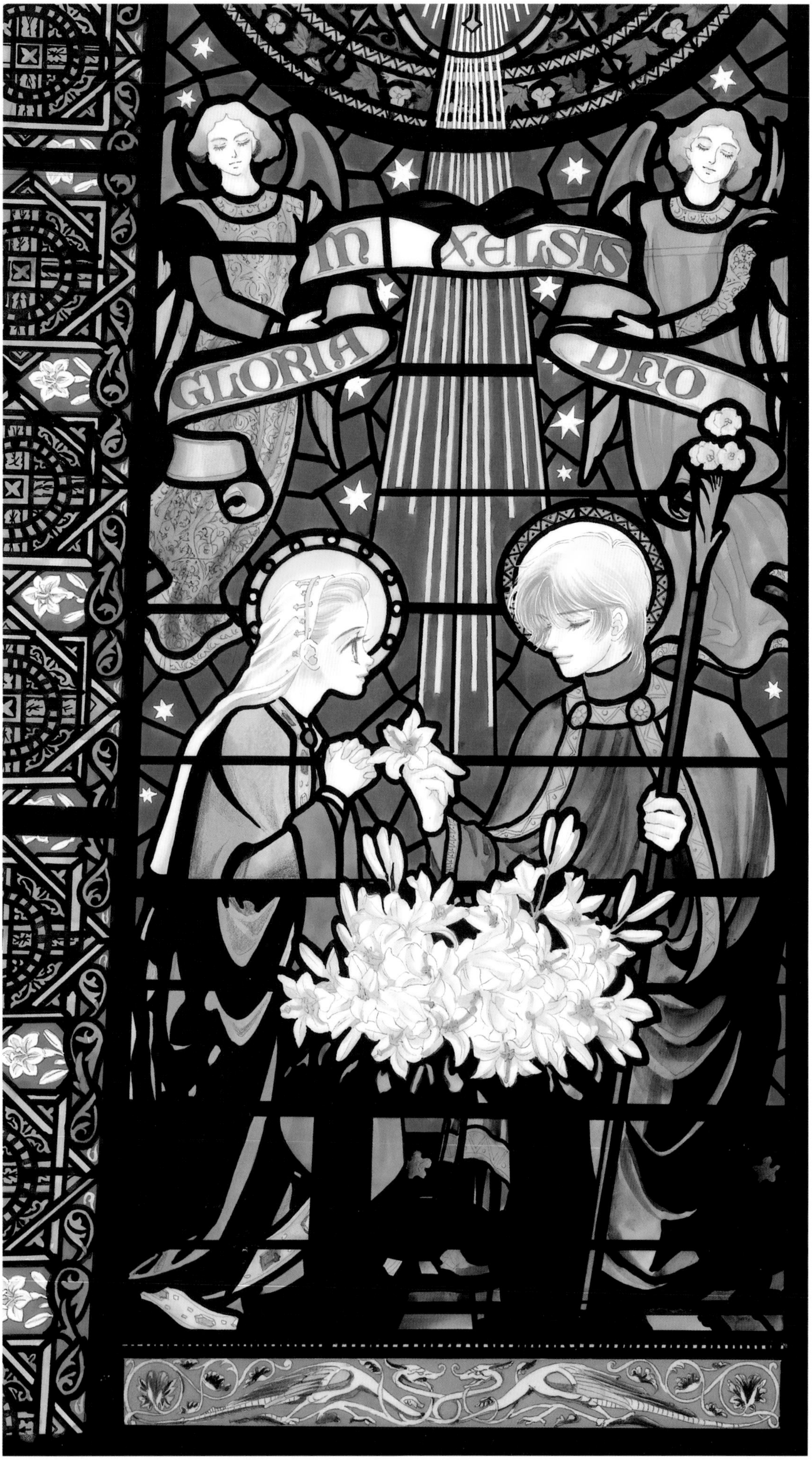
IN
XELSIS
GLORIA
DEO

別冊フレンド1995年6月号「エンジェル★ウォーズ」扉用イラスト［388×230mm］

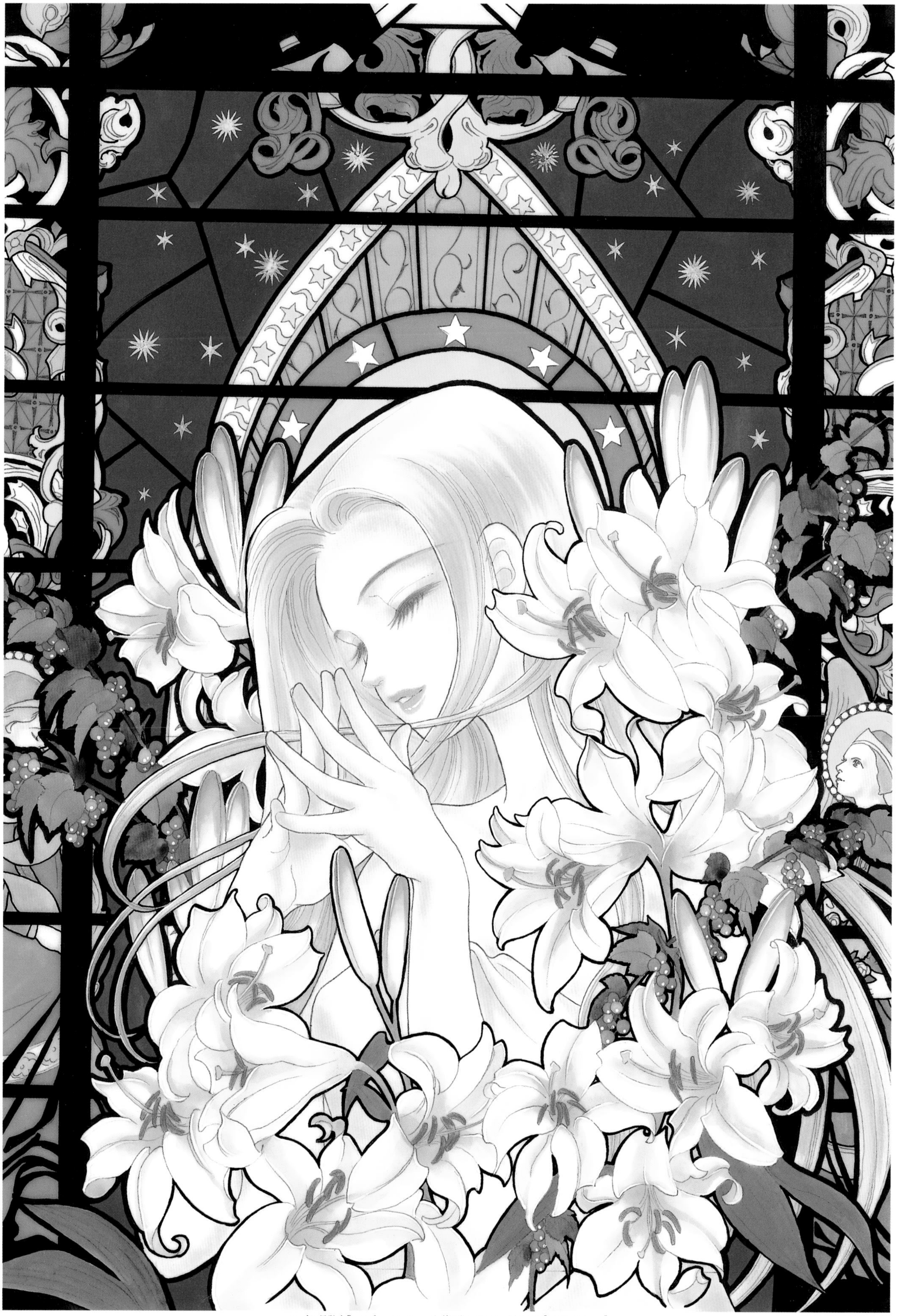

1995年6月発売「エンジェル★ウォーズ」第2巻KCカバー用イラスト[352×255mm]

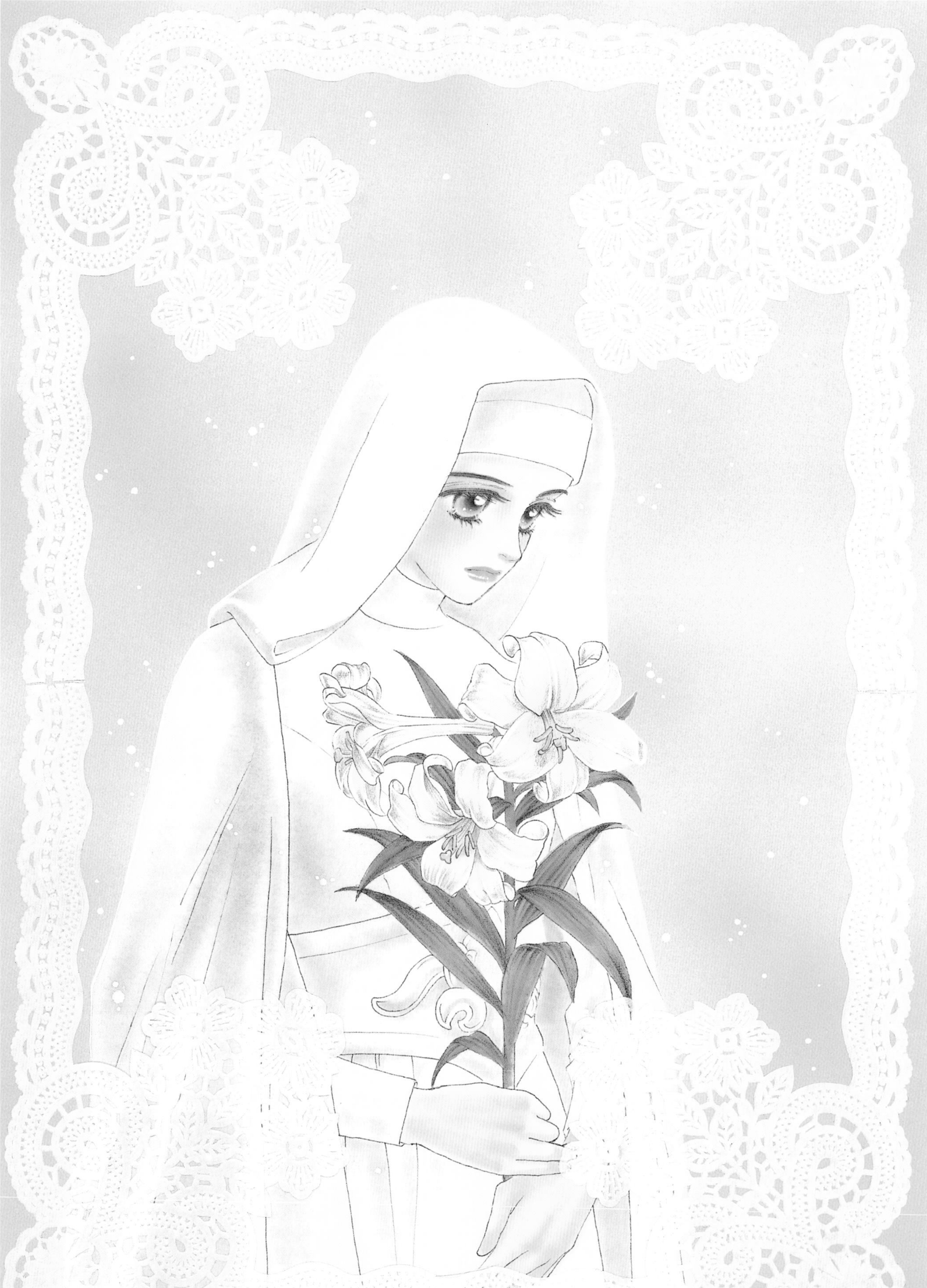

別冊フレンド1995年11月号「エンジェル★ウォーズ」本文用イラスト[382×282mm]



別冊フレンド1995年11月号「エンジェル★ウォーズ」扉用イラスト[373×282mm]

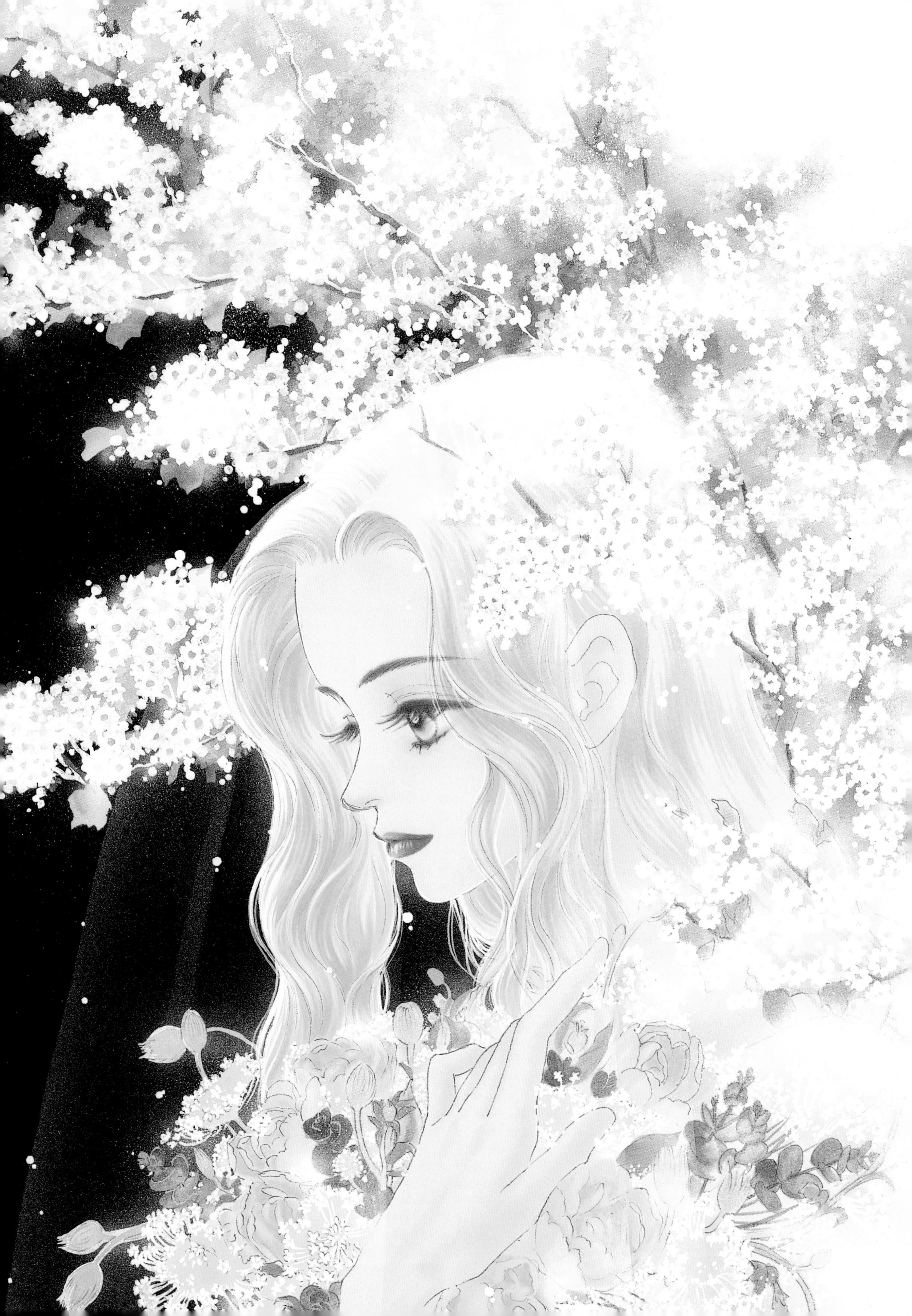

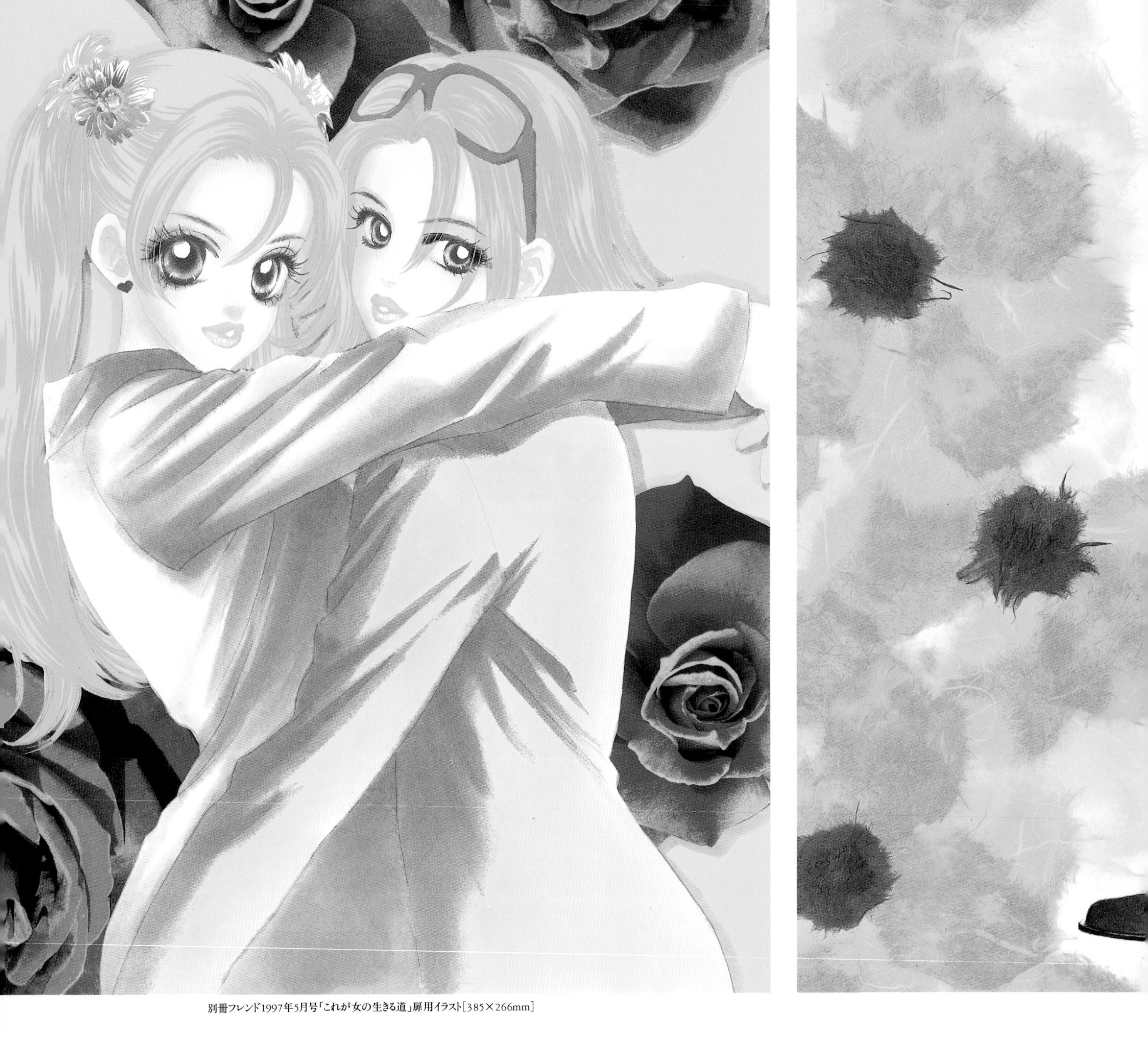

別冊フレンド1997年5月号「これが女の生きる道」扉用イラスト[385×266mm]

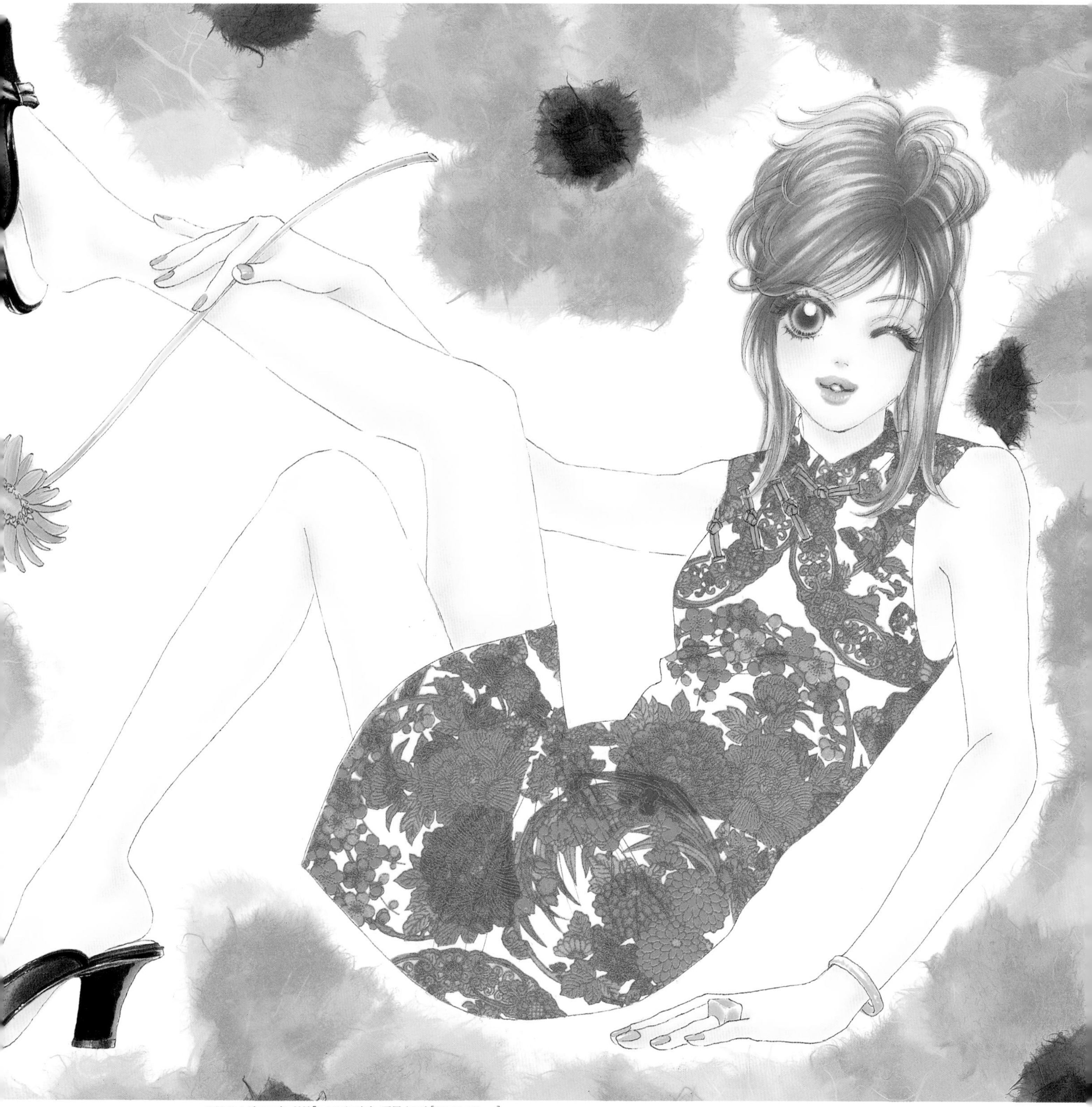

別冊フレンド1997年7月号「レンアイの自由」扉用イラスト[388×537mm]

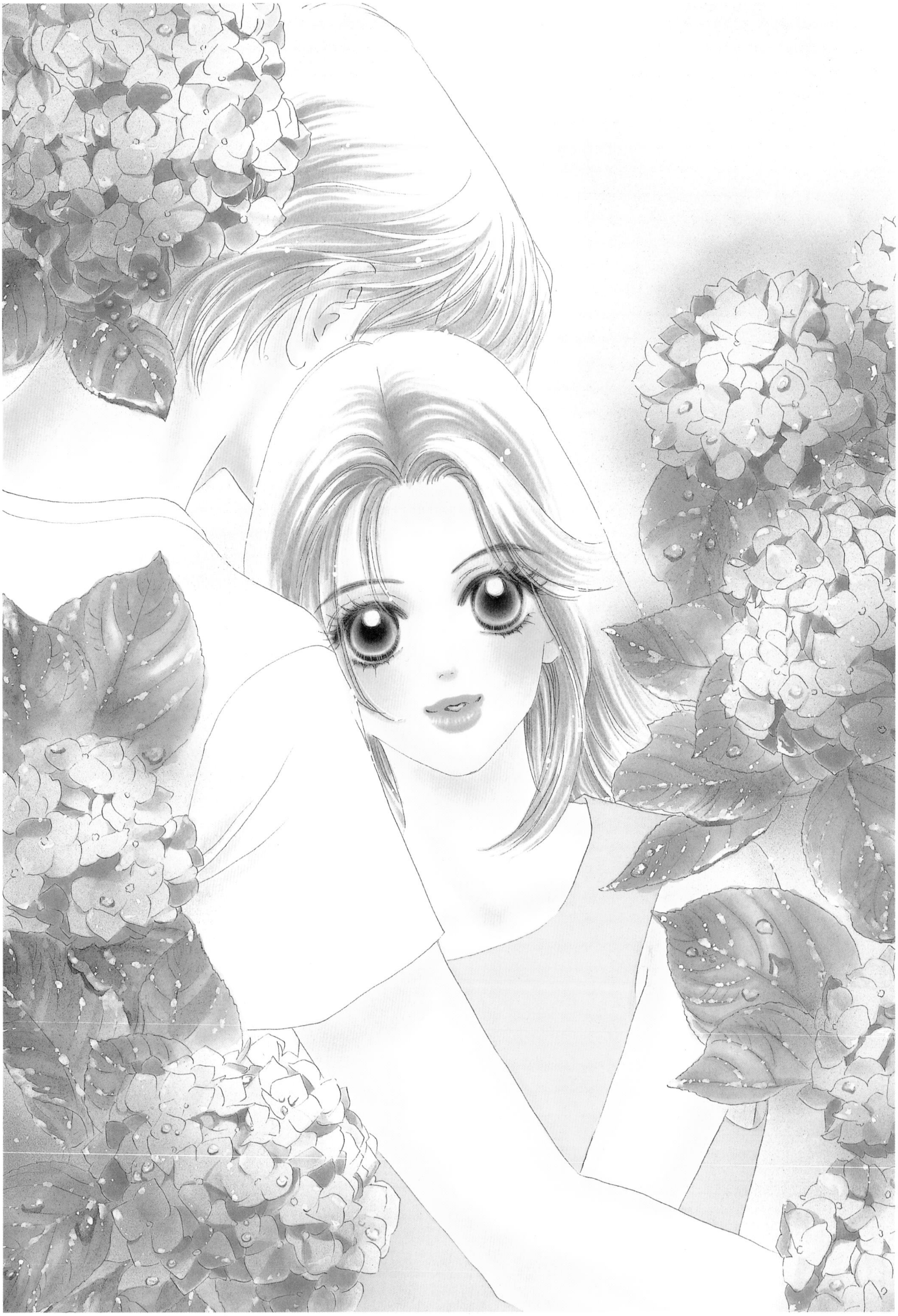

別冊フレンド1997年7月号 表紙用イラスト[379×271mm]



別フレDX Juliet 1997年3月号表紙用イラスト[384×273mm]

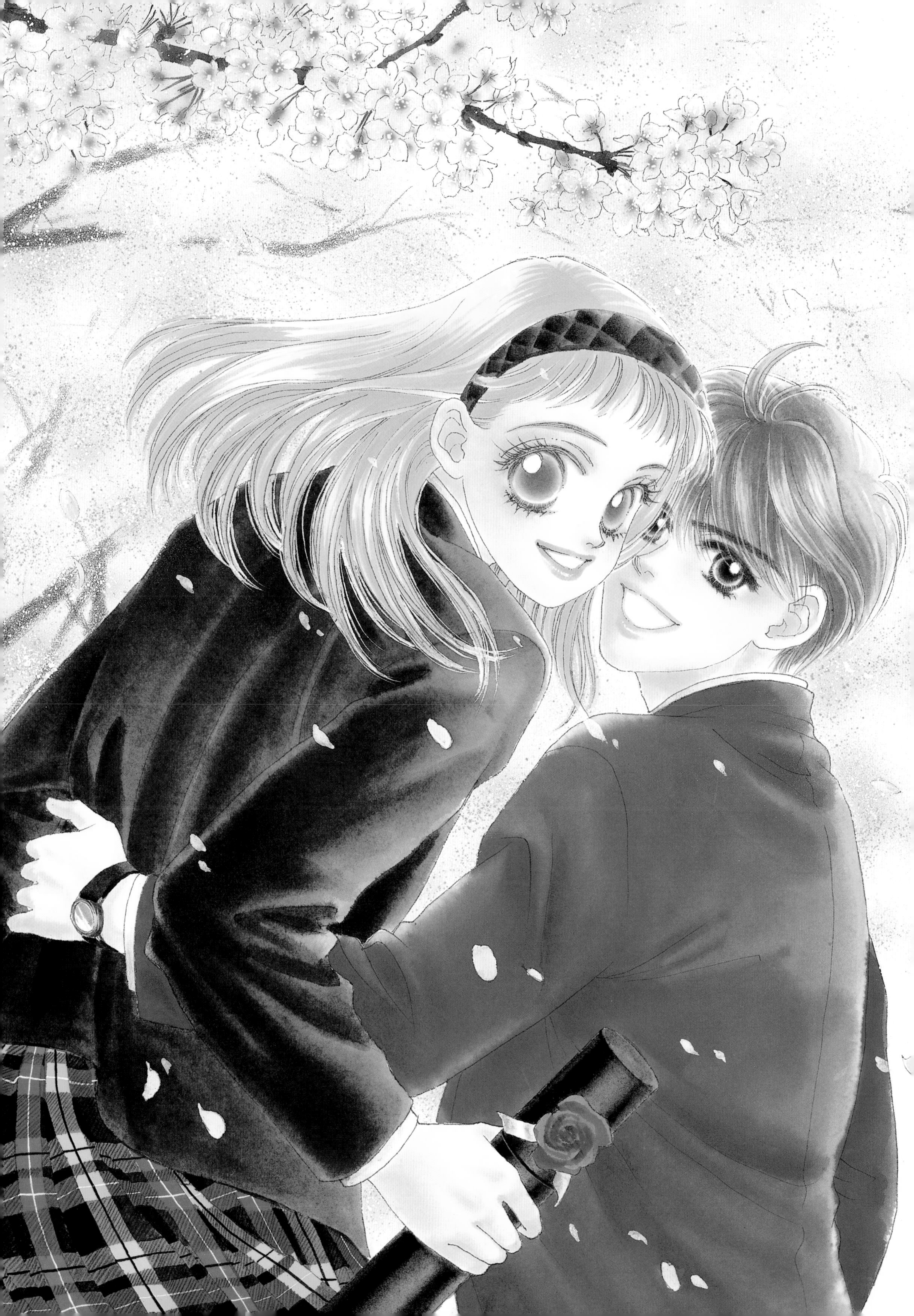

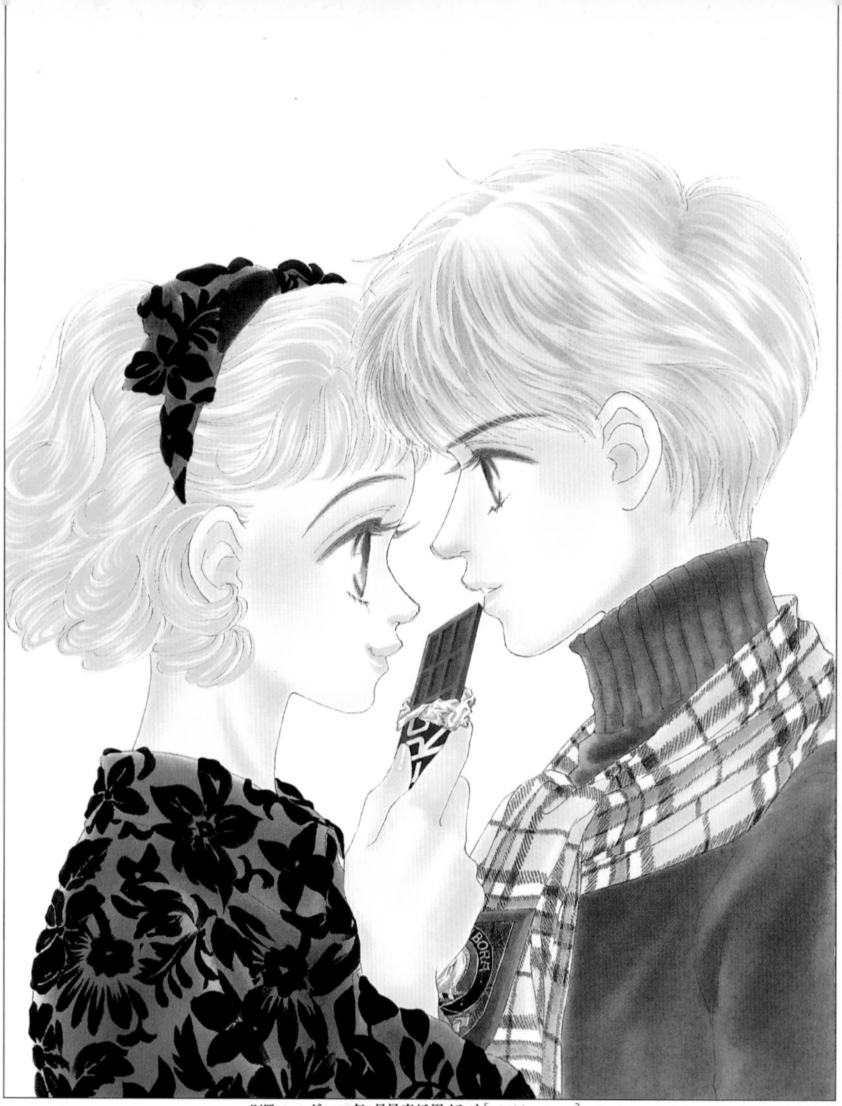

別冊フレンド1995年2月号表紙用イラスト[321×282mm]

別フレDX Juliet 1999年11月号表紙用イラスト[302×252mm]

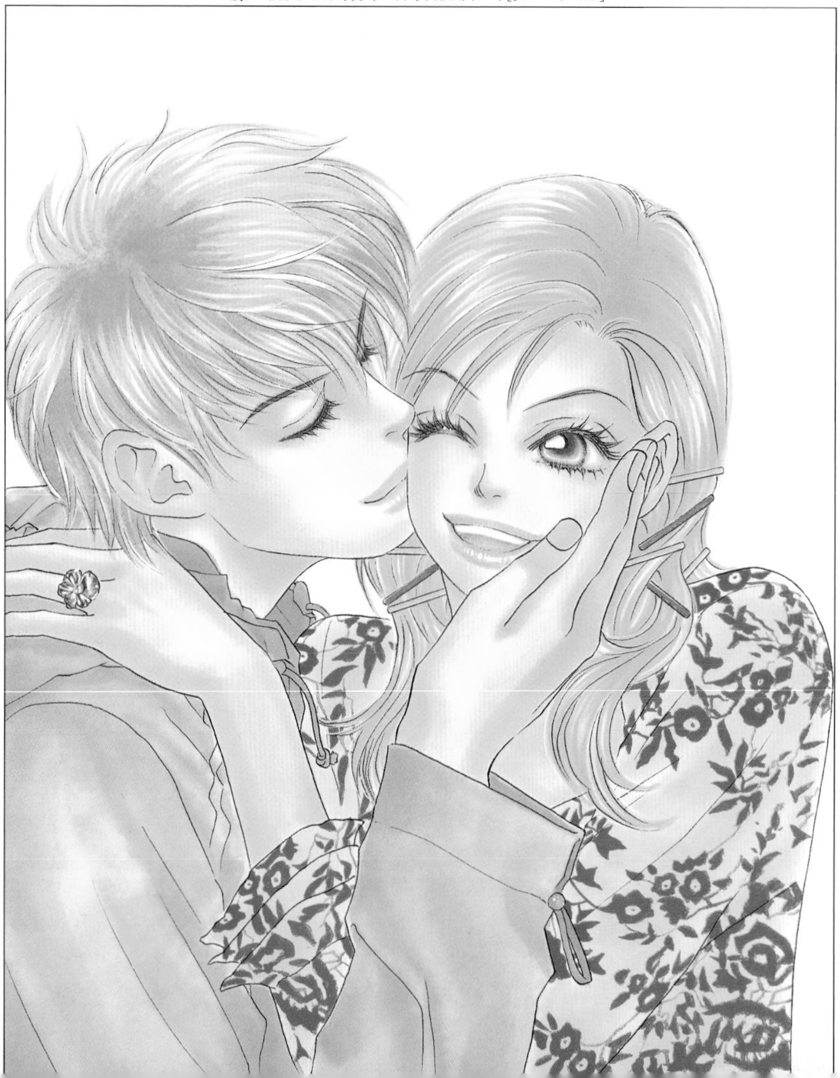

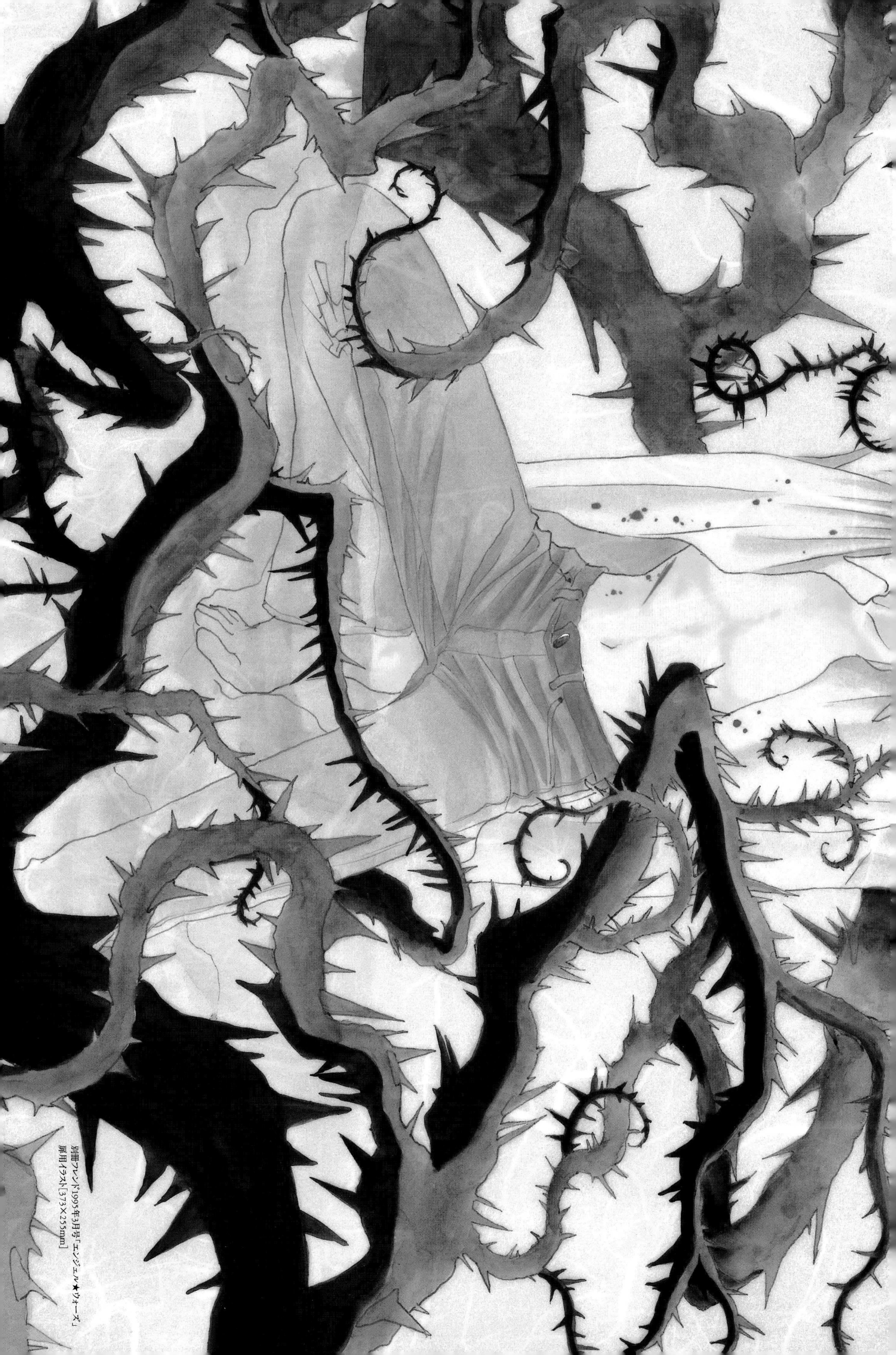

別冊フレンド1995年3月号「エンジェル★ウォーズ」
扉用イラスト[373×255mm]

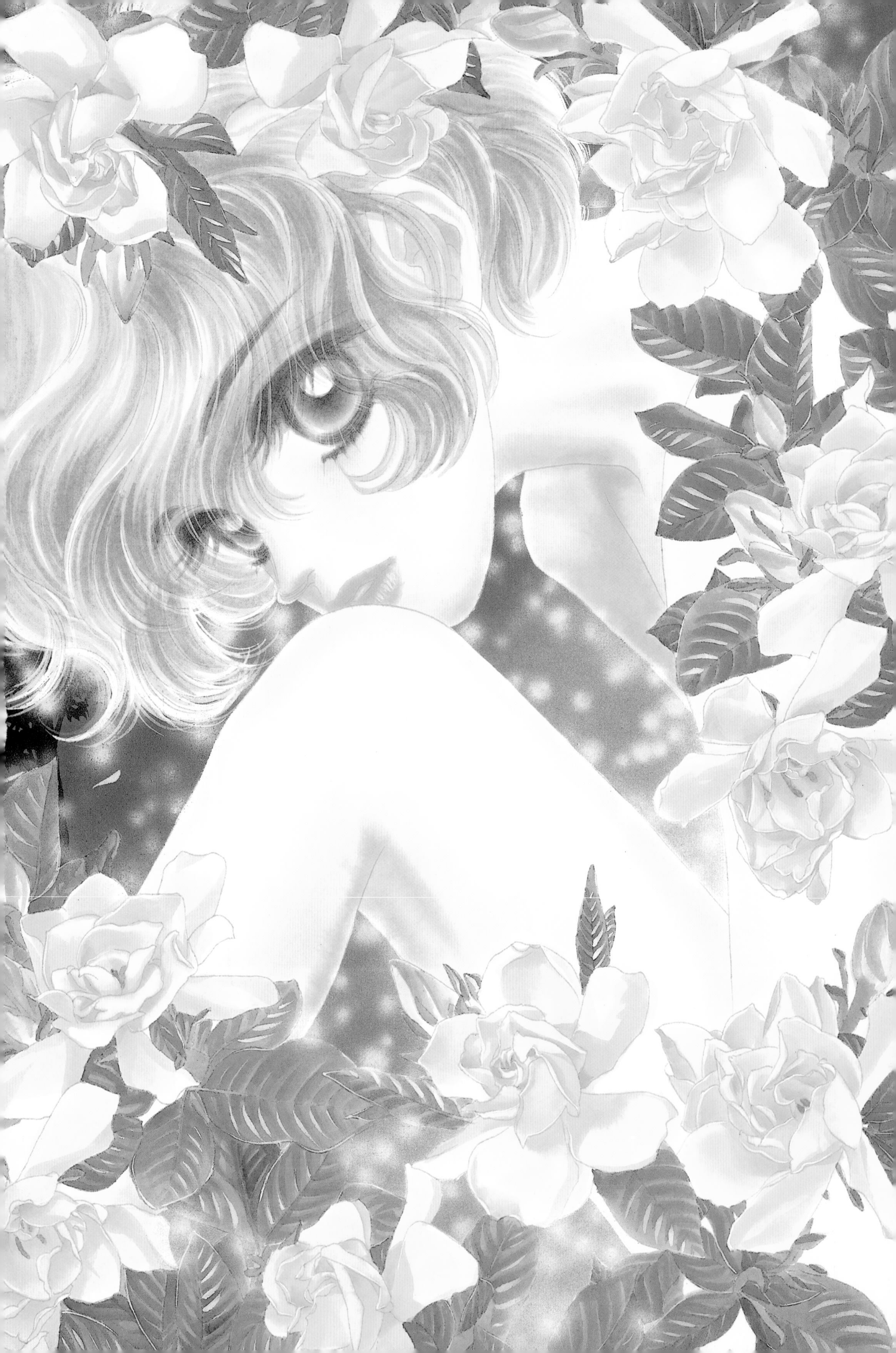

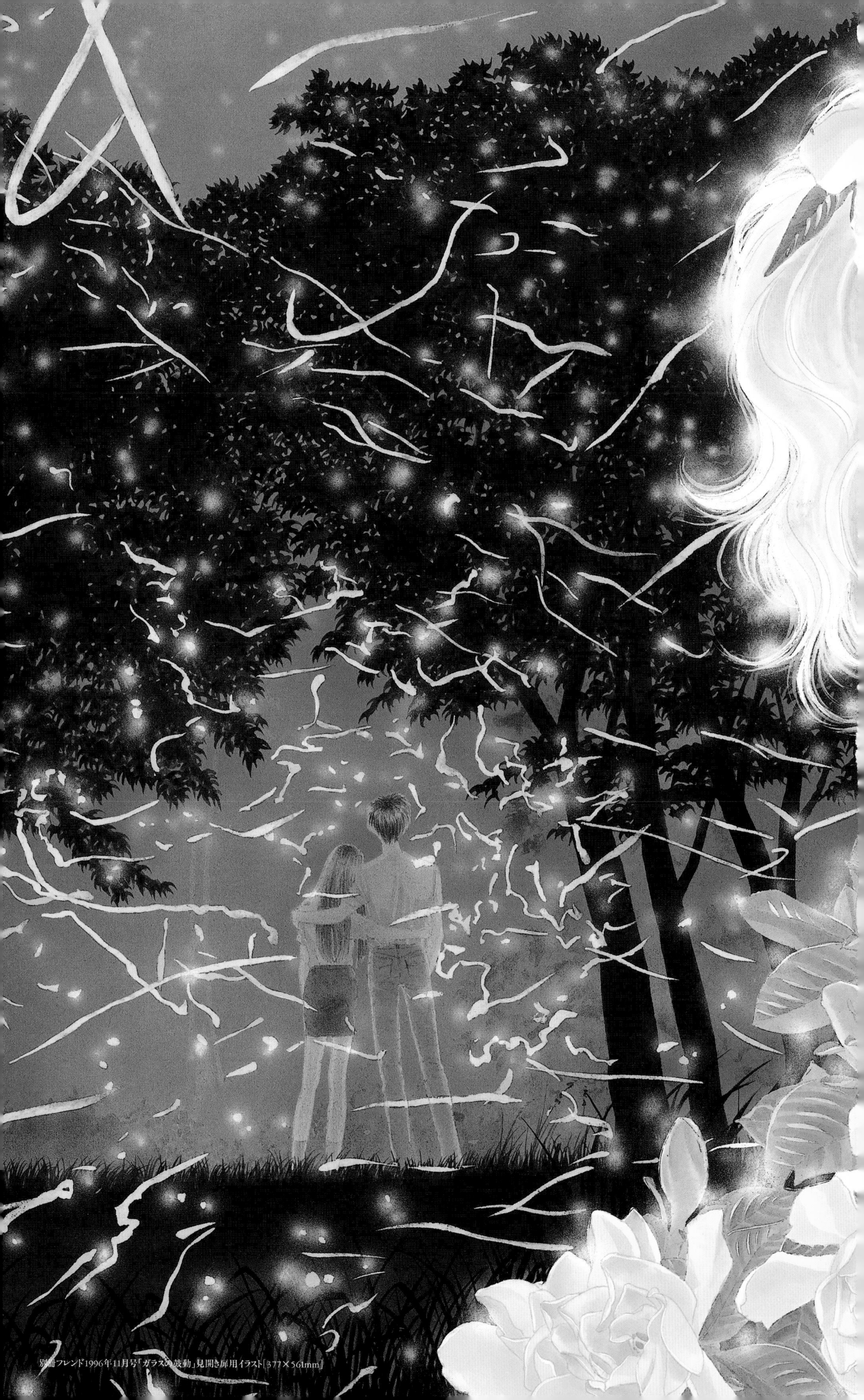

別冊フレンド1996年11月号「ガラスの鼓動」見開き扉用イラスト[377×561mm]

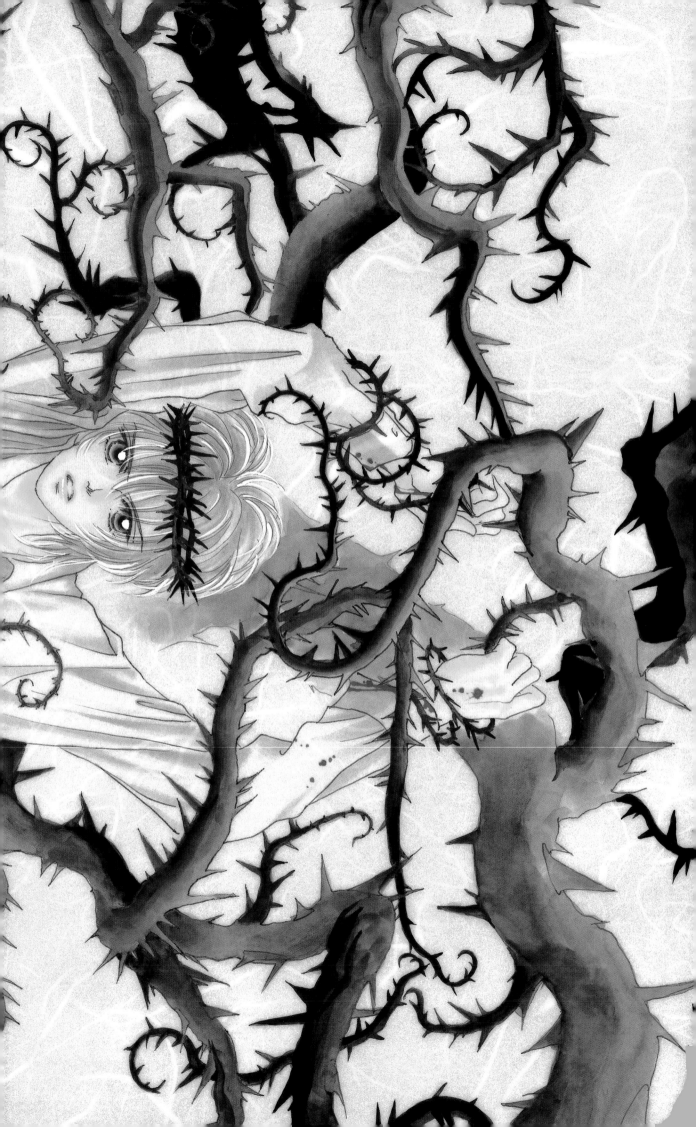

# PEACH PLUS

## Miwa Ueda Special Interview

MIWA UEDA

## Miwa Ueda created this work based on her own personal experience with the Sae's in the world!

**Interviewer:** How did Peach Girl come about?

**Ueda:** I've had the idea in mind for quite some time and wanted to do some drawings on it. Originally, I planned on just turning it into a short story, but since I didn't have any other ideas for a new series (laughs), I ended up going ahead with it and actually doing it! When it comes to Sae's attitude and actions, there are certain people out there who can say really nice things in front of you, then turn around and say something totally different to someone else. Looks can be deceiving so I wanted to depict the characters as being blind-sided by Sae's true personality.

別冊フレンド1998年3月号「ピーチガール」
1色扉用イラスト[354×242mm]

**I:** Was Sae part of the story line from the get go?

**U:** Well, I didn't really have a specific model for Sae. It's just that I've met a lot of little Sae's out there. I've always thought of those encounters and it's always bothered me, so I thought I'd try to create a manga out of it. Quite surprisingly, a lot of people really identified with this series, so I thought to myself `Wow, a lot of people have gone through this too!' (laughs). So, I first began with Sae's conniving ways and once I sorted that out, I created Momo, Sae and the rest of the characters.

別冊フレンド1998年1月号「ピーチガール」
1色扉用イラスト[361×255mm]

**I:** How was Momo created?

**U:** Well, as far as her dark skin color and the shape of her eyes, that was influenced by the way I was when I was a student who used to tan very easily. I thought it was kind of fun (laughs) to color her skin dark but since there wasn't anything out there with that kind of a heroine, it was worrisome.

**I:** What?! Momo is influenced by you?

**U:** It's definitely a coincidence that I tan so easily. I also had a complex about people being scared or intimidated when they saw me (laughs).

**I:** So does Momo's character reflect your personality?

**U:** No, not at all (laughs)!! A story with a dull heroine wouldn't work at all. That's why I created this manga with that in mind.

**I:** Does Kiley and Toji have any real-life role models?

**U:** None at all.

**I:** In terms of Kiley and Toji's image, was there a particular actor who you wanted them to emulate?

**U:** Well, now that you mention it, I really like Sorimachi Takeshi, the actor who played Onizuka in the *GTO* Japanese TV series and movie. But, I'd like to think that I managed to make them totally different from the beginning.

**I:** Between Toji and Kiley, which one is your type?

**U:** What?! I'm for Toji (laughs) but if I were going out with one of them, it'd be Kiley, but if I were going to marry one of them, I suppose I'd choose Toji. But my readers all seem to be total Kiley supporters now.

別冊フレンド1999年9月号「ピーチガール」
1色扉用イラスト[362×254mm]

## What about the war between Momo and Sae? What about Momo's love life?

**I:** Sae is such an intense character. What do you think about the readers who support her?

**U:** There aren't many Sae fans out there (laughs)! The fans get so mad at her because they really put themselves in the story. I thought I was drawing something really scary, but the letters I received from my readers were even worse. I couldn't go that far but I really sympathized with how much they suffered and how patient they were in dealing with their Sae-like experiences. I could die (laughs)!

**I:** Is there a part of you that's similar to Sae?

**U:** Ah, well, yes I think so. I wouldn't do the things she does, but I'd probably think about doing them. I think people tend to hide that side of themselves. If I were illustrating the series when I was younger, this manga would've focused more on the victim because when you're young, you tend to be more self-centered. That's just the way things are, I guess. But I really do like Sae except she really shouldn't be doing those things (laughs)!

**I:** Why is Sae such a catty chatterbox?

**U:** Well, that's because when drawing a manga it's difficult to include a monologue of all the characters other than the heroine. I wondered if there was any way I could draw Sae's emotions as picture icons rather than the actual dialogue to illustrate what she's feeling. Oddly enough, even when she's acting a bit strange or distant, I end up making her very talkative anyway! I had no idea I would do it all the time, but now I do it on purpose (laughs)!

**I:** Will the war between Momo and Sae escalate?

**U:** Yeah, well Sae hasn't grown up yet and unless she learns a lesson on all the bad things she's done, but I don't think she will (laugh)!

**I:** Have you already decided on an ending?

**U:** Nope, not at all (laughs)! I think that I really need to figure out the love triangle between the characters, like who Momo will lose her virginity to, but I haven't decided yet!!

**I:** Will you follow what the readers want?

**U:** No (laughs). Of course, I'm thinking about my readers, but I won't be compelled to follow exactly what they truly want.

**I:** Other than the coloring of Peach Girl, are there any other challenges?

**U:** In this series, I have to color Momo's skin, so that takes some time. It wouldn't look good smudged, so before I color Momo's skin, I use something called masking ink. This process takes quite a bit of time. When I first began the series, I thought that I had colored her skin dark enough, but when it was printed you couldn't see her tanned skin at all. I didn't know that would happen.

Miwa Ueda
Special Interview

# PEACH PLUS
MIWA UEDA

別冊フレンド2000年4月号「ピーチガール」
1色扉用イラスト[364×256mm]

## Whack-a-Sae is a game featured on the Peach Club official Web site. When will we see a 3-*D* Momo?!

**I:** Will you be using new materials or canvases?

**U:** I've used transparent paper before, but because color doesn't show up very well on it, I haven't used it recently. I've bought things to try out though, like watercolors and other mediums. I'd like to try using those materials as well as my computer. I think magazines only show hand-drawn images, so I'd like to create a 3-*D* Momo for my Web page. I used the game Whack-a-Mole as a model for the Whack-a-Sae game that I put up on my site.

**I:** Are you very involved with your Web site?

**U:** I draw icons and scan illustrations. My assistant's been really busy, so she hasn't been able to help out much (laughs). I put up what I've drawn on the site by myself but making icons is so difficult that I sort of want to master doing it on my own.

**I:** By the way, is there anything other than love stories that you'd like to try illustrating?

**U:** A comic featuring an evil nurse (laughs).

**I:** Finally, do you have a message for all your readers?

**U:** Well, Peach Girl isn't over yet and I have a lot of expectations for the next story development, so please continue to support me, okay?

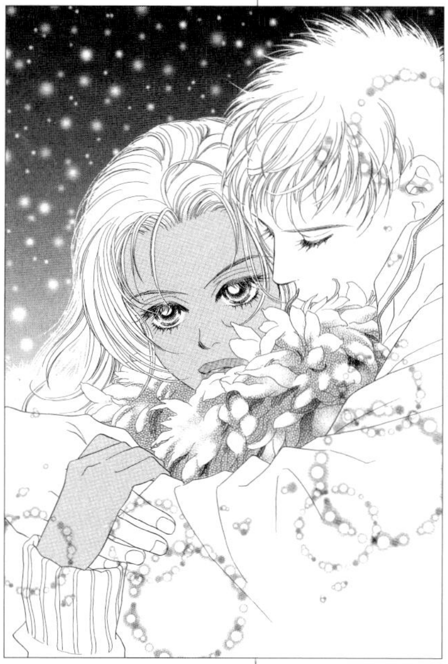

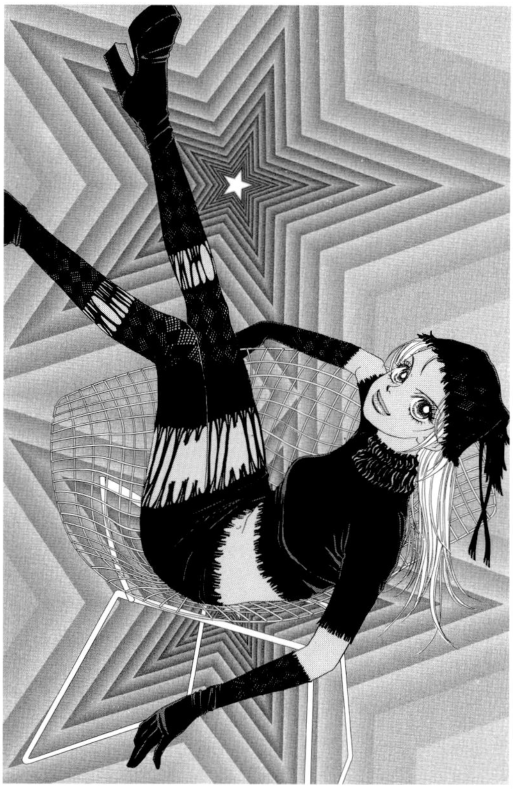

別冊フレンド1999年4月号「ピーチガール」1色扉用イラスト[349×229mm]

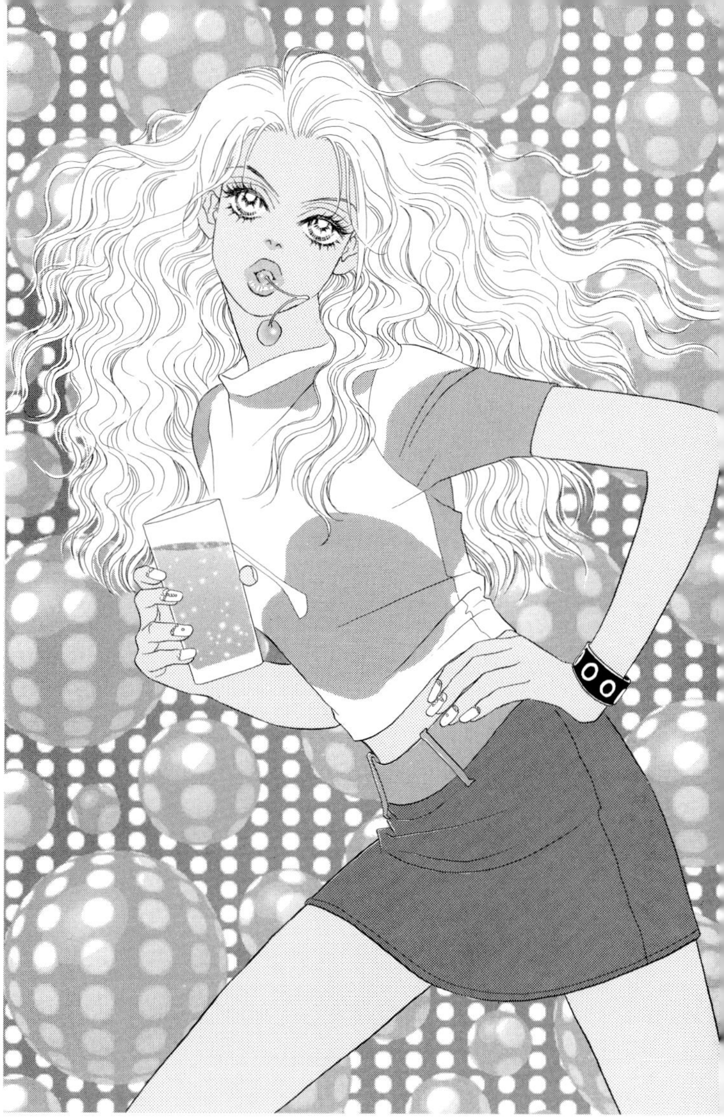

別冊フレンド2000年6月号「ピーチガール」1色扉用イラスト[349×230mm]

PROFILE

Born on September 29. Astrological sign: Libra. Blood type: O. Currently living in Hyogo Prefecture. Miwa Ueda made her debut in 1985 with "Peach Colored Elixir," which won the 162nd *Bessatsu Friend* award. Many of her best-selling works have appeared in *Bessatsu Friend*. She's very passionate about her computer and when she has time, she loves working on her Web site. You can check out Peach Club's official Web site by logging on to www.yomogi.sakura.ne.jp/~peach/.

| ▶ LIST OF WORKS | ▶ PUBLICATIONS |
|---|---|
| Peach Colored Elixir | *Juliet*, May 1985 - 162nd *Bessatsu Friend* award |
| Our Common Language | *Romeo*, Summer 1985 |
| Driving Boogie | *Bessatsu Friend*, September 1985 |
| The Puberty League | *Juliet*, January 1986 |
| That was the Only Sepia Colored Time | *Juliet*, March 1986 |
| Love at First Sight | *Bessatsu Friend*, April 1986 |
| Mirage Boy | *Juliet*, July 1986 |
| Please Don't Take Off Kupi's Underwear | *Juliet*, September 1986 |
| Caught in Alice's Tree | *Bessatsu Friend*, November 1986 |
| I Want to Give him a Lollipop | *Bessatsu Friend*, January 1987 |
| Lonesome Angel | *Bessatsu Friend*, April 1987 |
| Today I'm a Doll in Trouble | *Bessatsu Friend*, June 1987 |
| I'm Involved | *Bessatsu Friend*, August 1987 |
| Maria at a Battle Field | *Bessatsu Friend*, October - December 1987 |
| Imitation ♦ Gold | *Bessatsu Friend*, March 1988 & August 1998 |
| Midori's Sand Clock | *Bessatsu Friend*, October 1988 |
| Indian Summer | *Bessatsu Friend*, January 1989 |
| Moonlight Red Riding Hood | *Bessatsu Friend*, May1989 |
| Whisper of the Stars | *Bessatsu Friend*, June 1989 |
| Summer Valentine | *Bessatsu Friend*, July 1989 |
| Sign Cosign Love ♥ Sign | *Bessatsu Friend*, October 1989 - October 1990 |
| Jesus Christ! (short story) | *Bessatsu Friend*, November 1990 |
| Jesus Christ! | *Bessatsu Friend*, January - June 1991 |
| Oh! My Darling ♥ | *Bessatsu Friend*, September 1991 - February 1994 |
| Oh! My Darling ♥ Extra Story - The Reason Why I Love You | *Bessatsu Friend*, April 1994 |
| Angel ★ Wars | *Bessatsu Friend*, August 1994 - November 1995 |
| Glass Hearts | *Bessatsu Friend*, March 1996-March 1997 |
| This is a Girl's Life | *Bessatsu Friend*, May 1997 |
| Love's Freedom | *Bessatsu Friend*, July 1997 |
| Peach Girl | *Bessatsu Friend*, October 1997 – ongoing |

Translator - Panida Kamsingwong/Yuki N. Johnson
Cover Layout - Anna Kernbaum
Graphic Designer - Monalisa J. de Asis

Editor - Nora Wong
Managing Editor - Jill Freshney
Production Coordinator - Antonio DePietro
Production Manager - Mutsumi Miyazaki
Art Director - Matt Alford
Editorial Director - Jeremy Ross
VP of Production - Ron Klamert
President & C.O.O. - John Parker
Publisher & C.E.O. - Stuart Levy

E-mail: editor@TOKYOPOP.com
Come visit us online at www.TOKYOPOP.com

TOKYOPOP Inc.
5900 Wilshire Blvd. Suite 2000
Los Angeles, CA 90036

*PEACH: MIWA UEDA Illustrations*

ISBN: 1-59182-042-1

First TOKYOPOP printing: April 2004

10  9  8  7  6  5  4  3  2  1
Printed in Japan

Editor's Note: Captions under images have not been
translated as it is our intention to remain true to its original
content and quality. This art book has been reproduced
using special inks available only in Japan.